THE BEST OF
MODERN SCREEN

M·A·R·K B·E·G·O

Foreword by Debbie Reynolds

Columbus Books
London

All *Modern Screen* material reproduced in this anthology
is done so with full written permission, and is previously
copyrighted in the month and year indicated on each article
herein, under the magazine title *Modern Screen*.

Joan Crawford front cover issue date: *October 1933*
Back cover issue dates: Bette Davis: *August 1938*
                         Marlene Dietrich: *May 1931*
                         Clark Gable and Mae West: *September 1933*
                         Jean Harlow: *July 1933*

First published in Great Britain in 1986 by
Columbus Books Limited
19-23 Ludgate Hill, London EC4M 7PD

British Library Cataloguing in Publication Data
The Best of Modern Screen
   1. Moving-picture actors and actresses—California—Los Angeles
   2. Hollywood (LA, Calif.)—History
   I. Bego, Mark   II. Modern screen
   791.43′028′0922   PN993.5.U65

   ISBN 0–86287–304–5

Printed and bound by
R.J. Acford, Chichester, Sussex

MODERN SCREEN

10¢

APRIL

Claudette
Colbert

SCOOP!
NORMA SHEARER *talks about* JOAN CRAWFORD

CONTENTS

JEAN HARLOW
July 1933

CLARK GABLE & MAE WEST
September 1933

THE BEST OF MODERN SCREEN

by Mark Bego

he book that you are now holding, *The Best of "Modern Streen,"* contains many of the most exciting, the most glamorous, the most historic, the most humorous, and the most outrageous material from the pages of *Modern Screen* magazine from 1930 to 1960. Each article is presented exactly as it originally appeared in the magazine. The printing plates and most of the photographs have long since been destroyed, lost, discarded, or misplaced. The pages that are reproduced herein were taken from priceless, bound, original issues of *Modern Screen,* photographed directly from magazine pages, some of which are over fifty years old. The vast majority of these issues have long since yellowed and aged, so this book is quite literally keeping a piece of Hollywood history alive…a history that *Modern Screen* magazine was so much a part of.

The year 1930 was a difficult one for most of America. It was the first full year of the Great Depression, and most people were looking to motion pictures as a way to temporarily forget their financial troubles. It was also the first full year after talkies had taken over Hollywood. "Garbo Talks!" heralded advertisements for her first speaking film role, in *Anna Christie* (1930), making her one of the only established film stars from the silent movies of the 1920's to make the transition to sound productions. It was the first year of a new decade, and a new era for films. The movies were full of a new breed of stars, and to meet the demands of the cinema fans, a fresh new magazine debuted on the nation's newsstands; it was aptly named *Modern Screen.*

Volume 1, Number 1 of *The MODERN SCREEN Magazine* was dated November 1930. It was 132 pages long, it sold for ten cents, and the first star to grace its cover was Kay Francis. *The Virtuous Sin* (1930) was Kay's latest film, and *Modern Screen*'s debut cover

"I think I envy my children their childhood. Because what I really want is for someone to plan an Easter egg hunt for me."
—Joan Crawford
Modern Screen
July 1951

story about her was entitled "Lucky Thirteen." At this time, Kay was considered the height of chic, and her hairstyles and wardrobe were avidly watched and copied by women the world over. She was the perfect subject to become *Modern Screen*'s first cover girl. Also mentioned on the cover were the articles "Garbo's Hiding Place," "Eavesdropping on Will Rogers," and "The New 'It' by Elinor Glyn." Some of the interior features included "An Open Letter to Clara Bow," "Goodbye, Lon" a remembrance article about Lon Chaney, and "Hollywood Wardrobes," which peeked into the personal closet of Fay Wray. The "Portraits" section of the magazine devoted full-page "pin-ups" to Joan Crawford, Helen Twelvetrees, Robert Montgomery, Lewis Ayres, and Joan Bennett.

Within its first year and a half, *The MODERN SCREEN Magazine* had already proven an enormous hit. By spring of 1933 it was able to boast "Largest Circulation of Any Screen Magazine" on its cover, above the new, shortened name *Modern Screen.* It became the most famous screen magazine in the world, and over fifty-five years later, it has the distinction of remaining the *only* movie fan magazine from the golden age of Hollywood still in publication.

In the 1933 film *Dinner at Eight,* one of Jean Harlow's best-loved scenes finds her in bed eating bonbons, and reading the April 1933 issue of *Modern Screen,* with Claudette Colbert on the cover. In *Bombshell* (1933), issues of the July 1933 cover story on Jean Harlow are seen coming off of the presses and being avidly read by her devoted fans.

The different decades of *Modern Screen* are virtual time capsules defining the cinematic tastes of America—and for that matter the world. As television gained popularity in the 1950's, *Modern Screen* expanded its editorial scope to encompass the stars of the small screen as well as the host of new cinema screen stars. In the 1980's when music videos became popular on television, *Modern Screen* began to feature on its pages this brand-new breed of screen star as well.

Modern Screen has featured in its pages the biggest and most legendary film stars of seven decades—from Rudolph Valentino to Michael Jackson. How's that for scope? Every star from Mae West to Marilyn Monroe to Madonna has been on the cover of *Modern Screen*.

No less impressive has been the staff of regular writers and "special guest reporters" who over the years have brought their interviewing and writing skills to the pages of *Modern Screen*. The list includes Hollywood gossip columnists Hedda Hopper, Louella Parsons, Sheilah Graham, Dorothy Kilgallen, Ed Sullivan, George Christy, and Liz Smith; screen writers Anita Loos, and Elinor Glyn; novelists such as James M. Cain; biographer Bob Thomas; costume designer Edith Head; and even the stars themselves—Lana Turner, Judy Garland, Marilyn Monroe, and Joan Crawford all wrote for *Modern Screen*.

The Best of "Modern Screen" brings together the stars, the writers, the photographers, and the world of Hollywood excitement that the magazine has personified since its inception in 1930. Kay Francis, Clark Gable, Joan Crawford, Jean Harlow, Marilyn Monroe, and Rock Hudson are gone now, but the cinematic fantasies that they helped to create are still alive in the movies that they made, and in the pages of *Modern Screen* magazine.

Jean Harlow lounges in bed eating bonbons and reading the lowdown on all of her fellow Hollywood stars in *Modern Screen*. This photograph is from the Academy Award-winning 1933 film *Dinner At Eight*. (Photograph: Courtesy of MGM)

This is where it all began, the debut issue of *Modern Screen:* Volume 1, Number One, November 1930, with Kay Francis on the cover. The magazine has been in continuous publication ever since, featuring Hollywood's biggest stars on its cover, and bringing all the latest gossip and news to its readers.

THANK YOU

Thank you to the following people for making this book possible: Morty Tuller, owner of Sterling's Magazines, for allowing me to produce this book from original issues of *Modern Screen*; Jaine Fabian, librarian at Dell Publishing; Joe Beninati at Eljay Photo Service for photographing the original magazine pages; Joel F. Burton at Foto Screen for producing the veloxes; Lou Valentino, for the cover shot from his private collection of *Modern Screen*; Toni Lopopolo, my editor at St. Martin's Press, for believing in this project; Jim Pitula, for the layouts and expert book design on the chapter openings; Marc Raboy, for the fantastic photo; David Salidor, my publicist; Alex Kole, for invaluable production advice; Ted Greenberg, for working out the legalities; and to Bart Andrews, Jack Caravela, Andy Carpenter, Manuela Paul, Jim Pinkston, and Roy Wanner.

Special thanks to Debbie Reynolds for the Foreword. And to all the writers whose words have graced the pages of *Modern Screen*: I'm proud to be part of this distinguished group of "stars"!

This book is dedicated to my agent, Sherry Robb. You're my favorite "Modern Scream"!

Mark Bego
November 1985

PRODUCTION NOTES

The pages of *Modern Screen* that you will find in this book were reproduced from bound, original copies of *Modern Screen*. These copies have been kept in storage for all these years and are totally undamaged, as they were single copies that were never released to the public. They are as close to perfect copies as will ever exist.

The method of reproducing these magazine pages entailed having each page separately photographed and printed. From each print, an enlargement velox was produced and laid out on camera-ready boards. Many of the early photos were originally printed in a process known as rotogravure. To preserve the look of these layouts, all photo pages had to be subsequently "screened" into a modern dot pattern.

Since it was impossible to remove the individual pages from the original magazines, on some of the reproductions you will find some type irregularities toward the far right or left edge of the page. This was unavoidable, in an effort to maintain all of the original material. The type, the art, the photos, and the layouts are precisely as they appeared in those copies, as they were originally published.

NOTE: Do not attempt to order by mail any of the goods or products mentioned in the articles. These remain for historical authenticity only, and the original offers for goods and/or services have long since expired.

DEBBIE REYNOLDS
November 1961

FOREWORD

by DEBBIE REYNOLDS

The history and importance of publicity in the film industry and its first real home, Hollywood, has been told from the good and the bad...the real and the created gossip. But, no one can deny what a part the top fan magazines played in the great love affair between the public and the workers of the studio: the actors, actresses, directors, writers, "The Creators".

That is why I am most pleased for being asked to contribute to this book about *Modern Screen* magazine, and it's part in the years of the "Golden Era" of the motion picture industry.

From the time I made my first film at Metro Goldwyn Mayer (MGM), one of the most important aspects of being a young star was posing for photo sessions and giving interviews for articles that could appear in the important fan magazines. The job of being a movie star wasn't finished when the cameras stopped rolling. I couldn't even consider being seen in public places of importance or social events without false eyelashes, gloves, and shoes dyed to match the color of my outfit. Even for casual at-home photo layouts, every hair on my head had to be immaculately in-place before a shot could be taken. There was no such thing as a candid photo—every detail of a star's appearance, home, family, and children were carefully groomed to perfection before a photographer was allowed in the house!

Appearing on the cover of a movie fan magazine was serious business, and we regarded our exposure in them with great importance. Having been both a reader of *Modern Screen,* and one of the magazine's most popular cover girls, I can honestly say that *Modern Screen* has been an important part of my film career, and I say that with thanks.

Some of the most exciting articles from *Modern Screen*'s history are on the pages which follow. They capture the spirit of the Hollywood that I have devoted so much of my life to—both on screen and off. I hope that you enjoy this book as much as I have enjoyed being one of *Modern Screen*'s favorite stars!

Debbie Reynolds

SCREEN GODDESSES

t is an undisputed fact that Gloria Swanson was the world's first "screen goddess." Demure Mary Pickford and the willowy Gish sisters were indeed famous the world over through their films, but La Swanson gave new meaning to the term "movie star."

She began as an extra at Chicago's Essanay Studio. Moving to Hollywood in 1915, Gloria signed with Mack Sennett, and in 1918 she starred in eight films at Triangle Studios. When Triangle went bankrupt, she signed with Cecil B. De Mille. Through the six films that she did for him, especially *Male and Female* (1919), Gloria became an international superstar. Even the Prince of Wales was one of her fans!

Gloria was later to recount her incredible fame in the 1920's by admitting: "In those days the public wanted us to live like kings and queens. So we did—and why not? We were in love with life. We were making more money than we ever dreamed existed and there was no reason to believe it would ever stop." In 1926 Gloria's salary from Paramount Pictures was $900,000, and she bought the best of everything. Her bathroom was done in black marble with a gold bathtub. For her chariot, she drove a Lancia with leopard upholstery. Annually she spent $50,000 for gowns, and $10,000 for lingerie. On her way up the ladder to stardom, Gloria decreed, "I have decided that when I am a star, I will be every inch and every moment a star!"

For the June 1931 issue of *Modern Screen,* famed novelist and scenarist Elinor Glyn wrote "The Gloria Swanson I Know" (page 12). The two women first met in 1921 on the set of *The Great Moment,* Glyn's first screenplay, which starred Swanson. Elinor was the Jacqueline Susann of her era. Her daring novel *Three Weeks* was

> "Acting is, really an art form of ingenious lying. The more skillfully you lie, the better the acting."
>
> —Bette Davis
> *Modern Screen*
> February 1937

considered the most shocking book ever published. In it a noble woman seduces a younger man and has a three-week-long affair with him. Generally, if this sort of activity took place in literature, the woman would be struck by lightning for her sins. In Glyn's book the heroine proudly survives, with a smile on her face.

"I could not wait to meet Mrs. Glyn, and she was not a disappointment." Gloria recalled, "She was the first woman I'd ever seen wearing false eyelashes, and although she was old enough to be my grandmother, she got away with it!"

Swanson and Glyn were reunited for *Beyond the Rocks* (1922) which co-starred Rudolph Valentino.

Beginning with the initial issue of the magazine, Elinor Glyn became *Modern Screen's* first in a long line of reporters who were established writing stars from other media. This particular article appeared the same year that Gloria's *Indiscreet* (1931) was released. With the exception of *Sunset Boulevard* (1950), her talkies never matched the success of her silent films. In *Sunset Boulevard,* as fading movie queen Norma Desmond, Swanson protests, "I'm *still* big. It's the pictures that got small!"

"Garbo—Woman Without Love," from the June 1931 issue of *Modern Screen* (page 16), was reported by Harriet Parsons. Harriet was the daughter of famed Hollywood columnist Louella Parsons. Eventually they both wrote articles for *Modern Screen,* becoming the magazine's most famous mother-and-daughter team.

It wasn't until the Academy Award-winning film *Grand Hotel* (1932) that Greta Garbo uttered her most famous line, "I want to be alone....I just want to be alone." However, in this article we find that the die has been cast for the moody Swede to remain a solo act for life. Garbo made her film debut in the Swedish movie *The Atonement of Gosta Berling* (1924), which was spotted by Louis B.

Mayer on a talent-hunting trip to Europe. He signed her to a three-year contract and brought her to America. Her silent films for MGM are virtual classics, especially *Flesh and the Devil* (1927) and *Wild Orchids* (1929). She was one of the few stars of silent films who made the transition to talkies with ease. Her debut sound film, *Anna Christie* (1930), brought her an Academy Award nomination. This *Modern Screen* article appeared about the same time as her film *Susan Lennox: Her Fall and Rise* (1931) was released, co-starring Clark Gable.

"Why Jean Harlow Isn't on Her Own" (page 20), from the July 1933 issue of *Modern Screen,* needs a bit of explanation to grasp the full impact of what was printed about the stars in comparison of what was really going on in their lives. Jean would have been much better off "on her own"!

With her striking platinum-blond hair, Jean Harlow had no trouble being cast as a predatory dame and gun moll in films like *The Public Enemy* (1931) and *The Secret Six* (1931). But not even her title role in *Platinum Blonde* (1931) brought her the brand of stardom she sought. When both Joan Crawford and Norma Shearer turned down the role of Lil Andrews in the upcoming production of *Red-Headed Woman* (1932), over thirty actresses were tested. It was Paul Bern, vice president of MGM, who decided to personally coach and supervise a test of Jean in the role. With his tutoring, and a henna rinse, Harlow was a smash. She landed the part and became the star she longed to be.

At the time, Jean was still living at home (in the house she paid for!) with her pushy mother Mama Jean, and her slippery stepfather, Marino Bello. While Jean was busy at the studio all day, Mama Jean and Bello were busy spending her money quicker than she could earn it.

When short, intellectual, and protective Paul Bern took Jean under his wing, she found the surrogate father who was going to rescue her from her greedy parents. The world was shocked when Jean married Bern on July 2, 1932, but Jean was hopeful that she could make the marriage work. She was in for quite a surprise on her wedding night, when she found out that Bern not only was impotent, but was a sadist as well. When she fled her honeymoon cottage the next morning, she had sustained several bites, bruises, scratches, and blows about the kidneys. The scandal was hushed up—until two months later, when Bern committed suicide. Although he had married the sexiest bombshell in Hollywood, he still could not be sexually aroused. Unable to live with the fact, he shot himself in the head.

Why wasn't Jean on her own? Because as corrupt as her parents were, she felt safer with them.

Unfortunately for Jean, the beatings she had received from Bern had damaged her kidneys in a way that was not evident until 1937, when they failed and Harlow lapsed into a coma. Mama Jean fancied herself a faith healer, and in forbidding a doctor to see her daughter she in essence signed Jean Harlow's death certificate.

Kay Francis was the first actress to grace the cover of *Modern Screen* when it began publication in 1930. From the May 1933 issue comes the instructive "If You Want to Be Like Kay Francis" (page 25). When this article hit the newsstands, Kay was still riding the success of *One Way Passage* (1932), in which she played a terminally ill woman who has a shipboard romance with a convict on his way to the electric chair. She played a completely different role, that of a grasping wife, co-starring with Cary Grant and Carole Lombard in *In Name Only* (1939). "If you want to be like Kay" you'll unfortunately have to become a sad lush, because that is how her life ended in 1968.

Long before there was television or a show called *I Love Lucy* there was an actress and ex-Goldwyn Girl named Lucille Ball. When *Modern Screen* published "The Ball's a-Rollin'" in its April 1939 issue (page 27), Lucille was amid her first success as a wisecracking young actress in *Stage Door* (1937). In this article her "Annabel" films are referred to. They are *The Affairs of Annabel* (1938) and *Annabel Takes a Tour* (1938).

"Ginger's Getting Nowhere Fast," from the May 1939 issue of *Modern Screen* (page 30) is a bit misleading. Although she claims here that she has never set goals for herself, it wasn't long afterward that she won an Academy Award as Best Actress for *Kitty Foyle* (1940). She had made her mark in *42nd Street* (1933) and *Gold Diggers of 1933* (1933). Her teaming with Fred Astaire had already produced nine films by 1939, but it was as a dramatic actress that she wanted to establish herself.

You can act in dozens of movies, but if you don't get any publicity, you'll never become a star! So discovered Rita Hayworth; she reveals the ploy of the pearl-covered dress that put her in the headlines in the December 1941 article "Oomph for Sale" (page 34). That same year she starred opposite James Cagney and Olivia de Havilland in *The Strawberry Blonde,* but her two greatest successes were *Cover Girl* (1944) and *Gilda* (1946).

By the 1950's readers wanted more in-depth stories about the screen goddesses. Hence "What Really Happened to Doris Day," from *Modern Screen's* January 1954 issue (page 36), all about her breast surgery. When this article was published, Doris had just finished starring in *April in Paris* (1953), *By the Light of the Silvery Moon* (1953), and *Calamity Jane* (1953).

THE MODERN
SCREEN
Magazine
10¢
MAY
Marlene Dietrich

RUDOLPH VALENTINO
AS I KNEW HIM • By ELINOR GLYN

MARLENE DIETRICH
May 1931

THE GLORIA SWANSON I KNOW

In the warm and colorful style which is so undeniably hers, this writer gives you a fascinating picture of Gloria Swanson

By ELINOR GLYN

IT is now ten years since I first went to Hollywood—and what a change has taken place! Only by looking back can one appreciate the force in the personalities which have survived. For some who were famous then are now dead—think of poor Barbara La Mar and Alma Rubens—and some are married and happy, and some are out of the public eye, and forgotten, their stars set and their swan song sung; but Gloria Swanson is just as fascinating as ever!

In those long years ago movies were not the sophisticated, realistic bits of art the talkies are today. The clothes were ridiculous, the treatment of the stories bore no resemblance to real life. Hardly any of the actors or directors or actresses had traveled, and nearly all of them appeared to New York or European eyes a little grotesque in their fashions, having huge bobbed heads with masses of curls, when in Paris the heads were small and neat, and so on. Everyone in the movies, however, was entirely pleased with himself or herself, having no other standard to go by and all felt that outside opinion was silly and even impertinent. The bliss of ignorance and the power of gold kept Hollywood quite satisfied.

I REMEMBER well when I first saw Gloria Swanson in the Paramount Studio. It was just after the birth of her little daughter, and she was to return to the screen after a year of domestic bliss to star in my .first picture, "The Great Moment." I saw immediately that she was full of charm and magnetism, which emerged even through the queer clothes and "dressed" head which represented *chic* then in Hollywood. I was surprised that she was so tiny. I had thought she must be tall from her pictures. I have never seen such beautiful blue eyes—so full of meaning and character. I used to love to paint little pictures of them—just the eyes. Her mother-of-pearl skin was fresh as a tea rose, and her feet were a poem! I did not think her figure was very good then, and I remember trying to persuade her not to stoop, and to exercise her neck and shoulders. Her hair used to be dressed by "Hatty," a very clever colored hairdresser who did all the hair at the studio (one of the best hairdressers I have ever seen—it was not her fault if she had never been to Paris and only produced what was asked of her by movie notions!). But even when thus turned out by local talent, wearing what to me seemed impossible clothes and with a

some question of someone trying to cheat her. I remember being profoundly impressed by her most remarkable common sense—her arguments were all so logical and level-headed. I said to myself that I, a mature woman, could not have answered as cleverly.

At that period Gloria had supreme self-confidence. She had conquered her world, and as yet knew of no other.

WE had a delightful time making "The Great Moment." She entered into all my ideas, and made a perfect heroine. When the picture was finished and I left for Europe again I noticed a great change in her. She had gained poise, she held back her shoulders, and no longer stooped—her hairdress made her head a normal size, and her clothes came from New York. Gloria was exquisitely attractive now.

Even in those far-back days she had that rare faculty of absorbing the best of whatever atmosphere she was in. She had the great quality of perception.

It was not until we were making our second picture together, "Beyond the Rocks," with Rudolph Valentino as the leading man, that I discovered that Gloria was a sculp-

Elinor Glyn says of Gloria Swanson: "There is mystery and infinite possibility in the depths of the blue of her eyes, and a strange wistfulness. She could have been a Roman empress. She would have upheld the position. She has so many sides."

head almost as wide as her shoulders, Gloria just exuded charm, and I do not see how any man could remain cool about her! I must say that not many of them did! Gloria was the only case then, on and off the screen, of a woman expressing "It"!

SHE did not trouble much about books in those days. She was chiefly occupied in enjoying life and acquiring stardom. I grew very fond of her. I remember one day sitting in her dressing room—oh, how she must laugh now at the memory of the weird taste of it!—well, I was sitting in her dressing room while Hatty was conjuring those marvelous waves and coils into a structure, when the telephone rang. I could not help hearing the conversation. It was something to do with the lease of Gloria's house, or

tor! She showed me some of her work one day quite casually and I was amazed. It was full of talent. A head of her little child was truly inspired. This was a new side of her—a dreamy, poetic, lovable side. I could see the imagination working more profoundly in her than she herself realized. She had a natural exquisiteness emerging through everything she did. She read poetry now and only very rarely showed that wild streak which seemed to be a gypsy part of her nature that had to periodically break loose—and perhaps added to her attraction!

Her lovely eyes always had a message in them. They held possibility of sorrow and passion—and were always interesting and never banal. Gloria could never *bore* anyone!

ONE day when we were making "Beyond the Rocks" and were on location doing the Alps scenes, a great beam from the very high camera platform fell when we were eating our lunch. It might have killed us both if it had been two inches nearer. Gloria did not turn a hair or move. She had always great courage and nerve.

Below is an actual picture of Gloria in her dressing-room of the old Lasky studio having her hair done by "Hatty," the clever colored hairdresser whom Elinor Glyn mentions in this article.

(Above) Gloria and Elinor Glyn during the making of "Beyond the Rocks." The small picture at the left gives you an excellent idea of the sort of coiffure Gloria Swanson went in for in the old days.

We had a farewell dinner party when I was leaving again for Europe, and I remember Gloria's toast to me was one of the prettiest I have ever had. She said when she was as old as I was she hoped she would look just the same as I did!

By that time other stars were rising who might have been rivals for Gloria, but not one of them had her personality. She always seems the result of many lives—there is nothing colorless or "new" about her. There is mystery and infinite possibility in the depths of the blue of her eyes, and a strange wistfulness. She could have been a Roman empress. She would have upheld the position. She has so many sides. There is a scene in her picture, "What a Widow!" when she is supposed to be in a tantrum while having a fitting. She throws the dress on the floor, and I remember her telling me once how clothes going wrong annoyed her—a quaint little childish trait which perhaps she felt she wanted to laugh at on the screen. I wonder if she still gets annoyed when lines go wrong and fingers are clumsy?

Continued on page 26

14

PORTRAITS

Photograph by John Miehle

Gloria Swanson is now known professionally as Gloria Swanson, Incorporated. The rumors persist that Gloria is going to marry Gene Markey, celebrated writer, but Gloria herself will neither verify nor deny them. Here's something you didn't know about her: she usually eats lunch in her town car on the way to her various appointments.

GARBO—

Nils Asther and Greta Garbo made love on the screen in several pictures. But they never made love in real life. Theirs was a friendship born of similar natures and ancestry, no more.

Says this author: "Garbo knows — knows instinctively, I think, and has always known it—that the illusion of oneness of two beings which is created by a great love is an illusion and nothing more; that in reality these two must remain separate beings forever. . ."

WOMAN WITHOUT LOVE

In the days when Greta Garbo and John Gilbert were two names always linked together both on the screen and in real life. There were many reasons why Garbo could not love John.

It was through Mauritz Stiller, as you probably know, that Greta Garbo became such a tremendous success. She respected, admired—even worshipped Stiller. But she was not in love with him, ever.

A great many writers have told what they considered the truth about Garbo's love life. Here, for the first time, are the real facts

By HARRIET PARSONS

WHY has Greta Garbo never fallen in love? Why has she, who of all women seems created for love, been cheated of her birthright—the birthright of every woman from shopgirl to queen?

Is it fame, the merciless spotlight which plays upon her, which has cheated Greta Garbo of her share of love? Or is it the fundamental disillusionment of her nature which has kept her from falling in love as other women —even famous women do? Both, perhaps.

You can count on the fingers of one hand the men whose names have been linked with hers. There was Mauritz Stiller, the Swedish director who discovered her. There was John Gilbert, idol of millions, who wooed and lost her. There was Nils Asther. And young Prince Sigmund of Sweden. And Sorenson, who Hollywood whispered was a prince but who turned out to be the son of a Swedish box maker. Of them all only two— the first two—really touched her heart. And of those two one is dead because Garbo did not love him and the other broken in spirit—perhaps for the same reason.

ASTHER, young Sigmund, and Sorenson really do not count. After her split with Gilbert, Garbo used to see Nils occasionally. They were countrymen and

they shared in common a moodiness and a love of solitude. It was natural that they should sense a sympathetic understanding in one another—that they should meet and find things to talk about. There was never more than a casual friendship between them. But the press, robbed of the choice morsel which the Garbo-Gilbert romance had long offered, sought to present Asther as Gilbert's successor—sought to create a new romance where none existed. And Garbo lost a friend. Nils has since married the woman whom he loves.

As for the youthful and royal Sigmund—another bit of press whimsy. During her visit to Sweden after Stiller's death Garbo was seen in public with the princeling—which was quite enough to start tongues wagging. Garbo is so rarely seen in public with anyone—and when that anyone happens to be a prince! It was even whispered that the Swedish authorities had had words with her on the subject, according to report. Her own single and succinct comment on the rumor when she returned to America was, "I don't play around with kids."

Sorenson, the tall blond young Swede who wasn't a prince, was in love with Garbo. But Garbo wasn't in love with him. And it takes two to make a romance— everywhere, that is, except in the press. Son of a millionaire Swedish box manufacturer, he was drawn to

Greta Garbo—the woman so closely
associated with the expression of love
on the screen—has known remarkably
few men in her life. Mauritz Stiller,
John Gilbert, Nils Asther, Prince Sigmund, and Sorenson. Did she love any
of them? This writer tells us.

Hollywood by Greta's tales of that amazing colony. And quite possibly by Greta herself. During the months that he spent here he was constantly in her company, and it was apparent that she liked him immensely. Liked, not loved. And so when his passport expired he went back to Sweden and boxes. The prince charming legend subsided like a pricked balloon. And the world was thwarted once more in its attempt to construct a romance for its reigning queen of hearts.

But what of Stiller and Gilbert? Surely, you say, one of these two must have quickened love in that inscrutable, secret heart of Garbo's. I do not think so. Even though Garbo fainted at the news of Stiller's death. Even though she once almost eloped with Gilbert.

WITH Stiller it was the old Svengali-Trilby story. He was the master, she the pupil. Everyone knows how Stiller forced the Metro-Goldwyn-Mayer studio, because of their eagerness to secure his directorial genius, to accept his young acolyte also. Everyone knows how Garbo rose to world-fame through her achievements in the studios of Hollywood while Stiller returned defeated and humiliated to die in Sweden. It is already an old wives' tale.

Stiller's broken heart was not the result solely of his professional failure. He was jealous, hopelessly jealous of John Gilbert. Gilbert, handsome, young, gallant, could offer Garbo what he, for all his magnificent brain and wise, tender guidance, could never give her. It must have torn his heart to think of the two of them together. The sight of his own plain face must have filled him with an agony of loathing and despair. For the master had fallen in love with the pupil.

Garbo respected, admired—even worshipped Stiller. But she was not in love with him. The shadow of his lonely death still hangs over her, has deepened and pointed her fundamental sadness. And it is doubtless partly because of that shadow that she is unable to surrender her heart completely to any man.

SHE holds herself irrevocably and inexcusably account-able. One day a woman friend was visiting her at her home. Garbo insisted upon playing over and over a collection of melancholy Swedish records. "Why do you play that sad music?" asked the friend. "It must depress you frightfully."

"Yes," said Garbo. "It reminds me of one I hurt—one I murdered. But that is good—it is right that I should remember." No one else in the world would dream of saying that Garbo killed Mauritz Stiller. No one could possibly hold her responsible that a man died because she did not love him.

John Gilbert, too, was doomed to find only unhappiness in his love for Garbo. Garbo was drawn to him—he was her first real friend in America. His spirit of gaiety, his dashing good looks, his obvious infatuation for her, must have created in her at least the illusion of being in love. And yet, in the last analysis, Greta Garbo was not in love with John Gilbert. Once, it is true, he persuaded her to elope with him—but at the last moment she ran away and fled back to Hollywood alone.

The factors which kept Greta Garbo from surrender-ing to the man who came nearest of any to winning her were three. There was that ever-present shadow of Stiller—Stiller who hated John Gilbert. There was fame —the relentless, avid curiosity of the public and the press which has spoiled so many things for Garbo. A romance with John Gilbert could never be anything other than common property. Any romance of Garbo's would be that—but particularly so if the man happened to be equally in the limelight, equally the idol of millions. And Gilbert was then riding the crest of his popularity. What chance would those two have had for happiness? Ina Claire found out later the tragedy of *Continued on page 22*

The MODERN SCREEN Magazine's

GALLERY

OF

HONOR

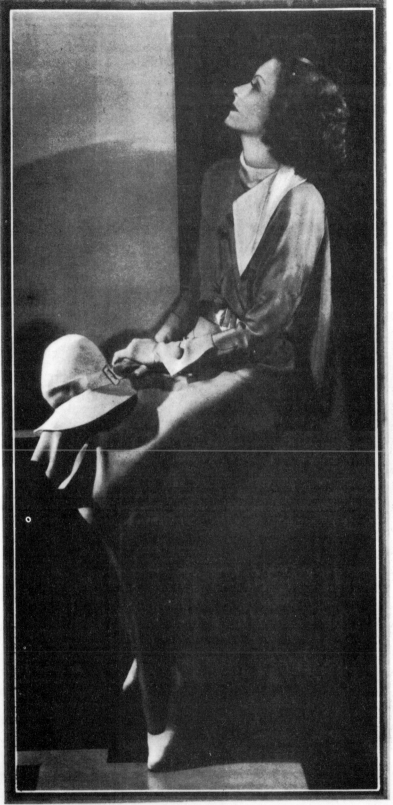

Photograph by Clarence Sinclair Bull

GRETA GARBO

—whose tenacity of purpose refuses to be weakened by the world's curiosity and who still goes her own way regardless—visiting the Mexican theater in the Latin quarter of Los Angeles and once a week having sauerkraut and beer in a little Hollywood restaurant.

WHY JEAN HARLOW ISN'T "ON HER OWN"

J. B. Scott

By CARTER BRUCE

THE stationery was pale lavender, slightly scented, and the ink that penned the discontented words was purple. The little square envelope was postmarked Kansas City. It was addressed in a round, almost juvenile hand to Miss Jean Harlow and it read in part:

"Gosh, if I had your looks and your money and your opportunity to meet swell men in Hollywood I sure wouldn't be hanging around home like you do. I'd have me a snappy apartment and a good-looking roadster and I'd come and go just as I pleased. After all, Jean, why don't you cut loose and have your freedom while you are young and beautiful and can enjoy yourself?"

"And that," said Jean Harlow herself, reaching for the letter she had just handed me, "is the question most frequently asked me by young girls. It was also the predominating query put to me in person when I was recently touring about the country meeting girls between the ages of sixteen and twenty-one. Boiled down to cold facts, whether we want to admit it or not, it merely amounts to this: Miss Modern America is straining at the home leashes . . . dying to get out and live in an apartment by herself or with another broadminded and equally 'free' girl friend . . . and this same Miss America can't understand why I'm still checking in under the same roof with my mother and stepfather when I have the means of

Wide World

whooping around on my own!" Thus spake Jean.

America's most famous platinum blonde was half-sitting, half-reclining against a divan corner in her own living room. Contrary to the popular idea that only one thing at a time can be done thoroughly, Jean was having plenty of success performing *three* important tasks. She was relaxing for the half hour prescribed by her doctor to follow her noon meal . . . she was reading over an assortment of fan mail . . . and granting me an interview . . . all at the same time, and doing a darn good job of

... Many young girls wonder why Jean Harlow—with her money and friends and necessities for enjoying freedom—still lives at home. Jean has unusual ideas about the business of going "on your own"

On the opposite page you will find Jean and Ivan Lebedeff at Lilyan Tashman's tea. Jean's mother has an interesting reason for knowing where and with whom Jean is. The other picture on that page is Jean with her mother. A miracle of understanding and tact—that mother.

all three. In fact, the entire angle of this story was Jean's own.

"I've often wondered," she had said, "why interviewers don't take the trouble to find out the questions that are most frequently put to a star by the public . . . which means an answer to the query that is of the greatest general interest. I think I have been interviewed on every topic under the sun except this one important thing that almost all the girls who write to me ask about." It was then that Jean had shown me the letter from Kansas City. She said: "It is typical. The same idea has been put to me thousands of times and I'd love to answer it."

SHE continued: "I think the answer, at least as it is true in my case, might be important. I think it might help.

"I'm not going to preach. And heaven forbid that I should sound like a moralist. The simple reason I have

never gone "on my own" is that I am happier, more contented and *have more freedom of action* under my parents' roof than I would have if I moved away. If that were not true then I would most certainly be in one of those ducky little apartments so avidly recommended as the seat of all freedom.

"Every time I hear this 'apartment' question I feel like soundly shaking . . . not Miss Freedom Questing Eighteen . . . but her parents, who seem to believe that the way to protect a daughter is to lock the doors after ten o'clock, supervise girl and boy friendships, and lay down house rules after the manner of a corrective institution. How silly that is. I know from my own experience that the quickest and safest and sanest way to keep the four walls of Home Sweet Home about a darling daughter is to open those doors so wide it is impossible to be conscious of them.

"I think my mother is just *Continued on page 22*

Why Jean Isn't "On Her Own"

Continued from page 21

about the smartest and cleverest and most interesting woman I have ever met in my life. But at the same time . . . like every other mother in the world . . . she wants to know where I am going, and with whom I am going when I leave her hearthstone at night. She not only finds out all that, but she also finds out what time I expect to return.

"But it is the way she trained me to volunteer this information on my own hook which is so smart!

MY mother has never made me feel that she was checking up on me because she was worried about my conduct, or my judgment in people, or the fact that I couldn't take care of myself. When I first started to go out with men, she merely made it clear that it was a matter of *my own* convenience that she should know where I was. Do you see what I mean? In case an important message should come for me, it was equally as important that she or my step-father should know where to reach me so that the message might be delivered. The hour I returned from my date had absolutely no bearing on Right and Wrong . . . but it *did* have a bearing on the hour breakfast was to be served in the morning.

"If I was planning to come in late, she invariably instructed the servants to grant me an hour's leeway. In other words, *where* I was going and *what* I was doing was made to be not only my own private affair . . . but my mother's as well. It had a definite bearing on her job which was the successful management of her household. Now I ask you," smiled Jean, "if that isn't a pretty cute idea? My mother knows where I have been almost every hour of my life. I have actually been checked in and out as rigidly as the most carefully guarded debutante, but never once have I been made to feel that my freedom was being cramped.

"My mother, bless her heart, once made the most generous statement ever made by a mother to her own daughter. She said: '*If what I advise you to do, Jean, is not perfectly clear to you . . . if it does not seem right to your own way of looking at the question . . . then I must advise you to use your own judgment!*' Never once has my mother given me advice I have not asked for. My mother has lived a free and interesting life. She is a sophisticated and charming matron. I think, as a girl, she was the same sort of person I am. Therefore I am more than anxious to seek her experience to help solve my own problems. If the mothers of America could only get it over to their daughters that they are not creatures apart . . . if they could only let them understand that they, too, have known the same thrills, the same temptations, the same joys and dangers and sorrows that their daughters regard as so *secret* unto themselves, what a great difference there would be in the homes of the girls who want to get away from

mother 'because she doesn't understand.'

"I smoked my first package of cigarettes when I was ten years old! Yes, mother caught me at it. I guess she was horrified but she didn't let me guess that. She merely put it up to me as a beauty tip . . . not a matter of slackened morals. She said: 'Baby, if you start smoking so young you will have awfully yellow nicotined fingers by the time you are grown. Why don't you wait until you are seventeen before you take up smoking seriously? If you find you still enjoy the habit, I won't say anything.' Well, I started smoking at seventeen. I've been smoking continuously ever since. My mother has never said a word. She made her bargain with me when I was ten years old . . . and she has kept her promise not to say anything.

"Of course it isn't possible for any three people in the world, no matter how broad their outlook, to agree on every subject. For instance, suppose I wish to spend a weekend at Caliente, or San Francisco. As a rule my mother and Bello are glad to accompany me. If there is some reason of theirs for our not going . . . they give in to me. As a rule it is a darn good reason and I will abide by it. But in one of those rare instances when we don't get together and my desire to go is so much stronger than their reasons for wanting to remain home . . . then we fall back on that agreement to 'use my own judgment.'

ISN'T it too bad that 'Freedom' to the average young girl has come to mean cocktail drinking, cigarette smoking, late hours, unchaperoned romances? Are they, then, so attractive?

"How can these things stack up against the authentic freedom which a well regulated home allows? If I lived alone I should be bothered with thousands of details I do not even know exist in my mother's home. After all, even the 'freest' cannot devote her entire time to smoking, drinking or love-making!

"I feel this way, too: If I lived alone I would not have the freedom of social life which I now enjoy. I should have to be careful of gossip wagging tongues about everything I did. A great many things would be denied me because I would have to be so careful of 'What People Will Say.'

"But all these reasons are unimportant as compared to the real true reason of why I make my home with my parents. I enjoy them . . . I like them . . . I can have more fun with them than with any other two people in the world. Twice in my lifetime I have been separated from mother, both times through marriage. Each time I have come back under her roof with a heart-felt thanksgiving that her love and her home is my refuge from heartbreak and disappointment and sorrow which the world has invariably dealt me when I was 'on my own.'"

Garbo—Woman Without Love

Continued from page 18

being married to a world-symbol—to a man who was known as the world's lover.

BUT there was something deeper than the thought of Stiller, more fundamental than her fear of publicity that shattered Garbo's nearest approach to a romance. The thing that made Garbo run away on the eve of her marriage to John Gilbert was the same thing that makes her walk suddenly out of the home of a friend. The same thing that makes her grow suddenly aloof and unapproachable in the midst of her most congenial moods. A sudden profound sense of the inadequacy of human companionship; a sudden desperate need to keep herself to herself. Garbo, in spite of the many childlike qualities of her nature, knows with a grim unhappy certitude the fundamental oneness of the human soul. Knows that in the last analysis we all walk through life alone and blindfolded. Knows that we may reach out gropingly to touch other human beings and seek to draw them to us—but that we can never, try as we may, make them part of us. Garbo knows—knows it instinctively, I think, and has always known it—that the illusion of the oneness of two beings which is created by physical love is an illusion and nothing more; that in reality those two must remain separate beings forever, however deep their love, however great their desire to partake of the essence of one another's souls.

And so even love—the common denominator to which all women can be reduced, has failed to bring Greta Garbo to the level of ordinary everyday existence. Whether she wills it or not she remains apart—lovely, mysterious and eternally the Unknown. Perhaps it is this fact, that she has never been in love, which is at the very heart of her mystery. The mystery which millions will worship and adore forever.

Jean Harlow keeps her stockings lovely looking this way

IF YOU WANT TO BE LIKE
KAY FRANCIS

By

FAITH

BALDWIN

. . . Any girl could be like her—if not physically, then spiritually or mentally. All you have to do is to learn how from this story

IF you want to *look* like Kay Francis you must be tall and slender with magnificent soft, shining black hair and gray-green eyes. You must have a wide, generous mouth and beautiful teeth, expressive hands, a fine textured fair, pale skin and the tiniest feet. You must have character in your face and good bones and a light, graceful carriage.

Most of these things you must be born with; some may be cultivated if your general build and coloring follow the Francis lines. So if you want to look like Kay Francis — and who wouldn't want to look like her?—you must look like this. But if you want to *be* like her, be like her in character and emotion reaction and attitude toward life, that's different.

The day I saw her we sat before a bright coal fire in the living room of her brother's charming New York house, and she wore a black negligée, very plain, with flowing sleeves, and I asked her if she'd mind if I sat and looked at her for a couple of weeks. For that's the way she affects you. And she laughed, and said she wouldn't mind; which was courteous of her. She said it in her low, pretty voice, which can't quite manage the R's and so slides over them, much to her horror.

We had something in common, for we had attended the same school, Miss Fuller's, in Ossining, New York, but, alas, at very different times. So we talked about Miss Fuller's and about the Cathedral School in Garden City to which Kay went afterwards. About her first

marriage at seventeen, and about her original birthplace in Oklahoma, which she doesn't recall, and small wonder, as her parents moved to California when she was a year old, and later to Denver. And, when Kay was four, to New York City.

The background of Kay Francis is bound up with the stage, for her mother, Katherine Clinton, was a well-known actress, and, I judged from the little things her daughter said about her to me, a wise and wonderful mother as well.

Kay's life has been colorful and varied. She has excelled in school athletics. She has in her school days written a play and played the leading male rôle in it. She has taken a secretarial course, travelled abroad, and been secretary to such important people as Mrs. Dwight Morrow, Mrs. W. K. Vanderbilt and others.

AND she has been on the stage, as the Player Queen in the modern version of "Hamlet," as a member of the Stuart Walker Stock Company, and on Broadway in such plays as "Venus," "Crime" and "Elmer the Great."

After that came Hollywood, and the rest is motion picture history. Her favorite rôle was the one she played in her recent "One Way Passage," a great picture, and she very much liked doing "Trouble in Paradise," as well. Her latest picture is called "The Keyhole."

As you know, she is married to Kenneth McKenna. And I know she likes books, airplane travel, sailing, tennis, sunshine, fresh air, and a clean face — which, besides being likes, are also beauty secrets — and watching all sorts of sports. She plays bridge and backgammon, and appears to possess a perfect menagerie of domestic animals. She drives a Cadillac—and a *Continued on page 26*

Want to Be Like Kay?

Ford—and sails quite a big boat.

As for her dislikes, they seem to include fittings—and this from a woman who wears lovely clothes more beautifully, I think, than anyone on the screen — interviewers, yet she was charming to me, and posing for pictures and portraits.

I am telling you all this because peoples' likes and dislikes are sometimes keys to their personalities. But it isn't enough to like and dislike the same things as Kay Francis in order to be like her.

To be like her, you must be vital. You must be interested in strange people and strange places, you must be ready to embrace change and adventure when they come your way. You must be ready for new fields of endeavor. Think of the variety and changes of her life. From schoolgirl to secretary, and from secretary to stage and screen! You must be alive, every inch of you, and you must be adaptable. You must be a hard worker. Only a hard worker could have accomplished as much in a time as comparatively short.

You must have a sense of humor, which laughs with others, and at yourself. There is a difference, you know. Kay Francis has humor which is like a clear cold spring of water, but not too cold; sun warmed, let us say. It ripples back of her laughter, and the light in her sea-gray eyes—stormy eyes, I think. It is very refreshing.

I ASKED her what quality in people appealed to her most. She told me promptly but thoughtfully, simplicity. I do not believe she means the simplicity of purely mindless, primitive things. She is not a primitive person. She is entirely of this world, poised, sure of herself, friendly, but not giving herself in intimate speech to every passerby. A good listener, an excellent conversationalist, as styled and chic and charming as one of the frocks Banton so brilliantly designs for her.

She has ideas. She knows which pictures she likes and which she doesn't like. She knows which parts she can feel, and, feeling, play. She has an excellent grasp of the mechanics of screen writing, the perfect construction which should go into the making of the perfect picture, and she is quick to see flaws in technique or characterization.

If you want to be like Kay Francis, you can't stop learning. You can't just rest on your laurels. You must set yourself a goal, and when you win through to it you must set yourself another goal and try for that one, too. Here is a self-contained person, quiet in gesture, restrained in speech but alive to her long finger tips, nothing inert about her, nothing phlegmatic. But a controlled person. I imagine that that control has been a goal and that she set it for herself.

If you want to be like Kay Francis you will have no use for swank. You will be faintly amused and more than faintly disgusted at the people who swagger in their talk, and who, having themselves won a certain position, look *down* instead of *at* other people, and who go suddenly high-hat.

If you want to be like Kay Francis you will be yourself. That is a paradox, I suppose, as perhaps you know your real self does not resemble Miss Francis in the least. But if you are yourself, you are like her in one very basic quality. For she is herself, quite perfectly, and does not try to be like anyone else. And how very wise she is.

In other words, if you want to be like Kay Francis you will be first of all your very own self, with a respect for the personality which is uniquely your own, a respect which isn't in the least vanity, and which is a very valuable thing to possess. For the rest you will be entirely natural. You will have no little affectations which, while they may be endearing for a time, soon become a bit boring. You will care for enduring things, the world which lies beyond your door, books, knowledge—and for simplicity.

I DO not mean simplicity of the "simple" sort. I mean a rather expensive simplicity. For it is, you know, the "simplest" clothes that are most expensive. The simplest dinner, which is the best, is generally prepared from the very finest materials. And in order to live simply one lives expensively. Nor do I mean expense in dollars. I mean that in order to live one's life as simply as possible, one must pay for it in a number of ways.

I remember that Miss Francis told me that when she is working she goes to bed at eight o'clock. If she consents to go out during the making of a picture she leaves a party at about nine-thirty. Ten is her deadline. Now, that is working hard and living simply, isn't it? And sanely, too, and wisely? But it costs her something, I imagine, in explanations and all the rest. We are cut so on a pattern that when any one deviates from it and makes his own pattern we are apt to be exclamatory about it. But when Kay Francis says she must go home at nine-thirty, she goes. This is her life. She intends to live it as she sees fit, and if she sees fit to be, for a time, a nine-thirty girl in a three-thirty town, she'll do it.

If you want to be like Kay Francis you must figure out where you are going and why, and when you have decided, you must go there serenely, as befitting a gentlewoman. With a little laughter back of your eyes, and with confidence in yourself and in your star.

In other words, if you want to be like Kay Francis you must be a very real person, and a person with not only genuine physical beauty, but genuine character.

If you *are* like her, I congratulate you. If you want to be like her I congratulate you also; it is a step in a very right and praiseworthy direction.

Gloria Swanson

Continued from page 14

AFTER making "Beyond the Rocks" I did not see her again for some years. She went to New York and made success after success. And then she went to Europe—and returned, having fallen in love and married a French Marquis. After this for a while her charm seemed dimmed to me. Her magnetism was submerged. The exquisite capricious Roman empress slept! And in her place was an ordinary wife and mother!

But now she seems to have stepped up into her own niche once more, expressing her old charm, with the added grace of cultivation and polish—only I do not want her ever to be "kinda cute," or to act a foolish, tipsy widow part again, nor that of a cart-wheeling flapper, but to be the graceful siren enslaving the hearts of men, while her blue eyes show the soul within, lovely, aloof, undaunted, its possibilities still a mystery, its desires unsatisfied by all else but eternity.

THE Ball's A-ROLLIN'

BY ELISABETH BADGER

Until the "Annabel" series, you mostly heard of Lucille in spasms of notoriety.

Yes, after years of movie-making, Lucille's now come into her own

AFTER FIVE halting years, the strange but happy career of Lucille Ball is beginning to gather momentum.

You all know Lucille. She's that tall, lanky girl with the sullen expression who looks vaguely like Ginger Rogers, wears clothes with distinction, takes pratt falls on request, and delivers lines with such stinging effect.

You know her now as "Annabel," of the pert series in which she devastatingly pokes fun at the movie queens whose ranks she is about to join.

You've known her in past spasms of notoriety, such as the time fashion-expert Bernard Newman pronounced her Hollywood's smartest woman, and dressed her in his own creations to prove it; the year her rumored engagement to Broderick Crawford kept Mother Helen Broderick busy issuing denials; her small triumph in "Stage Door;" and the several occasions when her marriage to director Al Hall has seemed imminent.

But between these flare-ups of publicity there have been long intervals when it seemed to Lucille that even her own studio didn't know she was there. Since her first day in Hollywood, she's been waging a private battle for recognition, with weapons sometimes comic and crude, sometimes painstaking and intelligent, but—at long last—successful.

"Annabel" has turned the trick. From now on Lucille is destined for more leading roles and fewer black and blue spots.

"What they don't realize," she said, happily settled over an order of cracked crab in the pleasant gloom of Lucey's restaurant, "is that though I've been around so many years, I've never really had any experience. I've still got a lot to learn about acting. The 'Annabel' series has helped a lot, but my chief function at the studio before

that was taking pratt falls when nobody else would do it."

Looking at her—small young face, deep blue eyes, and brooding mouth appearing intermittently beneath pulled down hatbrim and the year's longest feather—you might easily have mistaken her for a full-fledged movie star. But it took only a few minutes to discover the pleasant fact that she's still an ordinary mortal. As yet untainted with the upper-bracket idiom of rubies, racing stables and investments, she talks comfortably of bringing the family out by bus, of Chautauqua County picnics at Elysian Park and other such homely matters.

She's a realist, a strange mixture of dry humor, serious ambition, disillusionment and optimism, this veteran of the screen who hasn't had any *Continued on page 28*

Continued on page 28

experience. Lucille did more acting in her school days than she's done during her three years at RKO. Her career began before the mirror at home in Jamestown, N. Y., and flourished at school where, with her mother's help, she produced and directed plays for which she made the costumes, scenery and even the tickets and posters herself.

At the age of eleven, la belle Ball toured the surrounding countryside in one of her productions and became a local celebrity. At sixteen, she looked up dramatic school advertisements and chose John Murray Anderson's American Academy of Dramatic Art in New York, where Bette Davis was then the star pupil.

"I stayed there a year and a half," said Lucille, "but I thought there were too many lessons—music, singing, dancing—and too little acting. So I decided to get myself a real job on the stage.

"I got jobs all right. I was always chosen in chorus line-ups because I was so tall and conspicuous. But I just didn't have the knack of getting along with the other girls. Nothing was said, no one was actually nasty. They just froze me out, that's all. After I'd been forced out of several shows that way, I went home."

FOR several years she alternated between running home to mother, and running away from home to get back to Broadway.

"I got a job in a road company of 'Rio Rita' and rehearsed for six weeks—without pay, of course. Then someone announced that all the show girls had to be ballet dancers, so they fired us. That finished me. I decided the stage was a gyp, and that I wanted a job that paid regularly every week. So I got one as a model in a clothing house. Only $25 a week, but I knew I was going to get it. Those people are still my friends. I see them every time I go to New York.

"When I had learned a little more about how to wear clothes and how to talk and was beginning to know my way around New York, I got a job as a model at Hattie Carnegie's and stayed there for three years, doing photographic modeling on the side.

"In the meantime, I fell in love with a little guy who owned a silk business. He's very well known around New York. He was a pretty nice fellow. Anyway, I'd never known anything else, so I was contented.

"I almost got married then. But I used to see girls pushing baby carriages on Riverside Drive. You know, those black ones that look like you expect it to rain any minute. I hate those things! I think they were what decided me. So I planned to go away on a long vacation.

"Just then I was asked to make a test for a show girl spot in Eddie Cantor's 'Roman Scandals.' If they'd had a chance to see me in a bathing suit, they never would have picked me, I was so skinny then. Fortunately by the time I got there all the girls had been chosen, but one backed out at the last moment, so they signed me without a test, and shipped us right out to California.

"When Samuel Goldwyn saw us lined up in our bathing suits he looked at me and said, 'My God, where did they find *that?*' But it was too late to do anything about it. I played in 'Roman Scandals,' and then we were all signed for a year.

"I began figuring out ways of making

myself noticed. They were constantly lining us up for inspection by somebody. Gosh, how we hated it! I used to stuff things inside my bathing suit to make bulges. Then just as they'd get to me in the line-up I'd make some fresh crack. One day I had a piece of bright red paper and I tore it up and stuck little pieces all over my face and neck and arms and legs and stood there in the line-up, looking as if I had some awful disease.

"I kept on clowning around the set and gradually people began to notice me. Eddie Cantor took me aside and said, 'Lucille, you have a gift for comedy, a sense of timing that's priceless. Why don't you break away from this and try to act?'

"When Walter Winchell made his first picture 'Broadway Through a Keyhole,' he gave me the same advice. Lowell Sherman directed a picture over there and gave me more encouragement than anyone else. But I was afraid.

"All this time I wasn't learning much about acting, but I was learning a lot about myself. When you have to stand up against a bunch of girls like that it makes you analyze yourself and how you compare with the others in brains and beauty and personality. I had a chance to study a lot of big stars at close range, too. That gives you confidence. You see them acting up and you think, 'Well, if these great people really behave like that, I can't be so bad after all.'

"At the end of the year, some of the girls had married and some had found boy friends and mink coats. A few of us found ourselves still sitting up in the same little apartment where we'd started out—and we didn't know whether we were right or wrong."

Evidently the answer was "wrong," for Lucille left the Goldwyn lot and joined the stock company at Columbia, playing bits at $75 a week. With all that money to throw around, she decided it was time to send for her family.

"My young brother was already out here," she said, "but from the first moment I saw California I felt like I wanted to share it with as many people as I could. Why, there's a whole colony of people from Jamestown living in downtown Los Angeles, who came out here just because of things we wrote back home. Anyway, I sent for my mother and grandfather to

come out on the bus. Just before they arrived, I lost my job."

That didn't deter la Ball. She borrowed $500, rented a little white house that she knew her mother would love and borrowed a huge limousine in which to meet the bus. When the welcome was over, she started work as a dress-extra. Mammy and grandpappy had to be fed, no matter how her pride hurt.

"But it turned out for the best," said Lucille—and that's a phrase that keeps recurring in her conversation—"because as a result of that I got the job as a mannequin in 'Roberta,' and that led to my present contract."

THE studio, however, was even more apathetic to her talents than the rest of the world had been. Heroically, she tried everything. She abandoned her childish gags and studied acting in earnest, with Ginger Rogers' mother as her teacher. She worked hard to improve her face, her hair, her voice, her make-up. She acted in plays put on by Mrs. Rogers in a little theatre on the lot, and got an offer to appear in a Brock Pemberton play. But just as she was eagerly leaving for New York, the studio cast her in "The Girl From Paris," with Lily Pons.

"They gave me that part because the girl had to take a pratt-fall," said Lucille, undeceived, "and I did it."

George Kaufman promised her a part in the New York production of "Stage Door," but just then Mary Astor's diary made the headlines and Mr. Kaufman took to the woods, Lucille's contract with him.

The third time, she made it. Two years ago she went east for a role in "Hey Diddle Diddle," played out of town, got grand notices and was all set for the New York run of the play when she was recalled for the picture, "Stage Door."

One more wallop was waiting for Lucille. When she walked into the office, Director Gregory La Cava took one look at her and said, "No, that's not the girl I wanted." And that was that.

"He had taken a dislike to me, that's all," she explained. "I tried for weeks to get the part, but he wouldn't even give me a chance. At last I gave up hope, and one day I went to the hairdresser and had my hair dyed black, hoping it would change my luck. I was under the dryer and my hair was still wet when I got a call to come to the studio to help another girl make a test for the part I wanted. I was so burned up, I didn't even put on a dress—went over in a smock, with my hair wet, and read Ginger's part in the test. I was just as nasty and rude to Mr. La Cava as I could be. I was ashamed of myself afterwards, but that's the way you have to treat 'em, I guess. The next thing I knew I was given the part."

So it all turned out for the best. Lucille's career is rolling along. Her mother and brother and grandfather and cousin Cleo are still living in the little white house.

"I lived with them for a long while," she said, "but when Cleo came out there wasn't enough room, so I moved into an apartment. So you see we have a very happy little clique, all to ourselves."

On the subject of romance, she was typically forthright. "I've been going with Al Hall for two years," she stated without coquetry, "but I'm not anxious to get married now. I'm too interested in my career. I'm just beginning to get somewhere and I'm very happy. And besides —those black baby carriages still haunt me."

The Water's Fine!

Jane Russell, lovely star of the Howard Hughes production, "The Outlaw," poses in two equally flattering swim suits that are not afraid of the water

BY KAY PROCTOR

Without plan or purpose, she trips along and gives no thought to to-morrow

Ginger Rogers is a girl without ambitions. She just waits around and somehow things always happen.

THE NEXT time an ambitious mother of a dancing daughter points to Ginger Rogers to prove the sterling truth of the copy-book maxim about goals and hitching your wagon to a star, she had better check up on her facts.

Ginger never set herself a great or distant goal to achieve. She still hasn't got one. In a way she waits for the goals to come to her. That's rather amazing when you consider all she has achieved. And certainly it is unorthodox!

Ginger has a simple explanation for it. She illustrated it for me by drawing a square and a two-sided figure on the table cloth in the studio commissary where we were having tea.

"A goal is a plan," she said. "A plan is an outline. The minute you outline something, you limit it. Draw four sides of a square and that's it. It never can be any bigger or any smaller. But—draw only two sides, leave

GINGER'S

two open or blank, and what happens? There is no limit to the figure you can draw.

"It is the same with a career. Set a certain goal and you limit yourself to achieving that one thing. Leave it open, match progress with self-development and the world, not just one high peak in it, is yours to conquer if you can.

"Even people's abilities are not limited, except by themselves when they give up in the face of tough going or are content with what they have achieved. Time alone is limited—and that can be stretched to cover such a tremendous territory.

"The trouble with setting yourself a goal is that a career is like going to school. While you are in the first grade you know there is a second grade beyond it, and a third and fourth and eventually high school and college. But you must learn the lessons of the first grade before you can tackle the problems of the second. Setting a definite goal has a tendency to make you skip grades, or at least try to. If you have no goal, you are content to take each grade in its proper order.

"That's what I mean when I say I never have set myself a goal and do not have one now. I've concentrated on learning my lessons as they came along. It doesn't mean I do not *look* ahead. I do, eagerly. But I do not limit myself by formal plans. I never say, 'Next year I will do such and such and three years from now I will do the other.'

"I believe in living each day as it comes, to the best of my ability. When it is done, I put it away, remembering there will be to-morrow to take its place. If I have any philosophy, that's it. To me it is not a fatalistic attitude."

Ginger tucked her pencil back in her kelly green suede bag and smiled. She was a trifle embarrassed. "That was quite a speech, wasn't it?" she laughed. "I don't know that I've ever tried to put it in just so many words before, but it's true."

Her life and career proves it.

As far as she can remember—and she has an uncannily good memory—Ginger never had any childhood idea of becoming an actress, as most little girls have. She never dressed up in Mother Lela Rogers' high heels and long dresses and daubed on flour, strawberry juice and burnt match for make-up to play at being an actress. If anything, she wanted to be a school marm, maybe because she loved school and lessons or maybe, like most kids, because a school teacher's authority over others seemed pretty wonderful and desirable. It wasn't until she had her actual baptism behind footlights when she won the Charleston contest on a Fort Worth stage that the theatre held more than a passing interest for her. Even then she envisioned no great future as an actress or even a dancer. Setting such a goal for herself never occurred to her.

"I simply wanted to be the best Charleston dancer anywhere in the country," she said. "I never looked beyond that horizon."

When the four weeks' tour on a small-time circuit, which she had won as first prize in the contest, led to further vaudeville engagements and eventually to a spot with Paul Ash and his orchestra, vaudeville alone held her interest. Once again, she wanted only to be a top vaudevillian. In her professional "schooling," first grade and

In "The Castles," Rogers and Astaire do the famous "Castle Walk" of 1914.

post graduate work alike, no position but the head of the class would satisfy her.

"Next came musical comedy on the New York stage," she said. "Again I was fired with new ambition, but not beyond musical comedy. I worked like a demon, yes, but every hour of that work was directed at one thing only, supremacy in this new field."

One fact stands out clearly in tracing Ginger's steady climb to fame. Not once did she initiate the successive changes or make the first move towards effecting them. Others brought them to her, half-way thrust them upon her. So it was with her first motion picture work in New York where she made "Young Man of Manhattan" with Claudette Colbert and Norman Foster, the ensuing call to come to Hollywood, and eventually her present enviable contract.

"From the beginning, things seemed to work out that way," she told me. "When I was ready for something new, it seemed to happen, without my making a fuss about it. I guess that is what convinced me that doing one thing at a time and doing it to the best of my ability without looking beyond was the right idea. Each progressive goal seemed to come to me. Finally it forced upon me the conclusion that things come to us only when we are ready for them." *Continued on page 39*

GETTING NOWHERE FAST!

HEDY LAMARR

Why should the indiscretion of

BY LON MURRAY

Completely clothed, Hedy stole "Algiers" from such excellent players as Charles Boyer and Sigrid Gurie.

"Please forget my past," pleads Hedy Lamarr, "and let the Ecstasy Girl be buried. She has made life seem not worth living."

HAS HAD TOO MUCH ECSTASY !

a girl—whose only sin was ambition—be held against her years later?

SHE WANTS to forget she ever was the Ecstasy Girl, but the world will not allow it. A dark page in a young girl's life, a mistaken chapter that she hates, and from which, seven years later, she finds there is no escape.

Her name was changed from Kiesler to Lamarr. She is twenty-three and a woman now. She has literally cried her heart out. Those who truly know filmdom and its strange people stoutly maintain that she is one of Hollywood's better actresses. But notoriety and distasteful publicity still pursue her like the villain in an old-fashioned melodrama.

Only one thing will prevent the darkly tragic Hedy Lamarr from assuming her rightful place as a top-ranking star—the indiscretion of a sixteen-year-old girl whose only sin was ambition.

"Why can't I be judged by my present and future?" she pleads. The studio which holds her contract, has, ostrich-like, turned thumbs down on any references to the Ecstasy Girl in publicity releases. Hedy Lamarr must at twenty-three be reborn without a blemish on her reputation, without a history!

But, unlike the studio's most important foreign-born star, Hedy Lamarr will talk—or at least she recently did to me in the walled-in patio of her modest little Beverly Hills bungalow.

Hedy was born in Vienna of well-to-do parents. Her father, Emil Kiesler, was a big-shot bank director. An only child, she was given just about everything she desired.

She can't recall when she didn't want to be an actress —to go on the stage, or, better still, to act for the cinema. When Papa Kiesler learned of this wish, he became infuriated. Trude, her mother, patiently argued her daughter's case and eventually won the father's consent.

Hedy had small parts in two pictures after that. Then she was told that she was to be given her big chance— to be featured in "an artistic nature film." You can imagine how thrilled, how excited, was the girl of sixteen at this news.

She plunged into the making of that film with all the fervor of an impatient young body. Now many scenes in the picture, "Ecstasy," are without offense to the most Puritanical. Such scenes were photographed first and the sheltered girl suspected nothing.

Then the time came to make the sequences that made "Ecstasy" probably the most-discussed picture of recent years. They weren't long scenes and to many Continental minds, there was nothing wrong in them.

Hedy told me—and her eyes were clearly sincere—that she protested at the suggestion that she pose with all her clothing removed, but the director assured her it was necessary to the story and to the completion of an artistic endeavor. Beside it was then too late to withdraw. If she did, it was argued, she would be blackballed, her chances for a career ruined.

"In my ignorance, I was won over." A girl of good circumstances, little more than a child except in body, has little experience with the world and its panderers. After all, she thought, the sequences might not survive the cutting-room.

Likely you have seen "Ecstasy" and those much-talked-about scenes. Hedy is bathing in the nude when her horse senses the presence of a mare and takes chase, bearing the girl's clothes away on his back. Hedy leaves the swimming-hole and hurries after the horse. It is a scene soon over. An active imagination grasps more than one's eyes.

"I can't understand it," Hedy Continued on page 38

Hedy Lamarr in the much-discussed "Ecstacy." Did it shock you? She was assured this scene was merely artistic.

BY JAMES REID

Oomph
FOR SALE

Glamour is Hayworth's business and it ought to be a cinch—but life isn't all mink and orchids for this Hollywood career gal!

"I had to be sold to the public just like a breakfast cereal or a real estate development or something new in ladies' wear."

Rita Hayworth crossed one long, lovely leg over the other. Her full, generous lips curved in that smile that you've seen on more magazine covers lately than any other smile in Hollywood.

She had agreed to tell something that she hadn't told before—the deep dark secret, the *inside* story, of her sudden success.

"You see," she explained, settling back with that it's-a-long-story look in her eyes, "I made a big mistake right at the very beginning. I started as a dancer. After that, it took a lot of doing to persuade Hollywood to think of me as anything else.

"I was doing specialty dancing in a big hotel at Agua Caliente with my father, Eduardo Cansino, when Fox 'discovered' me. There was talk of putting me in the title role of 'Ramona,' and I was given a few dance numbers in 'Dante's Inferno' and a couple of other pictures.

"Then the studio changed heads. Mr. Zanuck wanted a big-name star for 'Ramona,' and they let me go."

Rita smiled wryly at the recollection of that day, five years ago, when she had walked out the front door of Twentieth Century-Fox and sat down on the concrete steps to cry her heart out—because she had been fired. It's hard to have your dreams crushed when you're only 17.

"I don't know how long I sat there sobbing. Probably an hour or more. Until suddenly it dawned on me that there wasn't a single person in all Hollywood who was going to take either the time or the trouble to feel sorry for little Rita Cansino. 'Crying isn't going to get me anywhere,' I said. 'The only way I'm going to get anywhere is to show 'em. Make 'em eat those words they spoke when they gave me the bad news. We're afraid your talents are limited—to dancing.'

"So, with grim determination, I made the rounds." Rita smiled again, in recollection. "And the only jobs I could get were in Westerns—at little out-of-the-way studios that nobody had ever heard of."

She has been under contract to Columbia for so long that people don't stop to wonder how Columbia ever happened to sign her. The untold story about *that* is: One day during the making of a gangster epic, Rita overheard the assistant director say, "Too bad that girl can't speak English." She saw red. So that was what was holding her back, was it? She steamed up to the director and said, boiling, "I want to get one thing straight. I can speak English as well as anybody on this set. I'm as American as anybody here. I was born in New York, grew up in the United States, and have a high school diploma." This outburst called her to the attention of the entire lot, including the Front Office. Result: a contract as a stock player and a switch to an American name, Hayworth.

"Then I married Eddie," Rita continued. She was referring to successful businessman Edward C. Judson (his specialties are oil and real estate) —older, wonderfully tolerant of her burning ambition to get ahead in films.

"After I changed my name, I expected wonders to happen. But my roles didn't become any bigger or any better. I came home one night, desperate, and asked Eddie to tell me what was wrong.

"He thought a moment and said, "You're trying to sell a product named Rita Hayworth. In business, a man doesn't wait for people to discover what he wants to sell. He advertises.

"He also pointed out that the most successful businesses spent money to earn more money. I was earning $175 a week then. So every week, half of it went into additions to my wardrobe, improvement in my personal appearance, and half into voice lessons and dramatic lessons.

The logical *Continued on page 38*

A fat raise jacked Rita's salary to $3,000 weekly. She squanders it on dresses ($7,000 yearly), shoes ($75 a pair) and chocolates—at least 5 lbs. a week.

Rita smokes, wears scarlet nail polish and has received 500 proposals. Lost 8 pounds while dancing with Astaire in Columbia's "You'll Never Get Rich."

story of the year:

what really happened to DORIS DAY

Behind the illness
of this beloved star
is a story that has never
before been told—
a tragic history
of struggle and
heartache for a
career she never wanted!

BY JANE S. CARLETON

■ For weeks now, the welter of rumor about D
Day has been rising and spreading.

Gossip, innuendo, exaggeration—everything
truth—has been advanced to explain her ill
and even her illness has been denied.

When *Lucky Me*, a Doris Day vehicle sc
uled to start at Warner Brothers last October
suddenly canceled, one studio spokesman off
this alibi: "The script isn't ready yet. A few n
weeks and we'll roll."

Simultaneously, a Los Angeles columnist wr
"Doris Day has had what practically amounts
nervous breakdown and chums claim that diffi
ties with husband Marty Melcher are a big
of her trouble."

Said husband Melcher when a newspaper
urged him "to level with me, Marty." "Nerv
breakdown? That's a lotta bunk. Doris is
tired. She'll be okay. There's nothing wrong
her. Just had a cyst or something removed fr
her back. Minor surgery. What are they mak
such a fuss about?"

"I read in the papers that she's going t
psychiatrist," the newspaperman continued. "S
posedly she won't be okay for months. Any tr
to that?"

"Of course not," said Marty Melcher. "S
just tired. She's done picture after pictur
fourteen pictures in a row. She's beat. Woul
you be?"

"That's on the level now?"

"On the level," Melcher said.

Marty Melcher is Doris Day's husband a
agent and business manager, and as president
Martin Melcher Productions, her new producer.
loves her very much. In her hour of need, he wa
only to help and protect her and if this seems
call for more tact than truth—well then, it's und
standable. But the truth has a purifying a
clarifying effect, and throughout the world, th
are thousands of Doris Day fans who are worr
about this tall, talented, freckle-faced blonde w
has given them so much joy and warmth a
entertainment.

The truth is that Doris Day is emotionally up
and that her neurosis may in part be attribu
to what physicians refer to as cancerphobia.

For some time now, Doris has been afraid th
she has cancer.

She belongs to a religious faith that holds th
disease may be cured by treatment which consi
basically of enlightened prayer.

In her own family and in her business circl
she has encountered some disagreement with t
belief.

Several weeks before *Lucky Me* was schedu
to get underway, Warner Brothers insisted th
Doris submit to a complete physical checkup. F
a while, Doris refused. The studio pressed its poi
The executives were *Continued on page 48*

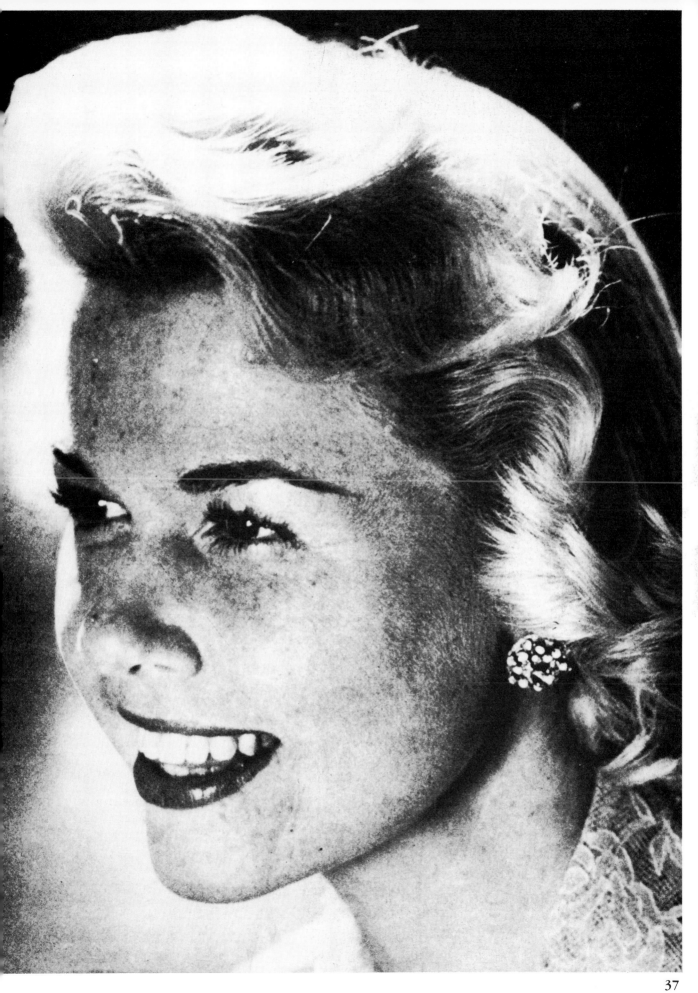

HEDY LAMARR HAS HAD TOO MUCH ECSTASY!

Continued from page 33

protested. "If I had been in a room with a man! But it was beautiful—artistic!"

Having lived in Paris and Nice, I could understand her point of view. I tried to explain the Main Street attitude, but only succeeded in adding to her bewilderment. You see, Hedy Lamarr has been damned seven long years for committing that which she can't believe is a crime.

"Ecstasy," when first released, was quietly successful throughout Europe—where the contours of the human body are treated more casually. But then, last year, the picture was revived by Barnum who gave it meaningful English titles and sent it to America. Highly exploited, there was difficulty with the censors, which only added to the sensational publicity.

MEANWHILE, when Hedy was eighteen, she had married Fritz Mandl, a millionaire munitions-maker. Of course, he knew about "Ecstasy" the first time it had been released, which was quite a different picture than it was to be in 1937. Perhaps he would have ignored even that in the ardor of courtship. Looking into Hedy's so big eyes, it is possible to forget many things. He too was young, not thirty.

Fritz gave her his name, a palace in Vienna, a mountain retreat in the Alps and a country hunting lodge. He would not allow her to act, but loved her greatly.

"I would drag him to a theatre or the opera," Hedy told me with a sad, small laugh, "and Fritz would be thinking of time bombs or gas masks. He was oh so much for business, that husband of mine."

I gathered that Fritz was very jealous. Hedy doesn't blame him now, for she realizes the havoc caused in 1937 when "that horrible picture" was shown to the far corners of the earth. Fritz Mandl was a man with a position to preserve and a right to his dignity.

Hedy's powerful husband sent agents, went himself, offering any price for the scattered prints of "Ecstasy." He spent what would have been a fortune to many, trying to bury the past.

Hedy too was happy each time a print was bought and destroyed, as though her freedom were being won link by link. But there remained one print in the United States which was not for sale at any price, and the specter would always be between Hedy and the sun. Incidentally, that print is still earning dividends for its owner.

There were many quarrels between Fritz and his wife. Hedy's father had died; her mother was distraught. Finally, the spirited young wife decided for herself. She would leave and go to America. Where none knew her, perhaps a new life awaited. So she left the things that wealth could buy and came to a new shore empty-handed.

But not alone. Her "reputation" had gone ahead of the Ecstasy Girl—as hard to ignore as her slim shadow. A civil divorce followed, but Hedy is still married to Fritz Mandl in the eyes of the Church.

For six months, the courageous Viennese sought a chance to show Hollywood that she could act. Night after night she cried herself to sleep. The papers still printed bits about the Ecstasy Girl. Studio executives looked at her oddly as though she were some creature out of a zoo.

Screen tests were made in routine fashion, and the verdict was reached that the girl decidedly had something, a streamlined Theda Bara, a youthful, impassioned Kay Francis, a cross between Garbo and the late Jean Harlow.

DESPITE these reactions, the producers hesitated. After all, this was the Ecstasy Girl. The Hays Office, mentor of the picture industry, must be considered—also, the Legion of Decency.

Metro had her under contract at a low starting figure, said to have been anywhere from $150 to $400 a week. The lower figure is the one usually whispered by those most likely to know.

Hedy played her victrola and went to the movies, learning English. She marveled that in America ice cream of excellent quality is sold at every corner drug-store. She ate it until her masseuse warned her that Hollywood doesn't want fat women.

And Hedy waited and still cried herself to sleep at nights. She was so alone. She was trying so hard to prove to the world that she could act—and with her clothes on!

"I am ashamed to admit it," she told me, "but there were times when I thought life was not worth living."

This girl from a strange land who had had everything was, in truth, distressingly near poverty. Her father had been wealthy before the world-wide depression, but had passed on leaving little to his widow. During her marriage, Fritz Mandl had always held the purse-strings. After leaving him, she had expected and received nothing. And the money paid her by her studio had to be stretched to take care of an agent's ten-percent commission, the wages of the housekeeper-companion who lives with her, the gowns required for a Hollywood front, hairdresser, masseuse, living expenses, etc.

And it's droll to note that Hedy's "ill-gotten gains" could not come to her rescue. Although "Ecstasy" made a fortune for its producers and exploiters, its young star was paid but the equivalent of four hundred dollars for her work.

HOLLYWOOD, however, specializes in happy endings. While Hedy Lamarr is still pursued by the shadows of her "past," there came a turn in events that may ultimately bring her happiness. She was loaned to United Artists for a featured role with Charles Boyer and Sigrid Gurie in "Algiers."

Grateful for the chance, Hedy assumed the role of Gaby, without guile, without any plan to steal the picture. It is not to her discredit that she committed high piracy in the opinion of many.

Cameraman James Howe knew that he had something very special when he viewed the first rushes. The girl's exotic beauty, her thick-lipped facile mouth with which she seems able to express any emotion caused Howe to insert additional close-ups. The result was that the capable Sigrid Gurie was left standing at the post and Hedy was triple-starred in the billing.

And the mocking fact is this: Although Hedy Lamarr does nothing shocking, although she is most modestly garbed, throughout the scenes in which she appears, she takes command and holds the audience's eyes by the sure fire device of personifying sensuous s-e-x. And she can't help it!

I didn't dare tell her as much after the premiere of "Algiers" at Hollywood's Four Star Theatre. I didn't tell her that she would number far more men as her admirers than women.

I didn't, for she had said, "Please, oh please ask America to forget my past. Let your article tell, if it must, all there is to know so that curiosity will be ended and the Ecstasy Girl be buried. You understand that I am one who has had too much ecstasy."

OOMPH FOR SALE

Continued from page 34

place to go in search of ballyhoo was the studio publicity department. "The press agents asked me if I had any violent objections to leg art. I said no. That was one thing I *wasn't* shy about, thanks to my background as a dancer. Willing subjects, they said, were hard for photographers to find."

Her first break in Life magazine was a bathing suit shot. And because she was so co-operative about posing, that magazine has since given her a half-dozen breaks and pictured her on the cover twice!

"But please don't get the idea," she went on quickly, "that I confined myself *exclusively* to leg art. I posed for layouts showing beauty treatments, the home life of a starlet and then 'how not to behave in a night club.' But," she admitted frankly, "the shots in bathing suits were what started the publicity ball rolling."

AND what set it catapulting?
"The studio," confided Rita, "had an idea that was a flash of genius. They said, 'Every time you hear of a best-dressed woman in Hollywood, she's always a star. Why don't we try something new—give *you* a build-up as the best-dressed starlet?'"

"Even before the fashion build-up started, Eddie and I realized the importance of always looking well-groomed in private life. That was how I got my first real break. After I acquired one $500 outfit, we went to the Clover Club, figuring that there would be more people there than anywhere else. At a nearby table sat Harry Cohn, head of Columbia, and Howard Hawks, who was going to direct 'Only Angels Have Wings.' I didn't know it, but Mr. Hawks was still looking for a girl to play Cary Grant's ex-wife. Even though he'd never seen me before, he said, 'That girl could play the part.'"

That role in "Only Angels Have Wings" meant a lot to Rita, but it didn't mean much to the public. She was on the screen for only about two scenes. And yet the public interest in her kept mounting steadily. There was only one explanation: Publicity.

"Eddie and I really went all-out in our campaign, invested $15,000 in clothes and made a practice of night-clubbing every Saturday night. The photographers took my picture. Columnists became Hayworth-conscious. People mentioned me in the same breath with stars.

"A couple of magazines asked me to pose for covers—space usually reserved for stars—and I did a few big billboard ads. A national picture magazine heard about the $15,000 wardrobe and covered a picture-story on it, calling me the best-dressed *star!*"

What single publicity stunt had paid the biggest dividends?

Quick as a flash, she said: "The time I put on the $250,000 pearl dress. No other publicity stunt in 1940 got the space that that did. Maybe you remember the dress. It was made of 40,000 pearls of seven different sizes—as an ad for the Imperial Pearl Syndicate. It weighed thirty pounds. It took fifteen dressmakers six weeks to make it. And at least fifteen guards surrounded it every time it was put on exhibition.

"The fashion editor of Columbia heard that I. Magnin and Company was going to show it here. She gave Magnin's a sales talk about having me model it—me, instead of Hedy Lamarr or Ann

Sheridan or Dorothy Lamour or someone else better known than I was. I'll never know how she managed that. And I didn't know she *had* managed it—I hadn't even heard about the dress—until I had a frantic phone call from her. I was at Catalina on a yacht, when she finally caught up with me.

"This was Monday noon. 'I've been trying to reach you since Friday,' she gasped, and told me about the dress, and how she had promised I would model it for newspapermen on Monday afternoon and for photographers on Tuesday. Only how was I going to get back to town in time? There wasn't a plane reservation

to be had. I camped at the seaplane landing, hoping against hope that someone would cancel out. Finally, at 3 o'clock, someone did. The fashion editor had gray hair by the time I arrived— but I did get there.

"The real ordeal, though, came on Tuesday. I stood in that dress from 4 to 7, posing for each photograper in turn. One photographer, for a national magazine, had been promised an exclusive shot showing me being helped into the dress. (The way I got into it, by the way, was to sit on the floor and then rise by degrees as two women unrolled it, inch by inch, down over me.) It took

a little doing to give him his exclusive shot. They smuggled him into the ladies' lounge, where his competitors wouldn't look for him, then escorted me there to pose for him. And all the while the matron was wringing her hands and moaning, 'Dear, dear, this is against the rules!' "

Couldn't she have made life simpler for herself by refusing to pose for three solid hours in a thirty-pound dress?

Rita smiled for the umpteenth time during our interview. "I loved it. *Any* time photographers gang up on me, I love it. And why shouldn't I? It's part of my business, my career, isn't it, now?"

GINGER'S GETTING NOWHERE FAST!

Continued from page 31

Continued from page 31

So it was with stardom. Maybe, as she looks at it, stardom came to her, but I know of no actress in Hollywood who has worked harder and more sincerely to justify and keep it. She still is following her one guiding light: the best you can do today and the future will take care of itself.

Only in one instance that I know of did Ginger deliberately alter the pattern of the present to safeguard the future. Knowing how securely she is established as the top dancing star of the screen, and knowing how fickle the tastes of fans can be, she insisted that of the four pictures she makes each year, two be dancing pictures and two be straight roles. Thus, having completed "The Castles" with Fred Astaire, her next will be a light comedy drama, tentatively titled "Little Mother," in which she gets stuck with the rearing of a baby who belongs to someone else.

After Hollywood, what?

"There will be something, of course," Ginger said. "We can never stand still. Frankly, I hope it will be the stage, but I am not worrying about it now or even particularly thinking of it. I'll know when the time comes. Until then—Hollywood absorbs my life."

If the stage is the answer, Ginger knows one thing. She won't go storming that citadel in the belief she is a second Bernhardt or Duse! She expects to go to "school" there too, beginning her "lessons" where she left off when she entered pictures—with light comedies or musicals. If it becomes apparent she is ready for stronger stuff, she'll tackle heavy dramas. But not until then.

It is interesting to trace her innate dislike of formal plans in her private life. She loves surprise parties above all other kinds and gets really angry over one thing, if someone in on the secret gives them away. She loves to take trips on the spur of the moment as she did upon the completion of "The Castles." On a Saturday morning she learned her last scene would be shot around four o'clock that afternoon.

HER secretary was dispatched for tickets. Her maid was told to pack bags. Her household of cook, gardener and steward was given its orders for the ensuing weeks. At six o'clock that night she was on a train headed for New York! And in the meantime, besides working in five different scenes at the studio, she had managed a portrait sitting, an interview, and a little quick shopping!

Little wonder it took so long to get her house finished. The architect and builder were about ready to throw in the sponge. Every time they met Ginger she had some new idea or change to be made. The playroom was all but finished, for example, when she decided to treat herself to the one thing she'd wanted all her life—a soda

fountain of her own. Unfortunately, the dimensions of the room were inadequate for the addition. Okay, Ginger told them, rebuild it. They did.

"Plans depress me," she explained. "They are so darned final."

She is volatile even in her hobbies. Her interest, and a tremendous interest, is caught quickly, but her enthusiasm seldom lasts any length of time. When she played badminton, she was an expert. When she went in for tennis, she became runner-up in an important Hollywood tournament. As a child she had a passionate interest in tiny dolls, but gave them up entirely for the commercial manufacture of fudge. Made it pay, too. This was followed by the piano. That lasted until she played her first public recital. Now in her spare time she'll play parchesi like mad for one week and change the next to volley ball.

In view of that, her attitude about golf is a strange one. She owns a fine set of clubs. "But I won't be a duffer," she said. "So I'm not going to play at all until I have the time to learn the game and play it properly."

There is one other thing she is not impulsive about—friendship. She endows the word with a deep and special meaning, reserving its use for the few who really hold a place in her sincere affections. But once she accepts you as a friend it is through thick and thin. Unless, of course, you betray her loyalty. That she will not forgive.

If only time were not limited, perhaps it would be a different story with Ginger and her hobbies for, basically, she wants to do everything well. Everything she cannot do well remains a constant challenge to her. But time is the one precious possession she doesn't have and covets most.

If she had time, for instance, she could do more of the thoughtful reading with which she is attempting to make up for the college education she missed while dancing up the road to fame. If she had more time she could become an accomplished pianist, painter and sculptress, for the talent unmistakably is in her. The one recital she gave, her charcoal and pastel sketches, and the bust of her mother she is modeling proves that. If she had time she could become one of Hollywood's loveliest hostesses, for her talent for hospitality is a great one.

BUT where other stars are given three and four months between pictures, she gets only six weeks at the longest, and that is a new concession on the part of the studio. Previously ten days or two weeks was her average rest period. It is the price she pays for box-office popularity. Rogers pictures, like the mail, must go through! When she is in production, particularly on a dancing special with its added arduous hours of rehearsal, she has precious little energy at the end of the day

to do anything but fall into bed exhausted.

Happily for her peace of mind, Ginger has the faculty for sorting the important from the unimportant and dismissing the latter from her mind as completely as a wave washes footprints from a sandy beach. On important things she concentrates with a driving force until they are accomplished. Then they, too, are marked "finished" and put away with yesterday.

Perfection in whatever she is doing is the only goal Ginger ever has set for herself. It is her only goal today. And it is the one goal, she realizes, that is given none of us to achieve.

"But I can keep on trying," she says.

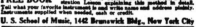

LEADING MEN

When Rudolph Valentino first came to Los Angeles in 1918, he found himself working as an extra in a series of films that did nothing to create the cinema image that he was later to represent to the world. He had a reputation in Hollywood as a gigolo who had slept with the right people to support himself and make contacts that would get him ahead in movies.

June Mathis, who was one of the principal powers at Metro, spotted Valentino as one of the leads in a film called *The Eyes of Youth* (1919). Mathis was determined to produce a film version of the best-seller *The Four Horsemen of the Apocalypse* (1921), and she cast him in one of the lead roles. The film went on to become one of the four top money-making movies of the 1920's. Films like *The Sheik* (1921), *Beyond the Rocks* (1922), *The Eagle* (1925), and *Son of the Sheik* (1926) made women swoon with ecstasy to see the gentle, passionate Italian cause his leading ladies to melt in his arms. In 1921, Valentino co-starred in *Camille* with the notorious Nazimova. He was the subject of much slanderous gossip when it was disclosed that both of his wives, Jean Acker and Natacha Rambova, were lesbian protégées of Nazimova's. When Rudolph died in 1926 at the height of his fame, thousands of his fans crowded the streets to get a final glimpse of the "great lover" lying in state. Valentino was indeed the screen's first major leading man. In the May 1931 issue of *Modern Screen,* Elinor Glyn wrote the remembrance "Rudolph Valentino as I Knew

Him" (page 42).

What was it that made Clark Gable one of the top leading men for three decades of movies? Writer Faith Baldwin tried to answer this question in "Why All the Mystery About Gable's Appeal?" from the March 1932 issue of *Modern Screen* (page 46). According to Baldwin, "Mr. Gable is something of a volcano. Volcanic men have a delightful danger for women." In October of that year, when Clark Gable and Jean Harlow's *Red Dust* (1932) was released, the lava sure flowed on the screen!

"Call Me 'Dutch'" (page 50) was the title of the September 1941 *Modern Screen* feature about young actor Ronald Reagan and his first wife, Jane Wyman. This is a rare classic, because today both Reagan and Wyman refuse to discuss their marriage.

In 1955 Rock Hudson was forced into marrying Phyllis Gates, his agent's secretary, for the sake of appearances. After acting in twenty-six films in seven years, when *Magnificent Obsession* (1954) was released Rock went from being a featured player to being a huge star. In 1956, his role in *Giant* garnered him an Academy Award nomination as Best Actor. *Written on the Wind* (1957) and *A Farewell to Arms* (1957) increased his stature as one of the most successful leading men on the screen. By the end of 1957 it was time to get out of the marriage that wasn't making anyone happy. "Why Rock Walked Out," from the February 1959 issue of *Modern Screen* (page 52), is filled with the emotional sense of the melodramatic that made *Magnificent Obsession* a hit. Rock didn't want to get into this marriage to begin with, but as it crumbled, *Modern Screen* was right there for the scoop.

"I know most of the Broadway mob and racket men. In my picture *Under Cover Man* I could have told those scriptwriters a thing or two."
—George Raft
Modern Screen
April 1933

144 PAGES IN THIS ISSUE!

Modern Screen

THE LARGEST CIRCULATION OF ANY SCREEN MAGAZINE

MARCH

10 CENTS

LOMBARD
CLARK GABLE

SPECIAL! EXTRA 16 PAGES WITH
GINGER ROGERS'
True **LIFE STORY**

CAROLE LOMBARD & CLARK GABLE   **March 1937**   41

Rudolph Valentino and Elinor Glyn—two names which many will always associate with romance and the poetry of love. It is not astonishing that Madame Glyn's description of the late Valentino is probably more understanding and vivid than any previous one.

RUDOLPH VALENTINO, AS I KNEW HIM

By ELINOR GLYN

With the indescribable charm and insight which is hers, this famous writer tells of the great romantic figure whose magnetism lives forever

IT was in 1922 that Rudolph Valentino played with Gloria Swanson in the second picture I made in America, "Beyond the Rocks." He had already appeared in "The Four Horsemen," and was spoken of as a promising young man. I thought he looked overdressed and rather like a handsome gigolo, I remember, the first day he was introduced. I felt a slight prejudice against him, but after half an hour's conversation I could see his great charm, and that he understood any subtle hints, and in fact had a sensitive and sophisticated mind. He was even then a fine actor and a sincere one.

He always said he liked the part of Lord Brackendale in "Beyond the Rocks," and certainly he played it to perfection. I think we put in a title to the effect that his grandmother was an Italian or French woman, to account for his very un-English type. He toned down his dress and took care to assume an English reserve.

WE all had a most delightful time making the picture: he was so easy to work with and understood all my aims about it, and was always on my side when utterly false psychology was suggested to us to inject into the story. In those days nothing true to life was ever shown in "society" pictures on the screen; they were the utterly grotesque imaginings of illiterate minds presenting what the public was supposed to like! Whether the public did insist upon this bunk I never really knew. I often talked with Valentino at our picnic lunches when we were on location, and we both said how wonderful it would be if we were rich enough to make a picture with everything truly as it would be in real life. He was full of dreams of greatness and very contemptuous of the lack of knowledge of the world in the majority of picture people in those days. I do not know how he had acquired this experience himself, nor from whence he had come. His Latin adaptability and intelligence had given him an easy grace and what the French call *savoir-vivre*. He had a wonderful sense of values and absorbed every smallest shade of the manner in which a grand seigneur would act, while he read and re-read the book of "Beyond the Rocks."

Gradually, as I began to know him better, he told me of a beautiful lady with whom he was very much in love and hoped to marry when he should be free.

She was "so different," he assured me, from anyone in Hollywood.

Alas—for the transitory nature of human emotions—and ties!

THE original ending of "Beyond the Rocks" was made as it is in the book—and it was the most affect-

ing and exquisite scene. Never have either Valentino or Gloria Swanson shown finer powers of emotion. However, the director thought quite another ending would be better—an ending which had an entirely false psychology. So some nonsense was substituted, and as the real ending was "ash canned" it was given to me and I have it now, and only the other day looked at the young and splendid Valentino and the exquisitely attractive Gloria in a true-to-life, heartrending episode.

I lost sight of Valentino after the picture was finished, and I did not see him again until some years later when he had become most famous, and I think had been influenced to quarrel with his producers. I happened upon him on the ship returning to England. I thought him very much changed; there was rather a snobbish arrogance about him which destroyed his charm. He was being fearfully civil to people whom he imagined were of importance in Europe. His sense of values seemed to have strangely deserted him.

This writer says that Valentino was always the master lover on the screen—except possibly in "Monsieur Beaucaire." In that, she feels, he lost something of his masculine charm.

After this he learned who was who and what was what, it would seem, for the next time I met him he really was with those who mattered, and much of his old charm had returned.

THEN finally, just shortly before he died, we met again in a beautiful country house, and the old Valentino, with a courtly, polished manner added to his old boyish fascination, seemed to be there. We had several talks and both rejoiced that movies could now be beautiful and true to life, not the trash of the old days. What a pity that he did not live to play in the talkies for his voice was delightful! It was resonant and deep and redolent with that romantic Valentino charm.

I remember especially one incident during the "Beyond the Rocks" picture. The lovers were upon a couch, and the director was instructing them in honest-to-goodness American slang how to "emote." They did not seem to be getting the spirit, when Valentino turned to me and whispered, "Oh! Do say the same words to us as are in the book," and so I let myself grow very emotioned and repeated the impassioned sentences, and lovely Gloria almost wept, and Valentino was deeply moved, and it became a wonderful scene! He was so sensitive to sound and the poetic aspect of things.

HE was always self-confident and really believed in himself. No man can have "It" on or off the screen without self-confidence and a firm belief in himself.

The secret of Valentino's great charm for women fans was his perfect love-making, a mixture of passion and tenderness with never any subservient mush in it. He had "ways" and was always a master. So the subconscious minds of women were satisfied. At home they had "good fellows," "sweet boys," indulgent daddies, kindly brothers, matter-of-fact, biddable, generous husbands, but their real-life lovers were seldom warm and poetic and romantic. Valentino awakened a chord in the being of many American women which had been asleep before. They suddenly knew what their lives had missed—romance—a glorious, beautiful master lover who gave tenderness because he loved and not because he placed all women indiscriminately on a pedestal. Their hearts beat, their blood ran—his kisses became almost real to each individual woman. They could go back to their dull homes, and duller male folk, full of dreams of bliss. A workaday world didn't seem so dull with those dreams. Valentino was the solace of many million female lives!

Only in one picture did he seem to lose his masculine charm, and that was in "Monsieur Beaucaire." There seemed to be a strong feminine influence there, it may have been the dress perhaps—but he was less of a god than usual.

THE mad vogue for him was not so great in Europe or England as in America, although he was highly

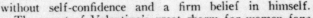

"His memory is still vivid . . . and he will always stand for

appreciated, because foreign women have not this lack of romance in their lives. They often suffer from an embarrassment of choice in Latin countries.

Valentino represented the polished, sophisticated lover. He gave no impression of an uncouth, simple fellow in love, whom any woman can wind round her little finger. They all sensed they could never dominate him in any way—he was the untameable. All their hunting instinct was aroused. He looked dangerous and not to be teased with impunity. He looked as if he knew everything about love. Who can forget the perfect scene in "The Four Horsemen" where Alice Terry came into his studio, and he took her shoes off and dried and caressed her damp little feet! Yes, he had "Ways with him"! Fascinating ways.

Then, too, his eyes expressed passion—they were bold and tender, and his every movement was full of grace.

Valentino set a fashion for screen heroes, and after him there appeared many dashing lovers—and if he could return now I wonder if he would hold the stage unchallenged? "Those whom the gods love die young," and beautiful and adored Valentino was no exception. Perhaps he might have lived had he not been smothered with quantities of nurses, and millions of roses, and the anxious thoughts of half America.

His memory is still vivid in many hearts, and he will *always* stand for what he so exquisitely portrayed—The World's Perfect Lover.

(Above) Many were the talks that Rudolph Valentino and Elinor Glyn had on the set during the making of "Beyond the Rocks." A fine friendship resulted from these talks.

Do you remember the impassioned scenes between Rudolph Valentino and Gloria Swanson in "Beyond the Rocks"? Elinor Glyn did much to perfect those fascinating love scenes.

ELINOR GLYN

has created a type of movie magazine feature which is refreshingly new and invigorating—a type in which she tells in her own vibrant way of the stars she has met and known.

These features appear only in

MODERN SCREEN

what he so exquisitely portrayed—The World's Perfect Lover."

WHY ALL THE MYSTERY

Clark's latest picture is "Hell Divers." It was made some time ago but has only recently been released. A story of airplanes and birdmen—both on and off duty. Dorothy Jordan is in the off-duty sequences—which gives Gable a good chance for both dramatic air scenes and thrilling romantic ones.

By FAITH BALDWIN

THE first time I saw Clark Gable—as the excessively unpleasant chauffeur in "Night Nurse"—I said to myself, "His ears stick out!"

It didn't seem possible to me that the new screen sensation could be, after all, so much of a sensation if his ears stuck out. But after five or ten minutes of Mr. Gable I no longer considered his ears—by that time his personality had gripped me so I wouldn't have noticed even if he were entirely without ears.

The extraordinary and rapid rise of this dark and dominant young man to fan favor has occasioned much interest and speculation and people everywhere are speculating on what it is that makes him so exceedingly popular.

He has become something of a "mystery."

I believe that Mr. Gable's astonishing hold upon the imagination is due, first of all, to the impression he gives of vitality, of virility. I believe that the feminine public is wearying of rather pretty and too polished young men and that Mr. Gable's brilliant mixture of suavity and brutality, his quite magnificent physique and his effect of arrogance, which is not the usual "debonair" arrogance, are some of the reasons why frail women swoon with admiration and strong men curse with envy when his name is mentioned.

Our mothers still remember their shudders of delight over such fiction characters as *Rochester* and *St. Elmo.* Most of us do not indulge in these outmoded thrills today but I am willing to wager that the modern novels which have proved the most popular among women—without benefit of critic or book club—are those which hold within their pages a very dominant and even domineering hero. Need I go further back than "The Sheik"?

I think that Mr. Gable would realize more deftly and truly the character of that fascinating pseudo-Arab than did the late Valentino!

Women, today, are "independent," they rejoice in their personal and economic freedom, they demand equal rights. But they remain women, for all that; or the majority of them do; and this majority remains susceptible to the extremely masculine.

Mr. Gable, on the screen, gives one the impression that, while he might adore the current heroine to the point of madness, he might also, if sufficiently exasperated, give her a very good beating—and get away with it.

I think that his general *leitmotif* is the hand of iron in the velvet glove—and very few women on this old earth are immune to such a paradoxical attraction.

MR. GABLE does not always portray astonishing—and, I hope, very rare—chauffeurs. He has been cast, and excellently, in gangster rôles and in more or less polished man-of-the-world parts. But the underlying strength is there.

Mr. Gable is something of a volcano. Volcanic men have a delightful danger for women. Women are always wondering just how far they can go with them—and still be safe. Women in their secret hearts like uncertainty. The man who is always courteous around the house, who puts his wife or sweetheart on a pedestal, who never forgets anniversaries and is consideration itself, may make, and does make, an excellent lover and a desirable husband, but his wife will attend the movies just the same in order to sigh over Clark Gable, and, when later in the evening her obliging mate helps her to wash the dishes, she may pray hopefully that he will throw one at her.

Women will deny this, of course. But it is pretty generally true.

Once, long ago, a very pretty girl said to me, "I want to marry the kind of a man who is quite capable of beating me if I annoy him *Continued on page 48*

ABOUT GABLE'S APPEAL?

. . . Brilliantly and charmingly this famous writer debunks the theories which have been built up concerning the secret of Clark Gable's tremendous success. Do you agree with Faith Baldwin?

"Mr. Gable is something of a volcano," says Faith Baldwin. "Volcanic men have a delightful danger for women. Women are always wondering just how far they can go with them—and still be safe." Is that the way Clark Gable impresses you?

Mystery About Gable's Appeal?

Continued from page 46

too much—but who really won't."

A lot of girls feel like that. And that is why they will make Clark Gable one of the biggest of the male box office attractions.

Mr. Gable does not appeal to the mentality, as do certain other motion picture stars. He does not, very much, appeal to the sense of humor. He does not even appeal to the purely romantic. His hold on the feminine imagination is the hold of life itself; exciting—vital, uncertain, stimulating. There is a little spice of fear in it and a wondering . . .

Strictly speaking, I do not consider him handsome. I can cite half a dozen stars who I consider better looking from a standpoint of feature. I do not even think that he has a great deal of charm, as charm goes. But he has a magnetism that is undeniable and very strong.

He has also, at moments, that bad boy appeal which is so very dangerous to most women. He is the kind of a man of whom women think . . . if he'd only met the right woman . . . if he'd only met *me!*

One of the curious elements in the impression given an audience by Mr. Gable—an impression so modern as to be reactionary—in his apparent lack of interest in romanticism. His love making is not romantic, it has not "glamor," it is of the earth, earthy. He appears on the screen, at all events, to regard women as conveniences rather than idols. Women may resent this but they respond to it, strange to say. He seems to be an entirely self-contained person, professionally at any rate. Too, so much has been written about his personal life, his two marriages to women older than himself. Writers appear to make a mystery of this also or else offer the opinion that it is because he wishes to be "mothered." However, it is hard for me to think of him as creeping home to be surrounded by maternal care. I venture to remark also, therefore, that Mr. Gable is not the only man in the world who happens to like mature, sophisticated and intelligent women. It does not in the least surprise me. I would be much more astonished if he had evinced a preference for flappers or schoolgirls.

BUT this lack of romantic emotion which is so dominant in his screen work makes him doubly interesting to all the women in his audience; for probably ninety-nine per cent of them feel that if he had met her—or her—or her—she, out of all the world could awaken the dream and the glamor and the romance which must, she thinks, lie dormant in his curiously and darkly secretive heart.

And there are probably thousands of women in the country today who, having seen Gable, have left the theatre thinking . . . if only I had the chance to reform him!

For a man to inculcate in women the desire to turn loving reformer is a sure sympton of his popularity.

There are several men on the screen who give their audience an impression of rugged strength. Wallace Beery is one, of course; and another is George Bancroft. Gable has this strength, it lies naturally in his physique but he has more than strength. He has the happy faculty of suggesting banked fires—and not too well banked, either. He has a manner which indicates that while he might kiss a woman's lips he might also under provocation slap her face, and with perfect ease. He has grace as well as strength, and a lithe, swift coördination of flesh and bone and muscle which is very attractive.

Absolute perfection of feature and too much polish would have caused him to fall short of the impression he has created. The first time I saw him I said to myself—aside from his superb build, he isn't particularly attractive. Five minutes later I was taking it back. Ten minutes thereafter I was saying, "He's ugly-good looking." And before the picture had reached the final close-up I didn't know what he looked like and didn't, particularly, care.

Most extremely handsome men have a monotony of feature and expression. Gable has escaped that, he has escaped the mould. Much of his attraction lies in the fact that he is ugly as sin one moment and devastatingly good looking the next, and perhaps, the third time you look at him he isn't out of the ordinary, either way. He has a changing and changeable face, and unless his producers rubber-stamp his pictures as he goes on, this trick of feature and expression will enable him to play as many diverse rôles as can be found for him.

Since the world war there has been a demand for charm, for romantic charm. It is beginning to lessen. There are far too many young men of romantic charm and not much else, in life as well as on the screen. There seems to be something of a reaction against them. The average fan is beginning to call for men of action, men whom the old trite term, "he-man," fits like a glove.

If the fans have called, Mr. Gable has answered. And how! He is not particularly mysterious, neither is his vogue. He is simply an unusual looking young man, with danger as his password, and women have always loved danger. They may choose security, in the long run, for their life motto, but they haven't forgotten danger. And that is why they will flock to the theatres to see Mr. Gable and in order to forget their personal security while they live, for an hour, and quite vicariously the exciting, the sometimes brutal and the always interesting life which Mr. Gable appears to embody.

Personally I have always liked a *bona fide* villain. And to find one masquerading as the most stimulating of the screen's heroes is something of a delight. Life may be a bowl of cherries to most people but to Clark Gable it seems to be a bowl of cherries—with a kick.

what really happened to doris da

Continued from page 37 worried about her. She looked drawn and tired. They didn't want to start a picture and have her collapse midway. After all, she'd been none too strong when she made *Calamity Jane* with Howard Keel.

The front office boys talked to Marty. Where Doris is concerned, her husband is the only court of appeal. A new contract was coming up. Why couldn't Doris be reasonable? The studio had worked her too hard. Everyone agreed to that. Yes, she deserved more money. No question about it. How about $150,000 a picture, two pictures a year, a five-year deal? How about Martin Melcher Productions to be released through Warner Bros.? Okay, only let the girl get herself checked over.

Doris went to a doctor, a great doctor, and she was given a complete physical. A tumor was found near the left breast. She was told honestly, but with tact.

You can imagine the thoughts that raced through her mind. She was sure, first of all, that the tumor was malignant, cancerous. She thought of Dixie Lee Crosby who had been killed by that disease. She recalled other people similarly afflicted. She wondered what would happen to Terry, her young son, if she should die. To die at thirty! Her emotions ran amuck. Tears ran down her cheeks and she cried in her heart.

But, her staunch faith in her religion brought her strength. She wondered if the answer didn't lie in prayer. Prayer has brought her great happiness in the past. Prayer has the power to conquer and rectify and cure. And she started to pray, but around her there were people, kind people whom she loved and respected and admired, including the great doctor, and he said, "Look, honey. There's only one way we can tell about the tumor, only one way we can find out whether it's malignant or benign. We've got to take it out. At least, we've got to take out a piece and have it analyzed."

You can imagine the conflict that raged in this lovely girl's soul—the conflict between her religion and medicine.

She was prevailed upon to enter a hospital and on September 24, she was admitted to St. Joseph's in Burbank. A biopsy was performed on the left breast. A small tumor, no more than two-by-four centimeters was removed and taken down to the pathology laboratory. Doris was kept on the operating table.

If they should find that the tumor was benign, then Doris had nothing to worry about. The surgeon would merely suture the incision and home she'd go, good as new.

If the tumor were malignant, a radical mastectomy would have to be performed to stop the possible spread of cancer.

In his laboratory, the pathologist took the tumor and placed it on the microtome, a slicing machine. A blast of carbon dioxide instantly froze the tumor so that it would be firm enough for dissection.

While he worked, the doctor, the nurses, and Doris Day, their patient, waited. They waited and they prayed. Doris, of course, was anesthetized. In the operating room, there was only silence and hope.

The pathologist took a glass rod and picked up a small sample from the tumor. He dropped it into a jar of water and stained the tissue with toluidine blue so that the cellular structure would be easier to determine.

Then he slipped the tissue fragments onto a pair of glass slides. Delicately, he placed them under his microscope. He looked at one, then at the other. Then he smiled. "Benign," he said. "Benign."

Continued on page 61

WHILE JOHNNY WASN'T LOOKING

When Johnny Weissmuller was staying at the Mirador Hotel in Palm Springs, the guests got a grand opportunity to view that million-dollar body. Scotty, Modern Screen's own cameraman, got out the trusty old photograph-taker and caught these fine pictures of Tarzan. Yes, that's Johnny diving off the top of the page.

EL MIRADOR

CALL ME "DUTCH"

RONNIE REAGAN BLACKENS THAT

BOY SCOUT REPUTATION OF HIS!

"Nice Guy" Reagan has pangs of conscience when he neglects his fan mail and has never refused an autograph in his life.

BY DAVID CHANDLER

Mrs. Reagan (Jane Wyman) was christened Sarah Jane Folks. Is nicknamed "Dynamite." She paints, plays tournament tennis—is writing the Great American novel.

The Reagan baby is blonde with china blue eyes. She's god-mothered by Louella Parsons who fostered Jane's and Ronnie's romance

This fellow Reagan is a hard one to peg.

He's been in Hollywood for three years, so you'd think people would begin to have a fairly definite idea of what he's like. But all you're sure about is that everybody is fond of him. "Reagan's a swell guy," they say. "Ronnie's such a nice boy," they declare. Or, "He is the sweetest lad."

Now these are mighty poisonous words to utter about any young actor in Hollywood; they make him sound so insufferably dull. It were better that it be bruited about that the guy breaks every promise he makes, drinks to excess, is unbearably conceited and beats his wife.

The "good boy" legend probably grew out of the fact that in all his early films he was inevitably cast as the spotless hero. He was so shining and virtuous that one captious critic maintained that the strongest thing Reagan ever drank was a glass of buttermilk in "Code of the Secret Service," and at that he left half the glass untouched.

This, of all the snide attacks on Ronald Reagan, is what hurts him most. It was not so long ago that Ronnie was known from coast to coast as Dutch Reagan, one of the National Broadcasting Company's top sports announcers, and in that capacity Ronnie not only had to broadcast the big sports events but hold his end up in the customary celebrations after the event. Pat Rourke, the barkeeper, in Jack Dempsey's bistro across the street from the Madison Square Garden in New York, still recalls how Dutch Reagan, shy three dollars and forty-five cents for his bar bill, insisted upon offering a slightly-under-the-weather companion as a deposit till he had returned from his hotel, where he had forgotten his wallet in another pair of jeans. Dutch thereupon calmly lifted up the friend as if he were as light as a Teddy bear and handed him over the bar to the cashier's high stool.

Part of the blame, Ronnie thinks, for his purity boy reputation can be placed directly on his name. "There's something about the name Ronald that tickets me as a nice boy even before people know me. When I went on the air as a sports announcer, I took the monicker Dutch. The trouble with Ronnie is that it suggests a lad in velve-teen knee-pants and a silk shirt with a dainty lace collar. But when I went to work for Warner's they wouldn't let me be billed as Dutch Reagan, so back I went to Ronald."

But most of the blame rightfully belongs to the man himself. Perhaps what Ronnie needs is a nice big dose of temperament. Maybe if he could storm into the boss's office one fine day and demand something outrageous—anything—and threaten to do something drastic and get himself suspended, it would help. He has never been known to turn down a part. "So-and-so is replacing Ronald Reagan in 'Saga of Tenth Avenue.' Reagan is now on suspension," is a story that has yet to be released. Ronnie has rated an A-plus in deportment at Warner's all his life.

And he deserves it. The afternoon we had lunch with him, for example, Ronnie had just spent a nice hot California morning posing in a full-length, fur-lined suit under a battery of lights for stills for "Flight Patrol." He had been living in the un-air-conditioned suit for the twelve weeks the picture was in the making, but now that it was over he had to make a few stills. All right. This is the end of it. Okay. So they kept him under the relentless lights for hours; they had him climbing in the plane, they had him climbing out; they posed him by the wings, by the tail, by the propeller and just looking up at the sky. And not a peep out of Ronnie Reagan. Well, at last it's over.

So along comes a photographer to Ronnie's table while he is munching a ham and cheese on whole wheat and says he's got an advertising tie-up picture he wants to shoot with Ronnie. "Why, of course," says Ronnie in that sweet, cooperative way of his. "What do I wear?"

"Your flying suit from 'Flight Patrol.'"

Ronnie uttered one tiny word of dismay, but one pretty-please from the photog and he promised to jump into that nice hot suit all over again.

Perhaps one of the reasons so few people know what Ronald Reagan is like is that he is not given to tooting his own bugle. If he got lost in Mexico Continued on page 54

The Reagans were married in January '40, after a whirlwind courtship. It was her third altar-trek, his first. Her engagement ring was a 52-carat amethyst.

Warner Brothers' "Million Dollar Baby," co-starring Dutch and Priscilla Lane, is his twenty-third picture in three years. It's his largest role to date.

All you've got to do is love each other, thought Rock and Phyllis, and all the rest takes care of itself. Just one problem. It wasn't to prove true.

WHY ROCK WALKED OUT

by Linda Matthews

■ The tall young man sitting on the bed put his head in his hands. "I don't know, Ma," he said softly. "Ma, I just don't know."

Across the room, the grey-haired woman stared at him. Then she got up and walked to the window. Outside traffic roared, voices drifted faintly up. Below her a sign flashed: Beverly Hills Hotel. She sighed. "I don't understand you, Roy," she said finally. "We're talking different languages maybe. You tell me you're getting a divorce. You tell me you're—you're through with Phyllis. You sit here in a hotel room; you've moved out of your house—and I ask you why—and you tell me you don't know." Suddenly, with surprising force, she crossed to him. She pulled his hands down from his face. "Look at me!" she ordered. "I'm your mother. Look at me. Tell me why!"

In the silence, a clock ticked. Defeated, the woman dropped her son's hands. She went back to the chair and picked up a jacket and a purse. She walked to the door and opened it. Then with her back to Rock, she said softly, "I'm going home. If the neighbors ask me why you left your wife, I'll tell them what I used to read in the magazines. You like your steak rare, she likes it well-done. So you're getting a divorce. I'll tell them that. Maybe I'll even tell it to myself." She turned her head. Her tired *Continued on page 55*

When we received this unusual story we worried and called Linda Matthews . . . "Are you sure your facts are right, Linda?" "Yes," said Linda. "But how could you have gotten them?" "That," said Linda, "is indeed the secret . . . but just ask this: have I ever sent you a false story?" Since the answer was "no," we print it with full faith that it is correct.
THE EDITORS

or at sea you would be pretty sure not to hear a thing about it. It is in the records, for example, that in his twenty-seven years to date Reagan has saved the lives of seventy-seven people from drowning. But an astute publicity department generally gives this figure out as seventeen persons. "I guess they figure people wouldn't believe it if you told them a movie star saved seventy-seven lives," is the way Ronnie explains it.

There is hardly a young contract player who is not publicly dunked in a swimming pool the first few weeks he is engaged, but for some reason no one ever thought to do body art for Reagan. Then quite by accident, one of the publicity boys happened to spy Ronnie emerging from the surf at the Santa Monica Beach Club. The publicity lad couldn't help uttering a long, astounded, "Whee!" And the next day there was an order for Ronald Reagan to make some pictures in trunks. Those shots brought oh's and ah's from fans the country over, as well as hundreds of offers for testimonials for everything from breakfast cereals to stretching gadgets for developing the Body Beautiful.

I DIDN'T know what that fellow was talking about that day down at the beach," Ronnie says. "I'd just come down for a swim, and he kept telling me that I should have told him I had a body. Well, what did he think I had anyway? I used to be a four-letter man at college, but I didn't think that that gave me an excuse to stick out my chest and expand my biceps publicly every time someone mentioned the word health."

Today, it must be told, there is more than a little chance that all this will be changed. Ronnie is married to Jane Wyman, and Jane is a little girl with a mind of her own and an aggressive ability that will be certain to leave its mark on friend husband. Besides, there are three Reagans and a fourth one reportedly on the way!

Just the other day something happened that would have been unthinkable last year. Ronnie had been called into Jack Warner's office for an important conference. Mr. Warner, the studio chief and the man whose say-so could rocket him to the top or doom him to another year or two of playing cops-and-robbers in the B's, was in a benign, kindly mood and was outlining his plans for Ronnie's future.

But did Ronnie pay grateful attention? No. All he kept watching was a clock on the boss's desk, eyeing it with increasing dismay as each minute passed. Finally he could stand it no longer. He stood up in the midst of one of Mr. Warner's sentences and said, "You'll have to excuse me, sir, but I can't stay a minute longer—I've got to go. You see, if I don't get home in fifteen minutes I don't get to bathe the baby, and that's my job. So long—I'm very late."

We asked Ronnie point-blank if he didn't think that being married to Jane had changed him a little. "I suppose it has," he offered tentatively, then deciding definitely, "I know it has. I used to be easy-going because I didn't have anybody to think of but myself. But now I always get to thinking about Jane and Maureen and, well, it does make a difference. You hate to let your wife think you're being made a chump of."

Ronnie is not ashamed to tell you that Jane is the first and only girl he has been in love with. "From the time I graduated from college back in 1932, till we got married I was too busy to think much about romance. First I got into radio, and it was a hard grind for five years. I started with a little fresh-water station in Davenport, Iowa, not knowing a thing

about sports announcing. Then the station got to growing bigger and bigger, and they towed me along. Then came the national hookups, the big football games, the Joe Louis fights, the World's Series—and I kept telling myself I wasn't good enough and being so worried I didn't have much time for girls.

"Then one spring I came out to California to watch the Chicago Cubs in their spring training and a Warner Brothers' scout screen-tested me, and before I could say boo I was playing in pictures! As my dramatic experience was limited to a couple of plays with the Eureka College Dramatic Society, you can imagine how scared I was. I was afraid that any moment I'd be called before someone, be told it had all been a dreadful mistake and get canned. It wasn't till 'Brother Rat' that I began to be sure of myself. And that's when I sort of started to take real notice of Jane. Oh, I'd seen her around, but I'd never thought much about her. When we were shooting 'Rat' I kept finding myself unconsciously on the lookout for her."

"Did she take to you at once?"

"Heck, no. She thought I was a snob. You see, I've got to wear specs because I'm so darned far-sighted I can't see anything less than a hundred yards away without 'em. Well, a couple of times I'd forgotten my glasses and had walked by Jane without so much as a cool 'hiya,' and for a while I was just plain poison to her.

"Then we both worked late one day, and we bumped into each other going home. I knew she hadn't had dinner so I suggested we have it together. I got to like her at once. So naturally at work the next day I suggested a return engagement and got an immediate booking. Then I found myself dating her every chance I got."

WHEN we finished the picture we were both in the mood for a long spree of dining and dancing and staying up till dawn. We'd both been working hard and needed a little bit of tooting around. I never had a serious thought about it.

"I think I began to realize I was in love when Jane went off to Santa Barbara with friends for a week-end and left me alone. I thought the world had come to an end. When she returned forty-eight hours later, I felt twenty years older. Soon after that we both got a chance to go on a personal appearance tour with Louella Parsons. Those weeks together cinched it. I was crazy in love and didn't care who knew it."

Jane, beside being wife and mother and actress in her own right, is now a combination of agent, business manager and publicity man for Ronnie. Given half a chance she is sure to tell you about her husband. He likes comfortable old things, so periodically Jane has to browbeat him into going to the tailor's and getting new clothes. If Ronnie thinks that nice banker-grey flannel in the corner is just the thing, not ostentatious and just right, Jane will tell the salesman in definite, firm tones that what the husband wants is a Glen Urquhart plaid and draped, please, to show off that manly chest.

The only thing that is Ronnie's domain without question is a threadbare armchair and ottoman that sits in a corner of the Reagan living room. The room itself is a decorator's item in dubonnet and yellow, and the sight of the faded, decrepit chair is a bit of a shock. But it's Ronnie's chair, and the earnest plea of no decorator is going to get it out, color scheme or no color scheme. As a matter of fact Jane tried once to get it recovered, just recovered—and had to call up to get it back untouched lest the master of the house really get angry.

This display of temperament and stubbornness, this evidence that Ronnie has a very definite mind of his own, is just what Jane is cultivating in her lord and master—and if it means a dirty old chair in the living room, why, so be it.

As we said, the Reagans now have a child,

Maureen Elizabeth, eight months old. For the public enlightenment, it might just as well be given out that Maureen is the spittin' image of mother Jane, with the same wide, curved forehead and the same charming nose. Dad just beams at her. If you ask the he-man if he wouldn't have preferred a boy, he gives you an emphatic "no."

"You know, the nice thing about having a girl is that you have a sort of picture of the girl you married, the girl you're in love with as a child and a young girl—you kind of watch her grow up. I know it's silly, but it gives you a kick."

RONNIE doesn't have any old-fashioned prejudices about his wife working. "I think the trouble usually comes from people resenting each other's success," he says. "This is especially true of actors. As for us, I can honestly say we share in one another's success, and we have fun talking about our work to each other."

The Reagans are both crazy about their work. Every so often they will get a yen to do the town, but mostly they spend their evenings in the movie houses. The big problem of their life is trying to find a picture they have not seen. The good ones they see two or three times (they love to watch the technique of a swell job of film-making), and the Bing Crosby pictures they see four or five times. Jane is an ardent fan of Bing's. (She owns every record he ever made.) Ronnie's pet enthusiasm is George Murphy, and at the last telling he had seen "A Girl, A Guy and A Gob" only three times less than Lord Beaverbrook has seen "Destry Rides Again," which, we are told, is thirty-seven.

The Reagans are sensible folk. They live on an allowance, and what they don't actually need goes smack into the bank every week and no nonsense. It makes it a little easier that Jane and Ronnie both work and they admit it. Those weeks when one or the other is on layoff, why, there's just that much less money to go into the bank.

The reason for all this saving is the new home they're building. Right now the Reagans live in a penthouse apartment off the Sunset Strip, but they are waiting for the day when their new house is ready for the moving in. Ronnie broke another precedent when he elected to build in Beverly Hills rather than the Valley where men's men are supposed to live these days. Doing the unexpected gives him a kick.

As for the future, it is right here in pictures. They are in his blood, and he knows of nothing so important or so much fun. The only thing that may get in the way is the United States Cavalry. Ronnie is a Second Lieutenant in the Cavalry Reserves, and he may be called up for active service any day. Not that he is grudging in his willingness to go. Anything but. It may give the studio bosses nightmares to picture one of their brighter hopes spending one full year in maneuvers in the gentle way of the cavalry, but if the truth be told, Ronnie would love it if it were not for that year of separation from Jane and Maureen. Ronnie has always soft-pedaled talk of his commission in the cavalry because the studio would get frightened. The cavalry's idea of a ride is not a gentlemanly canter on a smooth bridle-path. What they like is a snorting, spirited charger that cannot stand still and a terrain that is uneven, hilly and full of hidden brooks. The cavalry loves those plunges down practically perpendicular ravines, those lunges across rivers that have swollen dangerously overnight. The cavalry has a way of seeing to it that army post hospitals do not contain too many empty beds!

Some chaps who possess one tired old mare take so many horsey pictures you get the idea they themselves sup on oats and mash. But Ronnie doesn't talk about his riding ability. When he was making "Santa Fe Trail" there was a scene that called for dangerous, tricky riding, and Ronnie was anxious to do it. But when they were ready to shoot it, there was a double ready for the take. Ronnie begged to do the scene himself. "We won't hear of it," he was told. "You might get hurt and hold up production. Besides this calls for really expert riding."

Characteristically, Ronnie said all right and let the matter drop. The next day he had to go to cavalry practice and they had a pretty hectic drill. Seven riders were hospitalized, and the way the troop rode made that scene in "Santa Fe Trail" look like a slow motion study of equitation for a middle-aged ladies' riding class.

But Ronnie is not going to make a fuss because they won't let him ride a horse. If he ever does get temperamental, you can bet that last dollar it will be over something worth getting temperamental about. When you love making movies the way Ronnie does and you plan to spend your life in the industry, you're bound to be a little sensible. "I'll spend my life in pictures whether as an actor or what have you," he says. It looks like he'll have a long time before he gets into the "what have you" class because his future as an actor is brighter and more promising than ever. For his work in "Santa Fe Trail" he got a real part opposite Priscilla Lane in "Million Dollar Baby," and the preview audiences were so enthusiastic that he was given the lead in the picturization of the best-seller "King's Row," which promises to be one of Warners' extra-specials.

So it begins to look as though, in spite of himself and his modesty, people are beginning to find out about this guy Reagan. He'll never be found tooting his own horn, but from now on a lot of people are going to do it for him.

why rock walked out

Continued from page 52 eyes gleamed suddenly with tears. "Only I tell you this. While you sit here, you ask yourself something. You ask yourself why you and a nice girl couldn't get along. Why two people with everything in the world should make themselves suffer so. Why love dies out like this. Other people fight sometimes. They don't get divorced. So why you? Ask that. And if you really don't have an answer—you go home again, Roy. You hear me? You go home again."

The door shut.

"All right, Ma," Rock Hudson whispered into the empty room.

And for the hundredth time he began again the slow, painful search for an answer. Why two nice people, two people in love, couldn't make it work.

And there had been love—so very much. Alone in the room he could still remember those first weeks of dating Phyllis—the heady excitement of picking her up, being with her

"I'm crazy about you," he told Phyl one night. "I guess you know that. But we're so different, you and me."

"That's what makes it fun," she had said then. "That's why we'll never bore each other."

He had laughed and drawn her closer. "If I believed that, I might—just possibly—ask you to marry me."

Suddenly the laughter was gone. They regarded each other with serious eyes.

"Ask me," Phyllis said softly. "Go ahead and ask me."

And believing that love was enough, they were married.

Other people fight, his mother had said. *They don't get a divorce. But do other people fight as much?* he asked himself suddenly. *The way we do. Over—over nothing. Over anything—*

That fatal dress

The first one had happened six weeks after they were married. There had been the honeymoon, and then Rock was back to work. Evenings he would walk into the house exhausted, ready for dinner. One night, dinner wasn't ready for him.

"We'll eat in half an hour, sweetie," Phyllis had called from the kitchen. "I'm awfully sorry—but wait till you see what I've got—"

Rock sank down in a chair in the living room. "What?"

"The most beautiful—the most heavenly—the most luscious evening gown. It's black chiffon with a train—it's the most stunning—"

"Wait a minute." Rock sat up, raised his hand. "Look. You bought an evening gown last week. Five hundred dollars worth of gauze or something. You haven't even worn it yet. And now today—"

The smile faded from Phyl's eyes. "Honey, you don't understand. Sooner or later I'll wear the one I bought last week. And there's sure to be some photographer around to take my picture in it. And you don't want them to get the same gown again the next time we go out—I mean, **what would your public say?**" The grin reappeared.

"I don't think that's funny," Rock said. He didn't mean it to sound so abrupt, so cold. But he was tired and hungry and he wanted his dinner. "Anyway, I've told you and told you—I don't want us to start **dragging around to nightclubs and premières and junk all of a sudden.**"

Never go out

Phyl stared at him. She let the kitchen door swing shut behind her. "Rock, I thought we agreed we'd go out a little more. I thought you promised—"

"All right. I said we'd go out. I didn't say we were going to burn up the town, did I?" He got up from the chair. "Listen, I come home tired at night. If you think I'm going to sit back while you spend a fortune on clothes to wear to formals and then make me take you to formals so you can wear the damn clothes—"

"A fortune!" Phyl shouted. "A fortune. Oh, that's funny. That's a riot! Do you know what you're making a week? Why, if I spent twice as much a day as I spend in a month I couldn't start spending it all. I couldn't—"

"Well, you don't have to try!" Rock bellowed. "What'd this little shopping trip cost me today? Five hundred dollars—a thousand?"

Phyl drew herself up. "It cost three hundred and seventy-five—"

"Oh, my Lord," Rock moaned. "Three hundred—for a piece of nothing—for a hunk of cloth you'll never even get to wear—a—"

Suddenly Phyl's voice was very soft. "No," she said. "The dress cost a hundred and fifty. I also spent twenty-five on a cashmere sweater. With the rest I got you that new snorkel outfit you saw. I got you a sweater. I got you a—" the soft voice broke. With tears streaming down her pretty face, Phyl turned and ran from the room. "B-but don't worry," her voice floated back to Rock. "I'll take it all back. I'll give you back all your precious money!"

Who was right?

He had sat alone for twenty minutes in the living room, listening to his wife cry upstairs. Then he got up and climbed the steps to the bedroom. With his arm around Phyl's shoulder, with her sobs muffled on his chest, he had tried to explain.

"Phyl, it isn't that I don't want you to have nice things. I do, baby, honest. But I was brought up to—to be careful with money. It goes against my grain to see you throw it out on stuff you don't need."

And Phyl had said slowly, "Rock, if you were still delivering mail, making practically nothing—why, I'd love you and marry you, and I'd scrimp and save and make my own clothes and never mind or say a word. I swear it. But we *do* have the money. It's the one thing we do have, because heaven knows we haven't got privacy or time together or—anyway—we have money. So why can't I spend it? I'm not bankrupting us, not by a long shot. And it isn't just the clothes. It's that I—I love to shop. Like you love to swim. It makes me feel good. So isn't that doing something useful with it? Isn't it?"

In her arms, Rock nodded, bewildered. But the next week, when Phyl bought a coat, and the week after—something else, the fights got worse and worse.

But when you're the country's biggest box-office draw, when your yearly income runs into six or even seven figures—how can you go to your mother and say: *Ma—we fought about money.*

What's the reason?

You like your steak rare. She likes hers done. So you're getting a divorce, his mother had said. A bitter joke, she thought that was. But it was more bitter

Continued on page 91

ON THE SET

For the sake of ultimate efficiency at MGM Studios in the 1930's, there was an unwritten law of one star or one star couple per picture. Hence, in a Greta Garbo film, she must be the focal point, and in a Norma Shearer movie, everyone else on the screen must be a supporting player. There were three great exceptions to this rule: *Grand Hotel* (1932), *Dinner at Eight* (1933), and *The Women* (1939). These were the company's "all-star" productions, and when viewed fifty years later, they still stand up as a trio of the greatest films ever made.

To commemorate the filming of *Grand Hotel,* photo sessions with the great George Hurrell were set up to capture this mega-event: Greta Garbo, John Barrymore, Lionel Barrymore, Wallace Beery, and Joan Crawford all in the same movie!

Although Joan was fast becoming one of the studio's major stars, she was intimidated by the prospect of sharing the screen with these legendary professionals. Crawford had long admired Garbo, and unfortunately, they appeared in no scenes together. Since Greta was so aloof, Joan had never met her on the set either. One day, during the filming of *Grand Hotel,* the two women met on a staircase. As though she were appraising a sculpture, Garbo held Joan's face in her hand and surveyed its angles: "What a pity! Our first picture together and we don't work with each other. I'm sorry. You have a marvelous face." That was the only conversation the actresses ever had in over ten years together at

> Clark Gable:
> "Well, well. How's my little chromium blonde this morning?"
> Jean Harlow: "You big Ohio hillbilly. I heard what you said behind my back!"
> *Modern Screen*
> August 1933

MGM. On the opposite page are some of Hurrell's shots of Joan from *Grand Hotel,* in the role of Flaemmchen the stenographer. The page is from the May 1932 issue of *Modern Screen.*

"Behind the Scenes with Jean and Clark" (page 58), from *Modern Screen's* August 1933 issue, is especially effervescent. Reported by guest writer Anita Loos, it captures the real-life Harlow and Gable that audiences have long imagined existed when the cameras weren't rolling. Both Clark and Jean came from working-class backgrounds, and they clearly spoke the same language. Loos, who reports the story in a razor-sharp style, became world famous for writing the book *Gentlemen Prefer Blondes.* She also penned the screenplays and/or stories for five of Jean Harlow's films: *Red-Headed Woman* (1932), *Hold Your Man* (1933), *The Girl from Missouri* (1934), *Riffraff* (1936), and *Saratoga* (1937). Note in this story Gable saying about Harlow, "I am worried for fear Jean's sick." Four years later, on the set of *Saratoga,* Jean collapsed in his arms and within days was dead at the age of twenty-six.

Among the best-loved movies of the Depression era were a string of frivolous backstage musicals with dance numbers by Busby Berkeley: *42nd Street* (1933), *Footlight Parade* (1933), *Gold Diggers of 1933* (1933), and *Dames* (1934), to name a few. In the July 1933 issue of *Modern Screen,* the magazine went on location to capture *Backstage with the Gold Diggers of 1933* (page 62). Catch Joan Blondell in her gold coin outfit from the "We're in the Money" production number! You'll also find Leslie Howard visiting...on the set.

FLAEMMCHEN

. . . Joan Crawford's work as Vicki Baum's character in "Grand Hotel" is said to be a major triumph for the star

Vicki Baum's genius needs genius to portray it. And Joan Crawford proves her tremendous acting ability. Starting at the top of page and going clockwise: 1. Wallace Beery tells her she is beautiful. 2. A tense emotional moment. 3. She tells Mr. Kringelein (Lionel Barrymore) he's a good man. 4. "You aren't the same today," sighs Joan to John Barrymore. Have you read Vicki Baum's story on page 48?

Photographs on this page by Hurrell, courtesy M-G-M

BEHIND THE SCENES WITH
JEAN and CLARK

Below, Jean listens to the recording of a scene from "Hold Your Man," the picture which Anita Loos wrote for her and Clark (that's he at the right). "He'd be great as a lover," says Jean. "The type that always doesn't want to be mooshing about with you."

By ANITA LOOS

This popular writer knows her Hollywood thoroughly and she was actually on the set all during the filming of "Hold Your Man" which she wrote for Jean Harlow and Clark Gable. She also gave you "The Barbarian," "Ladies of the Night"—and loads of grand dialogue for other M-G-M films

ONE bright day in April I was sitting in my office looking at the new guaranteed earthquake-proof ceiling and speculating whether it would be better to be hit by chunks of plaster from an old-fashioned non-earthquake-proof ceiling or by the entire unbreakable one-piece roof which now protects the scenario brains of Metro-Goldwyn-Mayer.

Suddenly the telephone rang. It was Bernie Hyman, producer of the Harlow-Gable picture just starting production.

"We're ready to shoot," said Bernie, "and we begin with the battle stuff. Thought perhaps you'd like to come over."

"Battle stuff?" What was Bernie trying to put over

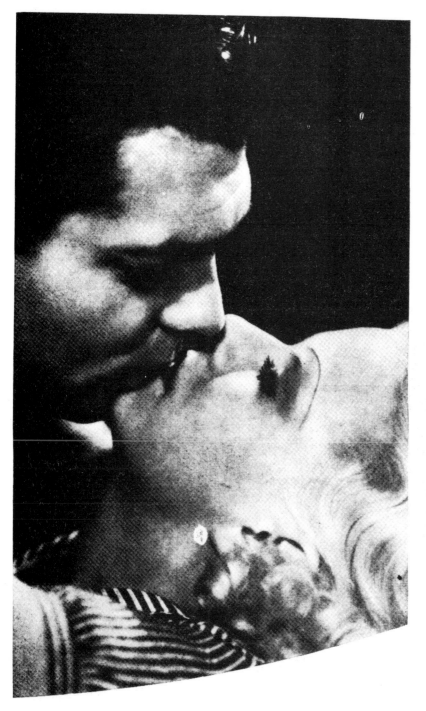

...Come to the Harlow-Gable set with the famous author of their latest picture! An intimate, breezy inside story by the girl who wrote "Gentlemen Prefer Blondes"

What happens when those "two red hot numbers" come out of an embrace? This story gives you the facts. Above, a snappy scene from "Hold Your Man." Remember them in "Red Dust"?

on me? I rushed to the stage and arrived just in time for the carnage.

Smack!

Dainty brunette Dorothy Burgess leaves the imprint of her open hand on the delicate cheek of Jean Harlow. Jean doesn't bat an eye. With studied deliberation she doubles up a fist the size of a blue point oyster, and—

Wham!

Dorothy takes it staggeringly on her dimpled chin. This was the "battle stuff." Just two Janes battling for the love of Clark Gable in "Hold Your Man." The scene is in Clark's bachelor apartment where neither lady had a right to be, according to the rules laid down in Hill's Manual of Social Forms, published in 1882.

This being the first day's shooting, a goodly crowd was there to see the girls fight it out to a clean decision.

HOWEVER, almost every day is a gala day on the set of a Harlow-Gable picture. Jean and Clark are such capable troupers and such good sports that work is play to both of them. Jean's phonograph, placed as near the "set up" as possible, plays every instant that the camera isn't going. A large, free-for-all jigsaw puzzle is on a nearby table in process of being "licked"—with every member of the company, from the "props" on up taking a go at it.

There is a lot of speculation on the part of the public as to just how actors and actresses differ from other human beings whose actions are not subject to keyhole scrutiny.

Not infrequently a mediocre actress tries to foist herself on the public as the real thing by having herself pictured in the Sunday supplements attired in dainty lounging pajamas, gracefully reposing on a chaise-longue with a volume of Wordsworth open on her horizontal stomach. Probably under her pillow, won on the pleasure pier at Venice, is secreted a contraband copy of Chic Sale's immortal work.

Mr. Einstein, who knows everything, will tell you that a pair of silk pajamas and a book don't make an actress. Other things are required in pictures nowadays—for instance, brains.

And of brains Jean and Clark both have plenty.

The public naturally longs to inspect its screen favorites in the "raw"; to catch them off-guard, that their whims, foibles and general characteristics may stand out like the weatherbeaten thumb of a hitch-hiker. It is on the set, between grinds of the camera, that the actor becomes more himself than he is at home or in his club. Having been keyed up during tiresome and exacting scenes, he welcomes a respite. Artificiality is tossed to the winds and he lets himself go.

It may be something of a revelation to see two of the world's most inflammable "neckers," Jean Harlow and Clark Gable, at their job of swapping sex appeal. What happens, for instance, when these two red hot numbers come out of an embrace? I'll tell you. They razz the face off each other. Underneath their sharp jibes lies deep friendship and respect, but one would never guess it from their incessant exchange of hot shot.

Jean and Clark are really enthusiastic in their praise of each other. If one should make a slighting remark about Jean in the presence of Clark, six foot one inch of masculine prowess would flatten him to the earth. Jean would resent any unfavorable criticism of her co-worker by hurling a shoe at the offender, as she sits around between scenes with her footgear off. (Jean, by the way, is not fond of being "dressed up." Beach slippers are her favorite footwear and her pet 'ensemble' consists of a pair of yellow flannel pajamas with a patch on the rear, and an old green turtle-neck sweater.)

"What about a dame that can't live without a gramaphone going?" Clark said. "Besides this one on the set she has one in her dressing room and three in her house . . . " But Gable seems to like to listen, too—and so does Director Wood.

One morning Jean was late in making her appearance on the stage. I happened to be there and Clark was plainly concerned.

"I am worried for fear Jean's sick," he said. "She's never late unless something's wrong. Do you know," he continued, "I can't understand how that tiny kid stands up under such strenuous work. She only weighs one hundred and nine pounds, but she seems to have the endurance of a prize-fighter. She is a brave little trouper—and can she act? Say, she sets a pace for me that keeps me on my toes every minute. It is a picnic to work with her. She anticipates every move and meets you more than halfway. When it comes to weighing dramatic values, Jean's scales need no adjusting. She ought to be a source of delight to directors—I know she is to Sam Wood. Sam says that she is a mind-reader and kidnaps his thoughts before he can express them. Gee, I hope the kid isn't sick!" And Clark heaved a genuine sigh.

I LOOKED up over Clark's shoulder. Tiptoeing toward us came Jean, forefinger to her lips.

While his back was turned toward her, Clark glimpsed her approach out of the tail of his eye but showed no indication that he was aware of her presence. He resumed his conversation in a louder tone.

"The trouble with Harlow is that she's mean. She plays her own stuff for all it's worth but she certainly crabs my best scenes. I can't call her down because she is a woman, but some day I'll forget myself. Have you noticed her sitting around with her shoes off? Well, she does that because she can't think without twiddling her toes. Her brains are in her feet."

Jean stopped and listened.

"And what about a dame that can't live without a gramaphone going?" Clark continued. "Besides this one on the set she has one in her dressing room and three in her house with radio attachments. She plays the record of 'Night and Day' day and night—until I'm going nuts. Thinks she can crab my performance! Huh! The poor sap—she doesn't seem to realize that if I *don't* give a good performance in this picture there won't be *anything* for the audience to see."

At this point Jean confronted her traducer, and with hands on her hips. "My pal!" she remarked.

Feigning surprise, Clark jumped to his feet. "Well, well, how's my little chromium blonde this morning? I was worried about you being late."

"You big Ohio hill-billy!" blazed Jean. "I heard what you said behind my back!"

"Well, did you ever hear that old crack about eavesdroppers never hearing any good of themselves?" he asked.

The he-man of the films dodged just in time to miss Jean's beach slipper as he fled.

"What a man, what a man!" grinned Jean as he left. "He razzes me every minute in hopes of getting my goat—and sometimes he does. In a big hot love scene the other day he whispered: 'Jean, you've got your eyebrows on upside down.' So I ups to him and said I could hardly wait for him to grow old and gray as I was just crazy about Gray Gables. If he *will* go in for ancient wheezes, I can not only take 'em—but I can hand 'em right back."

"Do you like working with Clark?" I asked.

"Well, I should say I do! I am never the least bit nervous with him. He is so *Continued on page 61*

Behind the Scenes with Jean and Clark

Continued from page 60

sure—and dependable. All the time."

"What would you think of Clark as a lover?" I asked.

"He'd be great," said Jean without any hesitation. "The type that doesn't always want to be mooshing about with you. But if you did get sentimental he'd break down and meet you halfway. However, he's in love with his wife and my big yen at the moment is for a Duesenberg car, so I don't think we'll get together *this* year."

At this instant up hove Clark.

"Well," said Jean loudly, "now I'll have to be pawed over by that big lummox Gable for an hour. If I get a chance I'll bite his ear off!"

EVERY day at tea time either Clark or Jean treats the company to tea and cake. While on a picture Jean scarcely eats anything, because she has an idea that food instantly makes her fat and can change her contour in the length of time it takes to swallow it. If she allows herself an infinitesimal cookie at tea, she swears that it can be seen in the following shot.

Jean has a "double" who is not on the payroll at M-G-M. It is her mother. Jean's nickname for her is "Angel." "Angel" generally shows up at the end of the day to take Jean home. They adore each other and are so much alike in appearance that any of Jean's fans would know her mother instantly if they should meet her. She has the same natural silvery blonde hair as her daughter and exactly the same features.

Incidentally, Jean rarely uses slang, except when she is scrapping with the gentleman she sometimes calls "Roughneck Gable." This is only one of her numerous pet names for Clark.

Both Jean and Clark are very agreeable to allowing strangers on the set while they are working. However, it is a studio rule for the guide always to ask the stars before they show visitors on the set.

One day during the shooting of "Hold Your Man," Jean had had a very exacting morning. She had been working with a bad case of the flu and was worn out. The guide came in and

asked her if she minded having visitors.

Jean, very weary, said, "Well I don't know. How many are there?"

"There are six of them."

"Six!" said Jean wearily.

"Yes," answered the guide, "but they are all very small."

Jean laughed so heartily that she couldn't refuse his request. When the guide came back he had six little Japs in tow.

THE Gable-Harlow set is noted for having no "yes" people. Everybody "no's" everybody else, making a very healthy atmosphere. Sam Wood, director, wields no blacksnake, but he gets what he wants by asking for it in a tone as gentle as he would use in asking for a cup of tea at a church fair.

Clark and Jean appeared together for the first time on the very stage on which they are now working. The picture was "The Secret Six," and the popularity they each enjoyed later might have had something to do with the public's desire to see them together again.

Jean is probably today the world's ideal of exactly what a siren should be. Her name has grown to be almost a synonym for sex. And in this—as in a few other weighty matters, I fear the world is wrong. Jean, as a type, is what I would call a mental tom-boy. Her attitude toward me is one of frank comradeship. She'd rather laugh than flirt any day. She'd rather be comfortable in old clothes than alluringly dolled up. She likes men better than women, I think. Women will always be a little resentful of Jean because of her striking beauty, and perhaps she senses this. Men are drawn to her, not only for her beauty, but for her unfailing comradeship and wit—and this she likes. A vampire she certainly is not, and does not want to be.

But when the cameras start to grind —particularly when she's playing opposite Clark Gable as in "The Secret Six" and "Red Dust"—it's different.

Just wait till you see some of those scenes I watched in "Hold Your Man!"

what really happened to doris day

Continued from page 48

The word was flashed to the operating room. Everyone was smiling. The doctor closed the wound. When Doris awoke she was told the truth. Absolutely no cancer. She could go home with peace of mind.

Physically, she was okay.

BUT peace of mind did not come easily, and at home she developed an anxiety neurosis, a constant apprehension, a psychogenic illness of sorts, and the doctor recommended that she see a specialist.

Doris complained of nervousness and fatigue and a tendency to be easily upset. To her, this was frightening, because all her life she has been an energetic, hardambition and a disinclination and partial

working girl and suddenly she had flagging inability to work or even to play.

Fatigability in girls like Doris Day rarely comes as a result of metabolic exhaustion, although Doris has frequently suffered from a marked anemia. More frequently, the fatigue is a result of emotional difficulties, the foundations of which can be traced to childhood conflicts.

I went to grade school with Doris Kappelhoff in Cincinnati, and while I never knew her well, I knew something about her family life.

The Kappelhoffs lived in the ground floor of a three- or four-story brick building.

Her mother, a sweet and thoughful woman, enrolled her in dancing school and later took her to Hollywood where Fan-

chon & Marco signed her and her youthful dancing partner, Jerry Dougherty, for a series of kiddie stage shows. I think she was thirteen, maybe fourteen at the time. Already she was becoming a bread-winner.

I am not a physician and I do not know the underlying causes of the psychoneuroses, but in the case of Doris Day I honestly think that this girl is unhappy because she doesn't want a career but is trapped by one. Against her own inclination, she has become big business. Recording contracts, her own radio show, TV rights, a new Warner Brothers deal, the leading light of Martin Melcher Productions.

Marty Melcher looks after all this with the superb competence born of experience. He has been an agent, he has worked in the music game for many years. He has had to learn all the angles, and he's learned them well.

According to some reporters there is no sharper man in Hollywood than Marty Melcher. Doris is indeed fortunate in having such a man to look after her finances.

UNFORTUNATELY, Marty looks after everything. When he was going with Doris, he helped move her furniture, he repaired things around the house, he made fast friends with her son, Terry. He advised her mother. In short, he became a father substitute, and psychologically, this may turn out to have been a very bad thing. As I say, it all depends on the childhood relationship between Doris and her father.

There is a psychological process termed, "recall," and it is hampered by another one termed, "repression," but in the weeks to come if Doris can look back into her youth and recall emotional experiences she has sought to repress, the answer to her nervousness and her current instability may be found.

Perhaps she will discover that she disliked her father because he refused to remain with her mother. Perhaps she disliked him for several other reasons. Perhaps in her subconscious, she has transferred that dislike to her fathersubstitute, to Marty Melcher, the overseer of her career.

Perhaps she refuses to admit any of this to herself and herein lies the basis for her personal conflict.

These are all possibilities and I suggest them because in similar cases they have been found valid.

To my way of thinking, Doris, in her subconscious, not only regards her husband as a father-substitute and a psychological crutch but as a figure synonymous with career. And her career, as I've said, has never been particularly pleasurable to her.

and I think the first-born child, a boy, died before Doris was born. She's the baby, and there's an older brother, Paul.

Her father was one of those rigid, toostrict fathers, a Teutonic mixture of sentiment and discipline. He used to teach music, and I think Doris was afraid of him.

I'm sure that practically all of her nervousness can be attributed to her relationship with her father. Her parents were divorced when she was eleven or twelve, and I think her youth ended then.

Her career was responsible for her meeting with Al Jordan who used to play in Jimmy Dorsey's band. They got married and soon she had a child. When the marriage went to pieces, she had to use her career to support her boy.

One time when she was flat broke, she begged the program manager of WLW to hire her at sustaining rates. He paid her scale, $64 a week.

Continued on page 107

Oh, it's a great show that Warner Brothers has made! The huge cast includes Ruby Keeler, Joan Blondell, Warren William, Ginger Rogers, Dick Powell, Aline Mac-Mahon and Glenda Farrell. (Immediately right) Joan Blondell, snapped on the set, in her coin costume. (Further right) Warren William and Ginger Rogers in a bit of byplay. (Below) Dance instructor Busby Berkeley gives Leslie Howard and Doug Fairbanks, Jr.,— visiting on the set—a violin lesson of a sort.

BACKSTAGE WITH THE

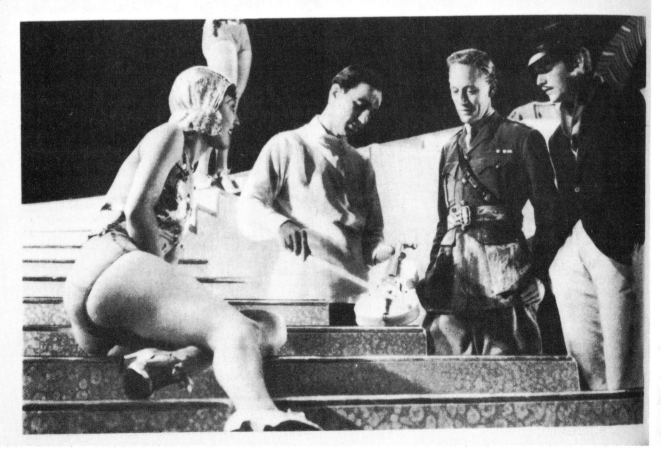

GOLDDIGGERS OF 1933

(Above) This just shows you how big those sound stages are. That is one of the most spectacular scenes of the show. The girls' costumes are very effective—three swirling tiers of wired white material. (Left) Ruby Keeler, in a white wig, Dick Powell and instructor Berkeley, rehearsing. (Further left) Ruby, Dick and Joan in a cute scene. The tremendous success of "Forty-Second Street" —and the success of Ruby and Dick in it—has been responsible for "Gold-diggers," you know.

Here are some of filmdom's famous with their stand-ins. A stand-in, in case you don't know, is someone with looks and ability, but little opportunity. Here is Ben Splane, who is "lighted" for George Brent.

Mary Lou Islieb is Shirley's chum and stand-in. Mary Lou got the job because her mother and Mrs. Temple are old friends. Everybody loves the star, but only her family and Shirley love her stand-in.

ME AND MY SHADOW

Helene Holmes is Alice Faye's "shadow." She is also her best friend and her personal wardrobe designer.

Sally Sage is prettier than Bette Davis, but she hasn't Bette's dramatic ability. That's why you've never heard of her while Bette ranks high among your favorites. So near and yet so far from fame and fortune!

Tyrone Power got his stand-in job for Tom Noonan, one of his most intimate personal friends. While they'd never be mistaken for each other, their build and coloring are the same. Stand-ins work hard, too.

Peter Lorre and Delmar Costello (left) are interchangeable on the set —as are Errol Flynn and Don Turner. When Turner is not serving as stand-in, he is the studio's chief stunt man.

ON THE SET WITH
"THE LITTLE FOXES"

Lovely, ruthless Regina Giddens (Bette Davis) is wife of Horace Giddens (Herbert Marshall), president of small Southern bank in year 1900. She has a daughter, Alexandra (Teresa Wright).

In lavish style for which he is famed, Goldwyn brought in top-flight portrait photographers George Hurrell (above), Maurine, Paul Hesse, James Doolittle, Charles Kerlee and L. Willinger to make publicity sittings of Stars Davis and Wright. Unit lenser was Bert Six. Since wild life conservationists ban birds on hats, studio had to borrow one from Louisiana Museum.

Chief trouble maker among authentic Edwardian period gowns designed by Orry-Kelly, this black velvet, bead-trimmed creation necessitated use of flesh-pinching corsets, brought on Davis collapse. Bette's wardrobe also included gown of black taffeta and lace, and one of white lace, both heirlooms. For stays, designers had no whalebone, used steel instead.

With her avaricious brothers, Ben Hubbard (Charles Dingle, above) and Oscar Hubbard (Carl Benton Reid), Regina plots to buy control of a cotton mill. Each one must put up $75,000.

To interpret morbid psychological nuances of Lillian Hellman's stage smash, Goldwyn gave camera assignment to thin, sensitive-faced Gregg Toland (kneeling), Hollywood's ace cinematographer. Toland lighting wizardry (see "Citizen Kane"), not elaborate make-up, made over-40, hard-faced Regina Giddens of 32-year-old Bette Davis. Candles were electric-lit.

Bitter antagonist of the greedy, arrogant Hubbards is David Hewitt (Richard Carlson), young newspaperman and son of the village dressmaker. Regina discourages his attentions to Alexandra.

Anxious to get the money needed for her share of the mill deal, Regina sends Alexandra to bring home Horace, ailing of a heart condition in Baltimore, treats him with unaccustomed solicitude.

Made up and costumed as Regina Giddens, Star Davis strikingly resembles more voluptuous Tallulah Bankhead, star of stage show. Becoming pompadour hairdress required 48-minute work each morning, helped illusion of middle age. Instead of conventional make-up, Warner artist Perc Westmore (above) depended on plain white base, very little eye shadow.

Nervous Bette smoked incessantly between scenes. Light-provider (above) is Prop Man Irving Sindler, who always sneaks his name into a Goldwyn film. In this one, it appears in newspaper insert. Bette's companion is Herbert Marshall, suave, 51, British—object of her hatred in the film, a warm friend in private. He played chess by mail with a British schoolmate.

Weak, disillusioned, Horace soon realizes her purpose, flatly refuses her demand for the $75,000. Coldly, brutally, Regina drops her mask, tells Horace she hopes he will soon be dead.

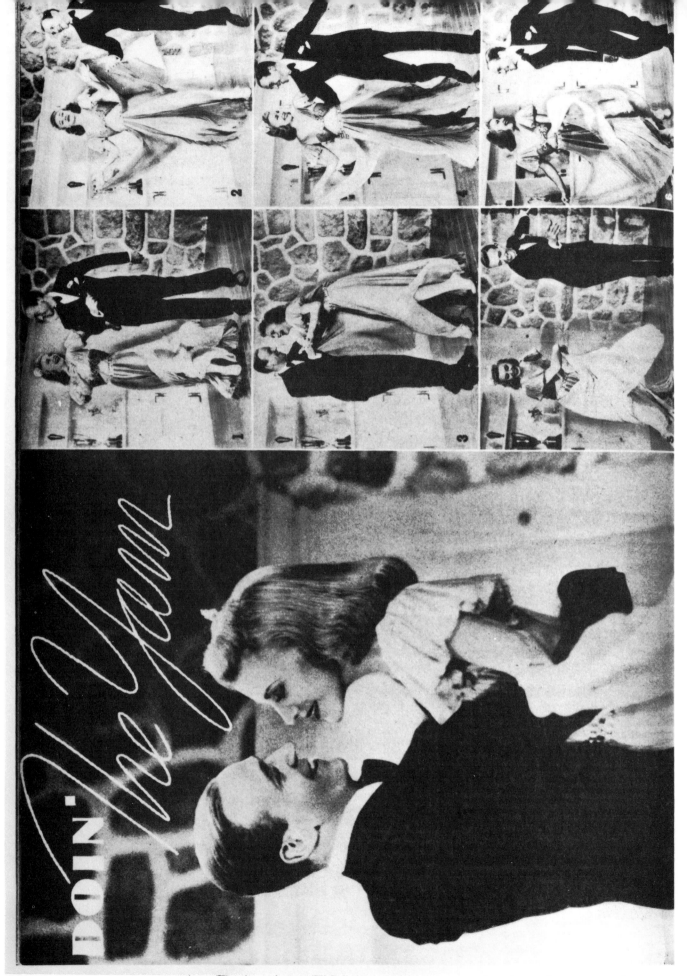

A scoop for you! Modern Screen presents an exclusive preview of Ginger Rogers and Fred Astaire swinging it again in "Carefree." Follow them as they breeze along in four-four time doin' the new dance that Fred himself created. 1. Let's go with a smooth swing stroll. 2. Break and strut your own. 3. Together with a "heel-and-toe." 4. Then Yam! (Heels together, toes apart, then a left, right, left, right). 5. Slide back with left foot forward. 6. Then pivot—so. 7. Right leg steady, hop in a half circle. 8. Knees raised, do a lowdown strut. 9. "Heel-and-toe" in a complete circle. 10. Follow the leader and strut. 11. The Yam again! 12. Raise your hand and sway. Did you get it?

AT HOME WITH THE STARS

aking its readers into the homes of the stars was always one of *Modern Screen*'s strong points. Exclusive room-by-room pictoral layouts of the stars' homes, movie star recipes, and details about how they ran their households were among the magazine's most popular features.

"Visit the Most Famous House in the World," about Mary Pickford and Douglas Fairbanks' mansion, "Pickfair," appeared in the May 1933 issue. The story was so dramatic that you would have thought you were touring Buckingham Palace!

In the March 1940 issue, in the article "Bette's New England Favorites," Davis shared her recipe for Boston Baked Beans—and, of course, Brown Bette for desert! In "*Modern Screen* Spends a Day with John Payne," the magazine showed him doing everything from cleaning his gun collection, to lifting weights, to hanging his laundry out to dry.

In the spirit of these intimate features: Come along with me, as we visit "Norma Shearer's New Home," from the May 1932 issue (page 72). This was the love nest of Norma and her husband, MGM production chief Irving Thalberg. Born in Montreal, Norma began her film career in 1920 in New York City as an extra in *The Flapper*. Following several films, she came to the attention of Thalberg and Louis B. Mayer, and they brought her out to California with a five-year contract. She made several silent "B" films, from *Pleasure Mad* (1923) to *A Slave of Fashion* (1925). Thalberg took Norma under his wing, and in 1927 they were married. In 1929, when talkies came in, actresses were watching helplessly as they failed their voice tests, and saw their careers disappear immediately thereafter.

"I like one grand vacation every year, usually a European holiday.... I think we should all get away from Hollywood once in a while."

—Constance Bennett
Modern Screen,
August 1931

Under Thalberg's supervision Norma Shearer passed her voice test with flying colors, and she was starred in *The Trial of Mary Dugan* (1929), which was MGM's initial "all-talking" production. Nothing like marrying the boss to ensure your future with the company! Norma won the best Actress Academy Award for *The Divorcee* (1930), and scored subsequent hits with *Riptide* (1934) and *The Barretts of Wimpole Street* (1934). Fancying herself an actress in the classic tradition, she convinced Thalberg to star her in two vanity productions: *Romeo and Juliet* (1936), playing fourteen-year-old Juliet at the age of thirty-two; and of *Marie Antoinette* (1938). The later film had been in the planning stages when Thalberg died in 1936. She surprised everyone and received Academy Award nominations for both films as Best Actress. She made only five more films after that. The two successes were *Idiot's Delight* (1939), co-starring Clark Gable, and the hysterical smash *The Woman* (1939). Norma, who died in 1983, had retired with several thousand shares of MGM stock.

Jimmy Stewart began his acting career when he was attending Princeton, with Joshua Logan's University Players. Other members of the company included Henry Fonda and Margaret Sullavan. Stewart and Fonda both moved to New York City in 1932, where they began theatrical careers. After Hedda Hopper saw him on stage, she suggested that MGM test Jimmy for films. He was perfect as the second lead in films like *Wife vs. Secretary* (1936), with Gable and Harlow, and in *Georgous Hussy* (1936), with Joan Crawford.

In its April 1939 issue, *Modern Screen* ran an article outlining the way to Stewart's heart—through his stomach—with "It's Pie for Jimmy" (page 76). That same year he scored three major cinematic successes with *It's a Wonderful Life, Mr. Smith Goes to Washington,* and *Destry Rides Again.*

Constance Bennett had a full social life and a varied career. She was considered by many to be the consummate star: she loved life and portrayed the role of a classy, fun-loving socialite in real life. David Niven once recalled that she could stay up till dawn for an all-night poker game at her house on Carolwood Drive, take an hour to freshen up, and leave the house looking as though she had had ten hours of beauty sleep! She is best known for creating the role of the sexy hostess Marion Kirby in *Topper* (1937), co-starring Cary Grant, Roland Young, and Billie Burke.

Constance was born into a theatrical family and like her sister Joan Bennett scored in many films. Her first role was in *Reckless Youth* (1922). According to silent star Louise Brooks, "Constance had just started her career, but her reputation as the best-dressed and haughtiest actress in movies was already established." In 1925 she co-starred with Joan Crawford and Sally O'Neill in *Sally, Irene and Mary* (1925). She sinned in *Sin Takes a Holiday* (1930), and was a kept woman in *The Common Law* (1931). She starred as a waitress-turned-star in *What Price Hollywood?* (1932), which was the prototype for Janet Gaynor's *A Star Is Born* (1937). During this era, Constance Bennett was the highest-paid star in Hollywood. The August 1931 issue of *Modern Screen* set out to answer the burning question of "How Constance Really Spends Her Money?" (page 77). At last you'll finally know for sure whether or not she really spent $250,000 a year on her wardrobe!

Like Johnny Weismuller before her, Norwegian-born Sonja Henie used the popularity and publicity she gained at the Olympics to pursue a movie career. While athlete-swimmer Weismuller ended up building a whole career as Tarzan on the silver screen, Sonja took her Gold Medal-winning ice skating dexterity and turned herself into a movie star. With her first picture for Twentieth Century-Fox, *One in a Million* (1936), she was a box-office hit, and she was hurried back in front of the cameras to make *Thin Ice* (1937) with Tyrone Power. She followed it with *Happy Landing* (1938), *My Lucky Star* (1938), and *Second Fiddle* (1939). She even skated to swing music when the Glenn Miller Orchestra joined her in *Sun Valley Serenade* (1941).

Sonja took the role of movie star very seriously. This was Hollywood, and she felt obligated to look immaculate at all times. At one point in her career, there was a fire in her home, and firemen had to come to extinguish it. When the fire was out and she was no longer preoccupied with fear for her own safety, she suddenly realized that the firemen had caught her without make-up, and off-guard, looking more like a frightened housewife than a star. She excused herself for a moment and disappeared upstairs. She reappeared at the top of her staircase a few minutes later, in a dramatic gown, full make-up, and a glittering array of her jewelry, looking every inch a movie queen. She then prepared a "thank you" meal for the firemen. Sonja wanted to be certain that when the fire department left her house, there was no doubt that they had been in the home of a movie star!

In the feature "Entertaining Ideas" from the December 1938 issue of *Modern Screen,* Sonja Henie shared her own Norwegian pastry recipes (page 81). According to Sonja, these pastries are perfect to serve with coffee. She however doesn't specify here whether or not that is to be hot coffee or, like her films, on ice!

Unfortunately, Sonja's career cooled down after *Iceland* (1942) with John Payne and *Wintertime* (1943), co-starring Cornel Wilde. When Fox declined to renew her contract, she signed to do two films at International: *It's a Pleasure* (1945) and a skating version of *The Countess of Monte Cristo* (1948). During the Second World War, her native Norway wanted her to give some of her money to their treasury, as they understood that she had made a fortune in America. Sonja loved Norway, but didn't feel that she was obligated to support the whole country. When she declined to surrender the bulk of her personal earnings to the war debt, she began many years of self-imposed exile from her native land. In the 1950's, Sonja was asked by the King of Norway to return to her homeland to skate in an extravagant ice show, and all was forgiven.

Gone with the Wind (1939) still holds up as one of the all-time greatest movies ever made. A lot of this has to do with the incredible cast that was assembled for this Civil War epic to end them all. As Mammy, Hattie McDaniel added warmth and humor to many of Vivien Leigh's scenes as selfish Scarlett O'Hara. McDaniel was always playing the humorously deadpan maid in films like *Saratoga* (1937) and *The Shining Hour* (1938), but she made history with her role in *Gone with the Wind* by becoming the first black actor to win an Academy Award. In the February 1941 issue of *Modern Screen,* Hattie shared some of her favorite recipes in "It's a Scoop!" (page 82). At long last you'll be able to make Plantation Chicken and McDaniel Dressing. Just think about it: dinner at Tara! Forget that diet; after all, "Tomorrow *is* another day!"

THE FINEST INTIMATE PICTURES OF YOUR HOLLYWOOD FAVORITES

MODERN SCREEN

MARCH

10¢

HOLLYWOOD HEARTBREAK by VICKI BAUM

JANET GAYNOR
March 1932

(Right) The lady of the house. (Below) The ping pong table and lounge on the north side of the house. Guests' bath-house in background.

NORMA SHEARER'S NEW HOME

By VIRGINIA T. LANE

ANOTHER great event has taken place in Norma Shearer's life. She has moved into a home of her own. A home that is the embodiment of all her ideas of what a home should be.

Not long after her marriage to young Thalberg she told me:

"Irving and I are vagabonds at present. We sort of roam around, leasing one house after another. It's a grand adventure. We're studying our reactions to each place so that when the time comes for us to build we'll know quite definitely what we want." They were living in Bebe

. . . Come with us and pay a visit to young Mr. and Mrs. Thalberg's lovely house-by-the-sea. The elegant simplicity of it will take your breath away

and transformed the rear of it into as lovely a patio as one could find anywhere. A rich topsoil was laid, rose bushes and green shrubs set in, full grown trees planted —and presto! she has a real garden. Separating it from the road is a high, painted brick fence.

The exterior is a combination of stucco and timber in the French Provincial style. The same style, together with the modern, has been used for the interior. I can't imagine surroundings more suited to the lovely star.

The terrace runs around two sides of the house and is what Norma calls "my concession to the beach." Since the Thalbergs intend to live in this home the whole year through, it had to have more of a feeling of permanency and stability than is usually given a shore home. With the exception of the terrace, it could very easily be a town house in some exclusive section of Los Angeles or Hollywood. But there *is* that terrace! Such an attractive, brick-paved one with a gay awning covering and sporting jolly swings and deep-seated couches and chairs. Out in the "front yard" of sand, scattered around the salt water pool, are unique Deauville chairs made of wood instead of straw. Brightly striped deck chairs and umbrellas lend a festive atmosphere. Norma's pride and joy is the Dubois fence on the north side that serves, too, as a wall for the ping-pong corner. "This is where we spend a good deal

The bright nursery where master Thalberg rules. It's done in pink, blue and white. There isn't a toy or a childish gee-gaw missing.

Pale cream walls are a delightful complement to the soft blue-green carpet in the living-room. The sofa is of yellow satin striped in blue. The fascinating coffee table is made of that interesting zebra wood.

Daniels' beach house then. Norma loved the upper balcony particularly. "At night, when we're sitting there watching the play of light from the Santa Monica pier on the water, it's almost too beautiful. It's as if a million stars had fallen into the ocean." I think it was that house which determined Norma to have hers built at the shore some day. That "some day" has come. The Irving Thalbergs have torn up their last rental contract and taken root.

As we swung along the road that skirts the blue Pacific, past Marion Davies' palatial Colonial mansion and director George Fitzmaurice's Spanish *casa*, I speculated about the type of house I was to see. What style of architecture would Norma choose? What color scheme for the interior? Of this I was sure—it would be a gracious house.

WE came finally to a residence that stood with its eyes on the sea and its eaves and outskirts shaded by trees. Trees are at a premium on these beach sites. Most of the people are satisfied to build their homes flush with the road and let a few hardy geraniums do for garden effects. But Norma has taken a good-sized strip of sand

The dining room is white with a fascinating blue-green carpet with which the curtains blend charmingly. The furniture is natural magnolia partly lacquered white to match the walls. The screen is white accented with blue.

(Starting above and reading counter clockwise) 1. The furniture in Norma's room is white, indelible blue and chartreuse—modernistic design, of course. 2. Another corner of Norma's room—it faces the ocean, 3. Norma's desk. It's magnolia wood—white. Isn't that blue barrel chair attractive? 4. Irving Thalberg's room is done in beige and blue. Neat but not gaudy. 6. The card room. It is panelled in bleached walnut. The tables and chairs are of magnolia wood with a white lacquer trim. Those caricatures are by Doumier.

All the pictures in this feature have been reproduced through the courtesy of H. W. Grieve, Interior Decorator

of our time," said Norma, catching up a celluloid ball. "Want to play a game?" We did. And she beat us badly. The hibiscus border, however, consoled us. We learned that the flagged path leads to the guests' bath houses and showers. If you haven't brought your swimming suit you'll find one handy in the locker.

THEN Norma showed us through the house. There were three things she stressed when she conferred with her decorator, Harold Grieve—comfort, "clean" colors, and simplicity. And there you have the keynote to Norma Shearer's home.

The entrance hall serves to introduce the other rooms, for there is a subtle blending of one room into another so that you have a sense of the remarkable continuity of the entire house. The hall flooring of induroleum composition (inlaid rubber tiling) is a rich terra cotta shade that offsets the parchment colored walls. A walnut console, with an old gilt mirror hung above it, and a settee are the only pieces of furniture. The settee is of a modernized directoire fabric in yellow and blue—a pleasing single note of bright color. Through double doors you pass into the living-room. Here, cream walls and a soft-blue-green carpet find a complement in the chintz toile curtains which have a cream background patterned in the blue-green, terra cotta and yellow shades. On the left as you enter is a screen, of the same material as the curtains, studded with large white lacquered nails. To the right stands a carefully disguised radio cabinet. It's of magnolia wood in a semi-circular design and it has a terra cotta marble top. You don't have to open the tambour front if you want it to play. You simply press a button.

That living-room is the kind that looks as well when it's flooded with sunlight and everybody is draped about on the chairs in crisp sport dresses as it does in the evening when luscious formal gowns trail the floor and the lamps spread a gentle glow. In the daytime the big windows become frames for beautiful marine scenes.

When you stay over at the Thalberg menage this guest room may be yours. The beds are walnut and the spreads quilted taffeta of honey color. Those quaint French plaques at the head of each bed are very intriguing.

MOST of the furniture is honey colored, the walnut baby grand piano providing the one deep tone of terra cotta. The sofa against the wall is yellow satin striped in blue and the ends are of zebra wood. In front of it is a coffee table of the zebra wood. Light wood columns on either side of the sofa support modern lamps with copper lustre bases. Several of the occasional chairs are blue and yellow plaid while the love seats by the fireplace are yellow satin pin-striped in white. They were specially made as were many of the other pieces. The yellow shade characteristic of the room is a very soft yellow, in no way flamboyant. Vivid colors would be impossible with the warm California sun streaming in.

The fireplace is very companionable and cozy. Norma designed it herself. Immediately above it is a great oval mirror and on the mantel are two blue faïence bowls and an ebony clock with ormolu mountings.

"I can hardly wait until my house gets a 'lived-in' air," Norma observed as we went into the card room. "It's all so new yet. The other evening we were having guests for dinner and I told Irving I hoped they'd spill coffee on that living-room carpet! At least that would have made it seem *used*."

We went into the play room. The walls are panelled in bleached walnut. Cunningly concealed behind one of them is—you'd never guess!—a projection booth. When the Thalbergs want to run a picture in their home they remove blocks of the panelling and "shoot" through apertures in the wall onto a screen in the living-room. Afterwards they'll probably draw up those magnolia wood chairs with their white patent leather seats to the bridge table for a game of contract. Both Norma and her husband are expert players.

The couch, arm chairs and curtains of this room are a pale brique color striped in white. The little cigarette trays that swing out from the legs of the table are Norma's own idea. That way the ashes don't get mingled with the cards. The clever Doumier caricatures—mostly of ladies with tipsy Eugenie hats and startling bustles and of strutting gentlemen in frock coats—lend a lively touch to the room.

THE Thalbergs' favorite way to entertain is to have small, intimate dinner parties. Just before their recent house guest, Lady Stanley, left, they gave one at which the Samuel Goldwyns, the Louis B. Mayers, Aileen Pringle, and Norma's sister, Mrs. Kenneth Hawks, were present. Brilliant talk—lovely gowns—highlighted by a *white* dining room. A blissfully cool room where the windows are hung with hand-blocked linen curtains that blend into the blue-green carpet. The furniture, of natur-

al magnolia wood partly lacquered white to match the walls, is modernized Louis XV style. Venetian glass fixtures, a silver urn holding flame-colored gladioli, the white screen accented with blue, the plain marble fireplace —all help to give the room a certain distinction that instantly attracts.

It was on the way upstairs that Norma said suddenly: "I think it's a great mistake for a woman to be a slave to her home. You know—always fussing about little things, re-arranging knick-knacks and continually puttering around. She simply wears herself out and succeeds only in making her family nervous. After all, you want to enjoy your home and not feel as if you were tied down to it."

In Norma's own bedroom the walls are a pale chartreuse color harmonizing with the upholstered headboard of the twin beds. This headboard is single and bordered by white lacquered nails. (Notice how often they're used in Norma's house? They are the newest quirk in interior decorating.)

There's nothing ultra feminine about the room. No laces. No sprawling dolls. However, even if you didn't know it belonged to Norma you'd *Continued on page 107*

IT'S PIE FOR Jimmy!

He'll take it every course—and no wonder, with these recipes

BY MARJORIE DEEN

The Stewart lad is strong for pastry as a main dish —or for any other course.

There's no excuse for a pie crust that isn't rich and flaky.

Courtesy Corning Glass

IF YOU were to try to find out all about Jimmy Stewart's favorite of all favorite dishes, you would learn immediately that it unquestionably is pie. But conduct your researches further, as I did, and you would soon discover that this statement does not begin to cover the situation—that is, if you take it to mean that Jimmy likes pies only as dessert.

True enough, he shares with most men the opinion that a good thick brown, spicy, apple pie is head and shoulders above all other sweets! But he also declared himself, over the luncheon table, as being strongly in favor of chicken pie as an outstanding main course dish—and forthwith ordered it, just to prove his point. He even went so far as to say that he had recently discovered that certain special rich pastry treats are an ideal accompaniment for still other courses of the meal! That statement I thought rather surprising until he explained it in this way:

A certain well known Hollywood hostess, it seems, is famous for the little triangles of flaky pastry that she serves with soups, cocktails and salads, sometimes at one course, other times at another, but invariably once on each and every special occasion. These pastry "bites" hold little dabs of some rich spread like devilled ham or *paté* and are served hot. This idea certainly has made a hit with the men folks at her delightful parties, judging from the glowing accounts of the engaging Jimmy Stewart.

Try these flaky tid-bits the next time you entertain. Just use your favorite pie crust recipe (it must be a rich one) and devise your own fillings. However, be sure that the pastry is of the melt-in-the-mouth variety. But then, that's the only kind you should ever turn out, whatever the purpose or occasion.

You'll see here, as a most important feature of both the recipes for Jimmy Stewart's favorite dishes, directions for making two kinds of pastry. One is a recipe to use in making the crust for meat pies. In this case it's chicken pie but it will work out as well with other fillings. The other pastry is delightfully flavored with cheese, that traditionally favorite apple pie accompaniment.

As for you amateur cooks who are just starting your baking efforts, I know no better last word of advice than that familiar jingle, "If at first you don't succeed, try, try again." Indeed that is "a lesson you should heed" if you are ambitious to turn out the sort of good pastry, and fine pies that all men go for!

CHICKEN PIE

1 large fricassee fowl	¼ cup cold water
1 sprig parsley	1 egg yolk, beaten
1 raw onion	¼ cup cream (or rich milk, or evaporated milk)
1 teaspoon salt	
1 teaspoon celery salt	8 small cooked carrots, quartered
⅛ teaspoon pepper	
1 whole clove	8 small cooked white onions
a small bit of bayleaf	½ cup cooked potatoes (diced or cut with ball cutter)
6 cups boiling water	
5 tablespoons flour	

Have the chicken cut in pieces, as for fricasseeing. Place in stew pan with raw onion, parsley and seasonings. Add boiling water, cover and simmer until chicken is tender. Take chicken from the pot and remove meat from bones, carefully, in as large pieces as possible. Return bones to chicken liquor and boil this stock until

Continued on page 83

This story tells you in fascinating detail just how and where the enormous income of Constance Bennett goes

Constance does not own a fleet of Rolls-Royces. She only has one car and trades it in for a new one about every two years. She figures that her automobile costs her about $5,000 yearly.

HOW CONSTANCE REALLY SPENDS HER MONEY

By WALTER RAMSEY

BREATHES there a girl with soul so dead who never to herself has said: "If I had a movie star's salary . . . !"

The very mention of those thousands per week conjures up a veritable strawberry-ice-cream-soda nightmare of shining town cars with uniformed chauffeurs and even footmen; a pink stucco palace in Beverly Hills with a marble swimming pool and tile tennis courts; a yearly trip to Europe in the royal suite of the largest liner; and as for clothes, well, closets and closets full of them. There's no doubt but what you and I and the other fellow could have a lot of fun with the average movie

star's salary. It's fun to think of it, anyway.

But even in our wildest imaginings I doubt if we've ever played very seriously with the idea of spending the amount of Constance Bennett's salary. It is one thing to imagine one's self spending from two to five thousand a week—but $30,000! Now there is a sum that takes a really first-class imagination to even start day-dreaming about. On top of that, when you stop to figure that the beautiful Constance was a million-dollar heiress before she began her career . . . and besides her amazing ten-week Warner Brothers' contract which pays her the $30,000 every seven days, she also holds a Pathé contract

If anyone imagines Constance Bennett spends money like the proverbial drunken sailor he has another—in fact, several—guesses coming.

(Right) Connie's gowns seldom cost her more than $350 each, and usually less. Connie points out, in this article, the absurdity of anyone believing that she could spend $250,000 a year on the clothes she wears.

said to net her several thousands more weekly . . . it makes you stop and wonder what this twenty-four-year-old girl does with so much money.

I KNOW you've read the wildest stories of the Bennett extravagance. For instance, that fabulous yarn to the effect that she spends $250,000 yearly on clothes alone. The very mention of that story makes Constance fighting mad! In an earlier issue of MODERN SCREEN she has already told us how that silly yarn got started. Someone walked up to her in a hotel lobby, you remember, and asked her how much money she spent on her clothes. "Plenty," was Connie's answer. Whereupon the ambitious and very imaginative reporter decided that $250,000 annually might be considered "plenty"—and quoted Connie's wardrobe expense at that figure. The svelte Bennett spent the next six months fighting down the bad reactions on that story. "How could I possibly spend $250,000 yearly on clothes?" she wailed. "They would have to be diamond-studded to cost that much money."

Because this and similar stories of her extravagance have been so far flung through print it was decided to really thrash out the question of her expenditures. What does she actually spend for her clothes? The upkeep of

Miss Bennett figures her California homes, one at Malibu and one at Beverly Hills (below), cost about $15,000 a year.

her homes? Her servants? Her vacations? What does it actually cost her to keep up the prestige of her stardom? Working on the idea that no one should know those answers better than Constance herself, the questions were put to her one afternoon as she rested in her bungalow on the Pathé lot between scenes of "The Common Law."

"I once swore," said Constance with a little frown, "that I would never mention the subject of money again for the press. The exaggerations of my extravagance are aggravating, to say the least."

"But if you settled the matter once and for all," we interposed hopefully, "if you really told just how you *do* budget your large income, there might not *be* any more of those exaggerated stories."

Constance smiled the smile that means so much at the box office. "Of course, that's one way of looking at it," she agreed. "But if I do talk about it this time, it will actually be the *first time* and the *last time* I shall ever speak of money and how I *really* spend it!"

Here was the psychological moment to bring out the pencil—before Connie had a chance to change her mind.

"FOR one who is accused of so much extravagance," she began, "it may surprise you to know that I am

EVERY YEAR CONNIE BENNETT SPENDS:

$15,000 for the upkeep of her homes.

$15,000—not $250,000—for clothes.

$10,000 for a vacation in Europe.

$6,000 for servants.

$5,000 for her automobile.

$5,000 for pin money.

budgeted down to the final cent of my income. Three-quarters of what I earn I never see. Of this sum (three-quarters of my total income) I use two-thirds for sound investments in either seasoned stocks or in bonds. The other third is used for careful speculation on the stock market or in other ventures which I feel to be sensible.

"That leaves me one-fourth of my total income to be spread over all the expenses I may incur, including the luxuries and the necessaries of life. I'll not quote a figure of my annual expenditures, but let me tell you that I consider it quite a good deal of money. And let me impress upon you right here that the amount is no more nor less than I would use if I were living in New York and not a part of the motion picture colony!

"While in Hollywood, I maintain two homes. One at the beach and one in town. Neither of them are large places. To the contrary . . . they are really small as compared to the homes of many others in the profession. The upkeep, food, insurance and incidentals of my two homes require about $15,000 a year.

"I have four servants in my employ—a chauffeur, cook, two maids——and a secretary. Their total salaries amount to about $500 a month—or $6,000 a year. $21,000 for homes and *Continued on page 80*

Continued on page 80

How Constance Spends

Continued from page 79

servants takes care of about one-third of my yearly budget. Isn't that a percentage recommended by our leading economists?

"For personal spending money I allow myself $100 per week. Ever since the time I was living with my family, before my marriage, I have allowed myself $100 for pocket money. I *still* do! If I had the income of millions, I would not increase this amount I have allotted myself. Out of this sum I take care of such incidental expenses as luncheons, theater or small café parties, tips to waiters, manicures and bridge debts. If I foolishly spend too much of my pocket money the first part of the week, I economize until the next 'pay day.' In other words, I don't borrow from myself beyond that figure. When it's gone . . . I'm broke!"

CAN you imagine Constance Bennett making a luncheon date at the Embassy Club with sister Joan and then having to cancel it because she had run out of money? "I'd do it," insisted Connie, "really I would. Or else I'd get her to take me."

And I believe she would . . . Connie's Scotch, you know!

We had worked down to the subject of automobiles by now. I had always thought she owned about a dozen of them in all sizes and colors.

"Not at all," she explained. "I buy a new motor car on an average of one every two years . . . and turn the old one in, of course. Figuring the cost, depreciation and upkeep I would say that this item costs me about $5,000 yearly. I also keep a car in Paris to be used while I am in Europe, but it is kept in 'dead storage' at a cost of about ten dollars a year."

Connie, who had been counting off the items on the fingers of one hand that peeked from the wide sleeve of a pair of pale-green lounging pajamas, said "clothes" . . . touched the fourth finger tip . . . and made a wry little face.

I'M sure modistes must have been more shocked than anyone else to read that I spend '$250,000 yearly on clothes'" she laughed. "They must have wondered where in the world I was getting them. As a matter of real, honest-to-goodness truth, my clothes run about $1,000 monthly. That would be $12,000 yearly . . . *not* $250,000! It is difficult to put an actual figure on one's wardrobe, for certain years it will run less than others. Shall we compromise and say that I spend between $10,000 and $15,000 for my clothes? And as I said before . . . that's *plenty!*

"The other day I purchased a very plain little sport ensemble. And while it cost $150, it maintained simple lines throughout. It could easily have been copied by a clever seamstress for about $17.50 . . . but as I am *not* a clever seamstress, I could never have remembered its lines well enough to enable me to tell a dressmaker how to duplicate it. However, once I have purchased such an item for my wardrobe, I very often have it copied in other colors for a fraction of the original cost. Thus from one expensive model, I may have three or four outfits.

"Of course, in comparing my budget for clothes with that of another, one must bear in mind several things. Women in both the social and theatrical worlds are often placed in the position of setting the styles . . . *not following them.* And whereas I have never had any particular desire to set the styles, it has always been my custom to wear original models. I buy almost all in Paris . . . and if other women like them, and want to copy them, all well and good. If *no one* copies them I am still satisfied . . . because I wear them merely to please myself.

"But, you say, original models cost a great deal of money . . . how do I do it even on $15,000 a year? That is a fair question and an easy one to answer. I buy nearly all my clothes in Europe. I am of the opinion that French designers are the finest in the world. Contrary to general opinion, gowns bought in France are not priced exorbitantly. Even original models are purchased at a figure far below their cost of purchase in America. One may buy a beautiful *original* evening gown in Paris for $350 and even lower. The duty brings the cost up . . . but here again one may use the seamstress to advantage. Copies may be made in varying colors and the average cost of the gowns so obtained is really quite reasonable.

The highest price I ever paid for an evening gown was $500. And the one time I spent that much was in New York! Each time I wore the gown I felt terrific remorse. I never really liked it. In order to cost that much money, a dress generally has a fur trimming or is heavily beaded. It is usually so unique that it can be worn but once or twice . . . after that it becomes a total loss, hanging in the wardrobe. Sometimes, however, a very simple gown costs quite a great deal . . . this is because of its new and clever lines. Personally, I would rather pay more for lines and less for beads and fur trimming . . . simplicity in line makes for the greatest smartness in my opinion.

"To the girl who has less money to spend on clothes, I can think of nothing better than 'looking around' in the smarter shops, remembering the details of the styles and having them copied by a dressmaker. *No girl earns so little that she need shop from the 'uniform styles' on the bargain counters!*

"Shoes, hats and bags have always been little pet extravagances of mine. I very often buy as many as three hats and as many pairs of shoes and bags to go with one ensemble. But the added accessories change the appearance of the ensemble and allow its use for a longer period . . . so they become a sort of an economy rather than a luxury."

Now that the subject of clothes was covered, Connie was holding up the last, the little finger, for what was supposed to signify travel expenses and incidental spending.

"I like one grand vacation every year," she went on, "usually a European holiday. It's a pretty expensive jaunt," she laughed, "but then I think we should all get away from Hollywood once in a while to get our perspective back. I usually set the $10,000 it

costs me to travel ten weeks in Europe down as one of the necessities of keeping one's balance. It costs almost the entire ten thousand for actual traveling expenses. I have a villa in Biarritz—a gift from my former husband, which is usually my headquarters while I am in Europe. If I should stay there during my sojourn, the cost is figured in the ten thousand used for the entire trip. If I do not, then it costs but $40 a month for a caretaker for the villa. The apartment I own in Paris is closed during the time I am in America and costs nothing except for care and taxes. Of course, insurance and income taxes come in for quite heavy amounts, but one could hardly call the money so used as 'spent.'

AS for jewelry—I have all of it I shall ever want—also gifts from my former husband. Occasionally I have a piece re-set in a more modern style, but jewelry is a very incidental luxury with me."

"There's one more item," I said as Connie tapped off the little finger signifying she had come to the end of her list—"and that is charity."

Connie shook her hand. "There are certain things I love to do that I don't care to talk about at all," she said firmly. "Of all the facts and figures I've given you—surely you'll let me keep that one little secret to myself." Just between ourselves, I happen to know that the "secret item" in Connie's budget would be a swell yearly salary for most of us!

So now . . . if we knew what Connie spent for insurance and income taxes, we might be able to figure out what she actually spends! If we knew *that,* we could multiply the total of all she spends—and get the approximate amount she *saves!*

Beautiful and dumb? Not *this* lady!

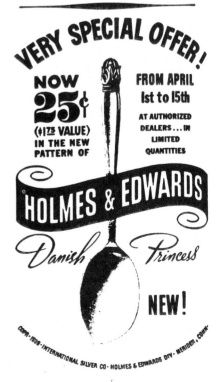

Sonja Henie suggests baked treats to serve with coffee

What is more tempting than Norwegian coffee cake with coffee?

Entertaining IDEAS

BY MARJORIE DEEN

Sonja says that, in Norway, coffee is served more frequently than here.

WHETHER YOU are a gay and golden picture star, like Sonja Henie, or just a charming, simple little housewife, one of the most becoming roles you can play is that of hostess in the realm of your own home.

If you have ever stopped to realize how important it is for you to shine in this setting of your own making, you have also figured out, I'm sure, that it is not enough just to be poised and gracious. Being a perfect hostess also involves serving the right kind of refreshments. This, of course, is equally true whether your guests have been invited in advance or have just dropped in unexpectedly.

The best way to prepare for these occasions—planned or impromptu—is to decide first on one certain thing around which to "build" your menu. And if you were to follow Sonja Henie's suggestion, that certain something would be coffee.

This popular custom can be directly traced to Miss Henie's

Norwegian "bringing up," for in Norway they drink even more coffee than we do. There the students foregather in "coffee rooms" for the stimulation provided by this fragrant beverage as well as for the exchange of opinions. And there housewives serve to their most honored guests coffee with whipped cream, accompanied by their most delectable baked treats.

What are some of these fresh-from-the-oven delicacies that go so well with a cup of steaming brew? Their name is legion. The question of choice is governed neither by type nor nationality but rather by personal preference. However, I think you will be especially interested in a couple of Sonja's suggestions which I tried out—with immediate success.

The one that takes precedence over all others, naturally enough, is coffee cake. Not the usual coffee cake, but one made according to our Norwegian star's treasured version of an "old country" recipe. Rich, spicy and decidely different, it is sure to impress your guests no end. The likes of it have never before graced my board but it is already booked for a return appearance!

Or perhaps you think your friends would prefer something more partified—a little more of the "Bridge Club" type of refreshments? Then by all means bake some Party Puffs, says Sonja. And in order to make the task simpler she supplied directions for making those most frequently served in her own home when folks drop in for a cup of coffee and a not-too-filling sweet. Nothing out of the ordinary about the Cream Puff shells, I noted immediately, but there's something pretty special about both the filling and frosting. The one is lighter than any I've ever tried, the other gleams like nothing I've ever seen. Where is that mixing bowl, and that coffee pot? For I'm expecting guests this evening—are you?

ALMOND COFFEE CAKE

¾ cup butter	3½ cups flour, sifted
¼ cup lard or vegetable shortening	2 tablespoons softened butter
1 cup sugar	4 tablespoons sugar
1 egg slightly beaten	1 teaspoon cinnamon
¼ cup cream	¼ cup seedless raisins
¼ teaspoon almond extract	¼ cup citron and candied cherries, combined
1 teaspoon soda	½ cup blanched almonds
1 tablespoon vinegar	white of 1 egg

Continued on page 83

Hattie McDaniel—in character

IT'S A SCOOP!

My, my! Here's Scarlett O'Hara's "Mammy" to tell us how to make her favorite Southern specialties

Now that "Gone With The Wind" has celebrated its first anniversary in such fine style down in Atlanta and is being released all over the country at popular prices, it occurred to us that millions of new admirers would soon be added to the countless people who already have enjoyed Hattie McDaniel's fine portrayal of "Mammy" in that epic of the old South. It seemed high time, therefore, to try and secure for our cooking columns some of those special recipes of "Mammy" McDaniel's we had been hearing about for years.

We finally caught up with her in the beauty parlor where, completely at our mercy, she promised to tell us how to prepare her justly famous dishes.

"Only you'll have to wait a while," she declared, "because, you see, I cook by instinct like so many of my race. But I know you'll want things all set down clearly, so's folks can follow them easily. I'll have to make some of those favorites of mine and write down how much I use as I go along."

She proved as good as her word for in a day or two along came these recipes, together with her favorite menu and some practical cooking suggestions.

So, if you have ever wondered what kind of a meal Mammy herself would have served to the O'Haras, here is your golden opportunity to learn—thanks to Hattie McDaniel.

Mammy's Southern Dinner Menu

Plantation Chicken with Dumplings
Corn Bread   *Onions in
String Beans   Cream Sauce
Cranberry Jelly
Tomato and Watercress Salad
McDaniel Dressing
Cracker Cake
Coffee
*or Sweet Corn Pudding

Chicken With Dumplings

Dress, clean and cut up a large (year-old) chicken. Put in a stew pan and cover with about 2 quarts of boiling water. Add 1 small onion, sliced; 2 stalks of celery, chopped; 2 sprigs of parsley and 4 peppercorns. Cover and cook slowly until tender. Add 2 teaspoons salt the last hour of cooking. Remove chicken, strain liquor and skim off any excess fat. Measure chicken stock—there should be 6 cups, so either add water or boil down stock to make required amount. Thicken with ½ cup flour (directions for thickening gravies will be found in the Special Suggestions at the end of this article.) Cook until smooth and thickened, stirring constantly. Return chicken to this gravy, add dumplings and continue cooking as directed in dumpling recipe.

Dumplings

2 cups flour
4 teaspoons baking powder
½ teaspoon salt
1 teaspoon shortening
¾ cup water

Sift flour, measure, sift again with baking powder and salt. Rub in shortening with your fingers. Add water gradually, mixing it in with a knife. Drop dumpling dough from tip of spoon into stewpan, an inch apart and resting on the chicken so they don't drop down into the gravy. Cover pan and steam dumplings — without removing cover—for 12 minutes.

Corn Bread

1½ cups flour
4½ teaspoons baking powder
1 teaspoon salt
2 tablespoons sugar
¾ cup cornmeal (yellow or white)
1 egg, well beaten
2 tablespoons melted shortening
1 cup milk

Sift flour, measure; add baking powder, salt and sugar and sift again. Mix in cornmeal. Beat egg until light, add melted and cooled shortening and the milk. Stir into dry mixture, beat thor-oughly, and turn into well-greased shallow, square pan. Bake in hot oven (400°F.) 25 minutes, or until done.

Sweet Corn Pudding

Chop fine 2 cups whole grain canned corn, or cooked green corn when in season. Add 3 eggs, slightly beaten, 1 teaspoons sugar, 1 teaspoon salt, a dash of pepper, 1 tablespoon melted butter. Stir in 1½ cups scalded milk. Turn into greased casserole; bake in slow oven (350°F.) until knife inserted in pudding comes out clean—about 40 minutes.

Cranberry Jelly

Pick over and wash 1 pound (4 cups) cranberries; add 1 cup boiling water and boil gently for 20 minutes. Rub through a sieve, add 2 cups sugar, cook 5 minutes, stirring constantly. Turn into a mold which has been rinsed with cold water. Chill, unmold and serve.

McDaniel Dressing

Grate an onion into a bowl. Add 1 teaspoon each of salt, paprika and prepared mustard, ¼ cup sugar and ½ cup vinegar mixed with ½ cup water. Stir in 1 can (condensed) tomato soup and 1 tablespoon Worcestershire sauce. Add 1 cup salad oil gradually and beat with egg beater until thick. A clove of garlic also may be added, if desired. Keep in covered quart jar in refrigerator.

"And here's just the dessert to have when you expect company and don't mind being a little bit extravagant," suggests Hattie McDaniel. However, since this recipe of hers serves 12 people you can divide these amounts in half, still have enough for the average size family and not feel extravagant at all.

Cracker Cake

1 (pound size) box graham crackers
1 cup butter (½ pound)
2¼ cups powdered sugar (1 pound)
6 eggs, separated

Fine foods were traditional on plantations like "Tara."

By Marjorie Deen

1 cup coarsely chopped pecans
1 cup (½ pint) whipping cream
1 teaspoon vanilla

Roll out or grind crackers to make fine crumbs. Melt half of the butter and mix it with crumbs. Cream the remaining butter, add sugar a little at a time, creaming well. Separate eggs, add yolks to sugar mixture one at a time, beating thoroughly after each addition. Fold in stiffly beaten whites. Add pecans and the cream which has been whipped until stiff. Take a loaf pan, line neatly with waxed paper—allowing enough paper to have it hang over on each side of pan. Put a layer of crumbs in bottom of pan, then a layer of filling, then more crumbs and filling alternately until all has been used. Have the last layer of crumbs. Cover with waxed paper and chill 12 hours in refrigerator. Lift out of pan carefully by grasping paper at the sides. Top with additional whipped cream.

Special Suggestions

"There are some little cooking secrets of mine I want to give you, too," Mammy wrote, "and here they are:

"To thicken gravy—when making the chicken dish I gave you, and stews and pot roasts as well—put the necessary amount of flour in a small jar, like a salad-dressing jar. Add enough water to cover it, put top on jar and shake about 1 minute. Results are perfect.

"Here's the way I do onions to keep the odor from penetrating my fingers. I either grease my fingers or hold the onions under water while peeling.

"Be sure your oven is good and hot before you put in your biscuits.

"To flour chicken for frying, mix flour, salt and pepper in heavy brown paper bag. Add chicken pieces which have been wiped and dried. Shake the bag and chicken will be well floured.

"When you are going to cream butter it's always a good idea to let it stand at room temperature until it's soft. Makes it so much easier to work with."

SONJA HENIE
Continued from page 81

Continued from page 81

Cream together butter and lard (or vegetable shortening). Add sugar gradually, creaming together thoroughly. Add beaten egg. Add cream and almond extract. Beat until very light. Add soda dissolved in the vinegar. Sift flour into a bowl, make a "well" in the middle and turn first mixture into this depression. Mix together lightly until blended. Roll out gently on well floured board to make an oblong piece long about 18 inches and ½ inch thick. Spread with softened butter. Combine the 4 tablespoons sugar with the cinnamon. Sprinkle buttered dough with ¾ of this mixture. Rinse raisins in hot water, drain and dry; add to citron, cherries and blanched almonds. Chop well together. Sprinkle ¾ of this mixture over the dough. Roll up dough as for jelly roll. Place this roll in a circle (with both ends joining) in a large, round, greased cake tin. Brush with egg white. Sprinkle with the remaining cinnamon-sugar mixture and fruit and nut mixture. Bake in moderately hot oven (400° F.) 30 minutes or until a cake tester inserted in cake comes out clean. Should be served hot, plain, or with butter.

PARTY PUFFS

1 cup water   1 cup flour
½ cup butter   4 eggs

Place water in saucepan, bring to a boil. Add butter, stir until melted. Sift in the flour. Stir vigorously, while cooking over low heat, until mixture is thick and smooth, and will form into a ball that does not stick to the sides of the saucepan. Remove from heat, cool slightly. Add the eggs, one at a time, beating hard for several minutes after each addition. Drop by teaspoonfuls, or from pastry bag, onto greased baking sheet. Each puff should be about one inch in diameter and slightly higher in the center. Bake in moderately hot oven (400° F.) about 30 minutes. Test "doneness" by removing a single puff from the oven to see whether it will "fall." If not, the others may be removed at once to a wire cake rack, to cool. When thoroughly cooled make a small slit in the side of each puff with a thin-bladed knife. Carefully fill with cream filling. Top with frosting.

SCANDINAVIAN CREAM FILLING

1 cup scalded milk
   yolks of 4 eggs, slightly beaten
⅔ cup sugar
2 teaspoons gelatin
½ cup cold milk
4 tablespoons butter
½ teaspoon (scant) almond extract

Scald the cup of milk in top of double boiler. Beat together the yolks and the sugar. Slowly add the scalded milk. Return to double boiler and cook over boiling water, stirring constantly, until mixture is smooth and thickened and will coat a silver spoon. Remove from heat, add gelatin which has soaked 5 minutes in the cold milk. Stir until gelatin has dissolved; add butter, stir until melted. Add flavoring. Chill in refrigerator until thickened. Use as filling for cream puffs.

BITTERSWEET FROSTING

2 squares unsweetened chocolate
1 teaspoon butter
1 tablespoon glycerine
2 tablespoons water
½ teaspoon vanilla
1 cup sifted confectioners' sugar

Place chocolate, butter, glycerine and water in top of double boiler. Cook over hot water until chocolate has melted. Remove from heat. Stir until blended. Add vanilla. Stir in the confectioners' sugar gradually, then add a little boiling water, drop by drop, until frosting is of the right consistency to spread. Spread on puffs with a knife dipped in warm water.

JIMMY STEWART
Continued from page 76

Continued from page 76

it is reduced to 2½ cups. Strain off the bones and to the stock slowly add the flour, which has been moistened with the cold water to a smooth paste. Cook and stir until smooth and thickened, then slowly add the egg yolk beaten with the cream (or milk). Cook 2 minutes, stirring constantly. Add the chicken meat and cooked vegetables. Use this rich fricassee mixture for Chicken Pie, prepared as follows:

PASTRY FOR CHICKEN PIE

1 cup flour
2 teaspoons cornstarch
¼ teaspoon salt
⅓ cup shortening
3 tablespoons ice water, approximately
1 egg yolk, beaten
1 tablespoon milk

Mix and sift flour, cornstarch and salt. Cut in shortening until it is distributed throughout the flour in pieces the size of small peas. Add water—a tablespoon at a time—mixing it in with a fork until dough will clear the bowl. Chill dough. Roll out on floured board. Place a 3-inch-wide strip of this pastry around the inside of a deep baking dish, around the top and coming up over the edge. Fill baking dish with the previously described chicken mixture. Cover with pastry crust in which several slits have been cut to allow steam to escape during baking. Trim off surplus pastry at rim of dish. Moisten top crust around the edge with a little cold water. Place a 1-inch-wide strip of pastry on top of this edge and down over the rim of the baking dish. Flute with floured fingers to form a thick, upstanding rim. Brush with well beaten egg yolk mixed with the milk. Bake in hot oven (450° F.) until crust is well browned.

AMERICAN APPLE PIE
PASTRY

2 cups pastry flour
½ teaspoon baking powder
1 teaspoon salt
⅔ cup shortening
⅓ cup cold water (approximately)
3 tablespoons freshly grated cheese

FILLING

½ cup granulated sugar
½ cup brown sugar
½ teaspoon cinnamon
4 cups thinly sliced apples
½ teaspoon salt
   grated rind of ½ lemon
2 tablespoons butter

Sift flour, baking powder and salt together twice. Cut in shortening until pieces are about the size of small peas. Add only enough of the water—a tablespoon at a time—to make a dough that will clear the bowl. Form into a ball, wrap in waxed paper and chill in refrigerator while preparing the filling. Measure and combine the sugars, cinnamon, salt and grated rind. Pare, core and slice the apples, add the sugar mixture, mix well. Divide chilled dough into 2 parts. Roll out one part lightly on floured board with floured rolling pin. Line a 9-inch heat resistant glass pie plate with this dough fitting it in loosely, then fill plate with the apple mixture. Dot with butter. Roll out the other half of the pastry very thin, sprinkle one-half of it with the grated cheese and fold the other half over the cheese. Roll out again to right size to cover pie. Place upper crust over the filling, after first moistening the edge of the lower crust with cold water. Trim off surplus pastry then seal the two crusts together firmly around the edge with a floured fork, or make a fluting with the fingers. Cut slits in top crust to allow steam to escape. Place in hot oven (450° F.) and bake for 15 minutes. Reduce heat to moderate (350° F.), bake 30 minutes longer or until apples are tender.

FASHION & BEAUTY

One of the most familiar images of *Modern Screen* magazine is of women sitting under hair dryers in a beauty parlor thumbing through its pages. The magazine carried articles about "Katharine Hepburn's Style Secrets" (August 1933), "Jean Harlow's Trousseau" (January 1934), and "Claudette Colbert's New Wardrobe" (June 1933). In the article "Hurray for Lipstick" (November 1945) Rita Hayworth decreed, "Lipstick is a basic beauty essential!" In the June 1959 issue, Academy Award–winning costume designer Edith Head wrote a piece called "If You Are Under 21, and Your Clothes Make You Look Sick...See the Dress Doctor." Dr. Head declared to one young lady, "Your clothes are lovely. But you just wear them improperly!"

Only Joan Crawford could make a statement like, "The proper dress makes life an adventure, the wrong one makes it a dull bore!" She said that and more in "Joan Crawford's Wardrobe," from *Modern Screen*'s October 1931 issue (page 86). Joan took the role of Joan Crawford quite seriously. She had begun her career as an energetic "jazz baby." When she married Douglas Fairbanks, Jr., she was suddenly catapulted into the upper echelon of Hollywood society. Whereas she first became noticed as the winner of Charleston dancing contests, she instantly had to re-invent a new Joan Crawford—the chic sophisticate. This layout, with photos by George Hurrell, represents the butterfly of a movie star emerging from the frivolous flapper.

Have you ever asked, "What shade of lipstick does Norma Shearer wear?" or "How does Joan Crawford pluck her eyebrows?" Well, "Beauty Advice" from *Modern Screen*'s May 1933 issue (page 92) has the answer for you. You'll also learn Clara Bow's secret for her "look," which is described here as "a study in orange."

"Jean Harlow's Wardrobe," from the November 1932 issue (page 96), shows off the star in some of the slinky gowns that she made famous. "Notice the utter simplicity of these gowns in which she's pictured," says the writer. Notice also that controversial Jean never wore underwear...it ruined her gown's line!

Carole Lombard was one of the most popular stars of the 1930's. She was a brilliant comedy actress, she was beautiful, and if you ever crossed her, she would probably swear at you like a truck driver. Her fun-loving, no-nonsense manner is what attracted second husband Clark Gable to her. When "Carole Lombard's Wardrobe" (page 102) ran in *Modern Screen*'s June 1932 issue, Carole was still married to William Powell.

While she was in high school Carole had begun her film career under her real name, Jane Peters, in *The Perfect Crime* (1921). In 1925 she was signed by Fox for the lead in *Marriage in Transit,* and the studio changed her name. Carole met William Powell when they co-starred in *Man of the World* (1931) for Paramount, and they were married on June 26, 1931. That year they also co-starred in *Ladies' Man.* Carole and Powell divorced on August 16, 1933, the year that her film *No Man of Her Own* was released. She must have had a thing for her leading men, because her co-star in the film was Clark Gable!

> "I'd rather know that the seams of my stockings are straight than wear diamonds."
> —Joan Crawford
> *Modern Screen,*
> October 1931

Photograph by Clarence Sinclair Bull

Although almost everyone in Hollywood knows where Greta Garbo lives, the Swedish star hasn't moved for some time. Perhaps she's getting used to inquisitive fans peering through the hedges. She takes a long hike every day at sunset and is usually accompanied by a woman companion. She is now at work on "Susan Lenox—Her Fall and Rise," with Clark Gable playing opposite.

JOAN CRAWFORD'S

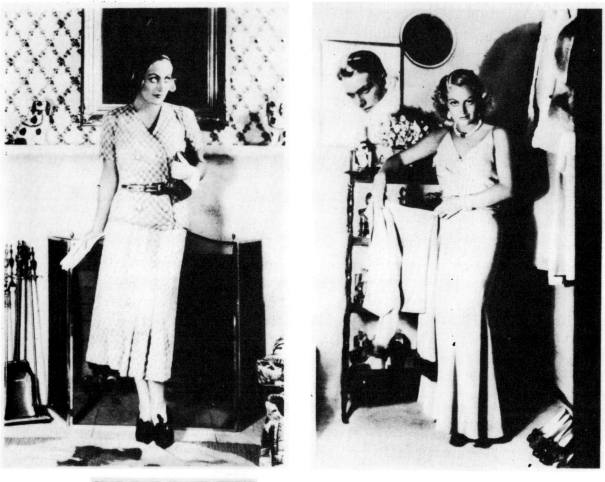

Joan looks very lovely in the brown and tan silk mesh sports frock, shown in the large picture at the left. It's double-breasted, belted with a chocolate brown and white suede belt, and has four unpressed pleats in the skirt front. (Left) Sun-tan mesh hose and brown oxfords complete it. Above, a simple and elegant ciel blue crêpe roma evening gown, with a matching jacquette trimmed with sable cuffs.

. . . Says Joan Crawford: "I'd rather know that the seams of my stockings are straight than wear diamonds.

"Girls today seek comfort as well as style in clothes. They dictate to fashion instead of letting fashion dictate to them! The proper dress makes life an adventure; the wrong one makes it a dull bore."

JOAN CRAWFORD typifies tomorrow. In thought, speech, manner—and dress.

She is the ex-flapper transformed into the charming young woman of today. The ex-flapper grown into a smartly intriguing person with a slightly amused, wholly tolerant outlook on things, and the ability to wear ginghams with as much confidence as she does satins.

Modern . . . dashingly chic . . . that's Joan.

"She's an example of the sophisticated, medium conservative 1931 girl," declares Adrian, M-G-M's wizard at

WARDROBE

By
VIRGINIA T. LANE

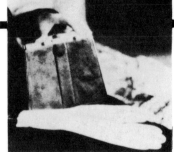

The indispensable black chiffon, the neckline banded with silver cloth. Joan is holding a silver velvet wrap bordered with black fox. The other wraps, left to right, are an ermine jacquette, a ciel blue lamé with silver fox, a full length ermine coat, and a mink coat. The large picture at the right shows Joan's black silk velvet fall suit, ermine cuffed. In the small picture, Joan's best black antelope purse.

dress designing. "Hers has been a natural evolution. First, like all very young girls, she longed to express herself—to make the world conscious that here, indeed, was a new being—and, of course, she tried to do it in her clothes. She first thought of herself in terms of a tight waist, a circular skirt and with bows on her shoes. That was her mental vision of Joan Crawford. Then, because she has an alert intelligence, she gradually acquired style sense. She dared new lines, saw that they became her and adopted them. Now she has a great variety of style.

• • • Here's a new department, combining our "Hollywood Wardrobes" with "Secrets of the Hollywood Stylists." Each month, Miss Lane will give you a delightful account of some favorite's wardrobe

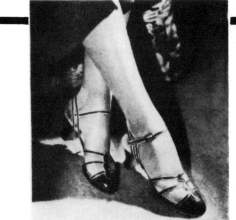

The three pictures on this page illustrate, from hat to shoes, an outfit that would be smart and sensible for the school girl or business girl this fall. The dress, directly above, is of navy blue wool crêpe. The lines follow the smart belted vogue. There is a peplum flare below the waist. The skirt pleats are stitched down to the knee. The large picture at the left shows the simple hat of rough white felt, banded with blue, which Joan wears with this frock. The collar and cuffs are narrow bands of white piqué. The diagonal bands which trim the bodice loop over the collar in a cute fashion. The small picture shows the blue and white sandals which Joan wears with this street dress.

There are very few creations she cannot wear . . . principally because she has the right mental attitude toward them.

"Joan has profited from everything she's observed. In a way, motion pictures have been to her a belated finishing school. They have taught her to distinguish between a tawdry fad of the moment and a lasting style. She is eager to accept the most chic thing I can give her. And if the design of a costume I show her is in blue," concluded Adrian, "she okays it without hesitation."

I HAVE known many women who were passionately fond of a certain color but I've never met anyone as devoted to blue as Joan is. She loves the entire range of it, from skipper to ciel and from navy to cornflower. Her reaction to it is immediate. Whatever the psychological explanation is—blue is definitely Joan's color. Her eyes are a bright gentian shade and when she's excited they

Another ensemble in Joan's favorite color—gentian blue corded silk, with a white broadtail scarf collar and deep cuffs trimming the coat (shown directly above). The skirt of the coat wraps and flares a bit and has the popular slightly uneven hemline. The large picture at the right shows the gored and slightly flaring skirt of the ensemble and the white wool lace blouse Joan wears with it. Those white woven leather oxfords would be appropriate for the summer days of early fall. In the small picture is a close-up of the little gentian blue hat Joan describes in the article. It has a ridiculous little broadtail bow right on top—you can see it on the chair in the picture above.

become very dark. They were dark as she sat across from me in her portable dressing room.

"Doug's coming back from location tonight," she said.

So that was the answer. We talked about her amazing husband, young Fairbanks, Jr., until, with the entrance of tea and delectable cheese wafers, I managed to bring the conversation around to clothes.

"When I look back I'm astonished, really, at the great number of blue frocks I've worn in the different productions," Joan began. "Fortunately, it's an excellent color from a photographic standpoint. In 'This Modern Age,' I wore a navy blue suit of rather loose mannish cut with raglan sleeves and a three-quarter length coat. It was trimmed with big silver buttons.

"Black is another pet color of mine, for the street as well as for evening. There's something so striking and chic about it. You know, it gives me confidence in myself.

(Above) Left, Joan's shiny black satin evening gown, with unusual intricate seaming. (Left) Slippers of black brocade studded with rhinestones, to wear with it. (Above right) Daisy patterned chiffon pajamas in shades from canary to chocolate. (Right) Gold satin slippers to wear with them.

Pictures on these pages specially posed for MODERN SCREEN and photographed by Hurrell, courtesy of M-G-M

You have to respond to a color to have it suit you, don't you think? And these days, colors are fickle as style itself. Those that we always thought clashed frightfully have been made to blend in a perfectly fascinating manner. And there's no such thing as not being able to wear this and that shade—you simply make up your face to blend with it, if you're bent on appearing in a forbidden tomato red or sea green or skipper blue. Personally, though, I'm loyal to blue, black and white. I have a touch of vivid color only in my sport costumes. Very bright shades seem blatant and harsh to me on the street. I invariably want to turn and walk in the opposite direction from them. They are like harsh, discordant voices.

MY hobbies in dress," went on Joan, "are shoes and hats. I've given more thought to them, studied them more carefully than I have my dresses. Because they *make* or *mar* an outfit. If a woman's shoes are clean, well-shaped and smart and she has on a becoming hat, you may be almost sure her dress will have style as well. I look at the feet first—perhaps because I'm a dancer—and they usually tell me a great deal about the woman. Whether she pays attention to the little things, such as run-down heels and scuffed toes and has them repaired; whether she's wise enough to wear shoes that fit so her feet will not become distorted.

"When I was in New York *Continued on page 91*

Joan Crawford's Wardrobe

Continued from page 90

and my money was limited considerably, I spent more on shoes than I did on my frocks. A number of my friends thought me foolish. Why, you could buy cute little slippers for one-third the price I was paying, they used to tell me. Cute, yes, but they seldom held their shape for more than a week and my shoes lasted about *four* times as long as those of my friends.

Do you remember the old lines that went—

'After all, what's in a hat?

'Oh, nothing, sir—only one's head!'

"Rather important if it's to decorate the head, the most prominent part of us! Hats can, and do, change the contour of a face. A dip here and your face has narrowed; a round, soft brim and you might be a cherub. I have a funny cap of gentian blue corded silk that sets on the back of my head and on the top of it is a white broadtail bow. (See page 89.) It matches an ensemble and when I put it on I feel excitement in the air. Why? For no reason that I can define."

I asked Joan how she shopped.

"Actresses are supposed to be models of fashion," she answered, "yet it seems to me we have less time for shopping than women in any other profession. I started out by employing a professional shopper. I'd tell her what I wanted and she would have it sent to my home, where I could make my selection at night. After a while, however, this proved unsatisfactory because I was too tired when I came home at night to choose well and I missed the fun of exploring about to see what the new styles were. So now I snatch hours to hurry to the Wilshire district where there's an assortment of small shops.

I SUPPOSE I'm very feminine in my desire for soft, luxurious materials—but fancy underwear has no attraction for me. All these be-laced 'foundation garments' seem to me to prevent a dress from having the smooth, flowing line that it should. I wear silk shorts—which I buy by the dozens in the children's department—and I walk straight by the crêpe-de-chine 'fussies'.

"Unfortunately, the clothes I get ready-made have to be remodeled because I require a size eighteen around the shoulders and a size fourteen around the hips." (Incidentally, it's her broad shoulders and slender hips that give Joan such a splendid figure.)

"The popular raglan sleeves are a boon to a girl of my proportions. Another trick to make the shoulders appear a trifle narrower is to set the sleeves high up. Necklines of a distinctive cut, and scarves, draped in all kinds of fantastic ways, serve to give a dress significance for me.

"The secret of successful dressing is to adjust new fashions to yourself. Change the way you wear your hair every month or so; try a new fashion and see if you can make it *yours*. Never allow yourself to be wedded to one style."

JOAN doesn't—that's certain. As Adrian observed, the styles she wears are legion in number . . . and you don't know which you like best on her. One minute she's particularly fetching in a youthful sport frock, like the one on page 88, and the next she's the gorgeous lady swathed in a black satin dress, like the one on page 90.

I believe the most feminine, fluttery type of garment Joan ever wears is the flowered chiffon pajama kind (see page 90). And she wears it only in certain moods. Usually she flies around the studio in tailored pajamas or in a short white skirt and navy blue coat.

Joan has very few fashion restrictions. I would say that panels or wide tuckings from the neckline to the hem are the solitary dress features it'd be best for her to avoid—because they would give her an elongated look.

HERE are a few hints on the care of clothes, several of which were suggested by Joan Crawford:

Air your clothes before putting them away. Always hang them so they will not become wrinkled.

Launder shirtwaists at home, if you can, to save the wear and tear on them.

Money can often be saved if spots are removed while they are fresh.

An old sheet or nightgown can be made into a bag to keep your good frocks in.

To give a garment longer life, worn spots should be darned and reinforced before they come through.

A double thickness under the arms of thin dresses and blouses saves them.

---

why rock walked out

Continued from page 55

than she knew. For there were so many things just as trivial—and just as dangerous—as those silly steaks.

"I've got a week off," Rock had announced one day. "There's a hold-up on the schedule and they've given me a week off!" He swept Phyllis into his arms jubilantly. "We can go away. Take a vacation. Do anything—"

Phyl crowed with delight. "Oh, honey—that's fabulous. I can get us packed in no time. There's a flight at noon tomorrow—"

"Hold on," Rock grinned. "We haven't decided where we're going yet."

Phyl's eyes opened wide. "But—we've been talking for weeks about going to New York. Seeing the shows—really doing the town. And there are people there I haven't seen in months."

Rock shrugged cheerfully. "Aw, honey, you don't want to go to New York. That was just a lot of talk—I mean, just kicking the idea around. I thought we'd take off for Hawaii or somewhere. Do some swimming—really relax—"

Phyl stepped away from him. Her voice was tight. "Rock, you know I hate the ocean."

"Yeah. Yeah, I know." He brightened. "But look, Phyl, this time will be different. I'll get you a snorkel outfit and teach you to swim. You'll be crazy about it once you get over being scared. I'll show you—"

The smile is forced

"That's what you said before we went on our honeymoon," Phyl said carefully. "Don't you think it's my turn to—to pick the place?"

"Phyl, you don't seem to understand. This isn't just our first time for a vacation. It's my first rest in a year. I need to relax. What—what kind of a rest would it be if we went to New York. Running around, seeing a bunch of people I don't give a hang about—"

"You'd rather look at a bunch of *fish*. You think it's fun for me, sitting on a beach waiting for you to drag yourself out of the water and remember I'm there? You think I like living in this house like a hermit, never going out, never seeing people?"

"We do see people! We have friends in—"

"*Your* friends," Phyllis wept. "Not mine."

A case for separate vacations

They ended up going nowhere. Angry-eyed and silent, they waited out Rock's precious seven days. When they were over, Rock went, with a feeling of sick relief, back to the studio. And Phyllis, her tremendous energy bottled up, ready to explode, thought that perhaps if they moved out of this tiny house, to someplace new, some bigger house that she could enjoy decorating and give parties in—maybe things would be better.

And so, for months, they fought over whether they needed a new house.

But you can't tell your mother: *We're getting a divorce because Phyllis doesn't like to swim and I don't like nightclubs.* She'd think you had a hole in your head.

Ask yourself, his mother had said, *why love dies. Ask that.* Lying on his back on the hotel-room bed, his eyes staring, unseeing, at the ceiling, Rock almost laughed. *Love—dead? Not quite, Ma,* he thought. *Not quite.*

For how many nights had there been when, after one of their stormy scenes, Phyllis had come into their room, into his arms. "Rock—oh honey, I do love you so much. What's the matter with us? What's wrong?"

And how many times had he stalked out of the house in fury, driven wildly into town—and found himself pulling over to the curb in front of a florist's window. And half an hour later Phyllis, at home, would answer the door to receive roses and a scrawled card—"Believe it or not, I love you, love you, love you—"

And for an hour, for a day or a week, they would tell themselves that love was enough, that two people who loved each other had to come out right in the end.

Continued on page 138

BEAUTY

By Mary Biddle

Above, on this page, Miss Norma Shearer—on the left, with, and on the right as she looks without make-up. Norma makes her lips fuller with a rather dark lipstick and enhances the depth of her eyes with the clever use of eyeshadow and pencil—read how in the article. On the other page, the two pictures at the top show Joan Crawford—on the left, with street make-up—on the right, in screen make-up. Joan actually scrubs her face for that shine—which is a chic, glowing shine. Now, immediately left, Claudette Colbert—a lovely model for brunettes to follow. All the make-up tricks Claudette uses are designed to play up her dark beauty without making it the least bit theatrical. And on the opposite page at the lower right, an exactly opposite type to Claudette—Constance Cummings—who strives for a most natural, unmade-up look for street wear.

FIVE FAMOUS MOVIE STARS TELL YOU HOW THEY MAKE UP FOR "EVERY DAY"

ADVICE + + +

Write to Mary Biddle about your beauty problems. Address her at MODERN SCREEN, 100 Fifth Avenue, New York, N. Y. Enclose a stamped, self-addressed envelope for your reply

I HAVE had a lot of fun this month. I've been finding out just exactly how five of the most famous movie stars make up. Not for the screen—for the street. After all, we may copy the gowns and the coiffures of the stars as seen on the screen—but their screen make-up wouldn't do us much good, would it? I've had many letters asking me such questions as, "What shade of lipstick does Norma Shearer wear?" "How does Joan Crawford pluck her eyebrows?" And I always promised myself that some day I'd find out and tell you. Well, I have found out the make-up tricks of Joan Crawford and Norma Shearer, Claudette Colbert, Clara Bow and Constance Cummings. All these girls are different types. They all offer helpful information which you will be able to turn to your own good uses. And they have all studied extensively this important business of make-up and grooming.

So—are you all set? We'll start with Joan Crawford.

Continued on page 94

READ ABOUT THEIR SECRETS—YOU'LL SURELY FIND SOME YOU CAN USE, TOO

If you saw Joan in person, you would notice that her face is shiney. No, I don't mean that the powder has worn off her nose. I mean that it is *intentionally* shiny. Like a little boy who has just been given a good scrubbing. And that's just what has happened to Joan's face, too. It has been scrubbed. And this is how she does it:

Before she goes to bed at night, Joan takes off all traces of make-up with a good cold cream. She removes the remains of this with astringent on a cotton pad. And that's that. In the morning, however, she washes her face with lukewarm water and a bland soap. Then she uses up an entire cube of ice on her face until it glows and tingles. Next, with a rough towel, she polishes it—and I mean she polishes it! Rubs her entire face all over until it gleams like an apple that has been polished on the grocery man's sleeve.

You may have heard about Joan's freckles. She has 'em all right. Lots. She makes no attempt to conceal them. Maybe you couldn't get away with this. After all, Joan has beautiful features, beautiful eyes and lovely hair. And when a girl is born with all those blessings, what's a freckle or two? Joan uses no powder in her daytime make-up. And there's another thing—to ignore powder you should have beautiful features and a very clear, clean outdoor-looking skin.

But Joan does use other make-up. She uses a light shade of lipstick and follows the natural line of her none too small mouth. She has never made up her mouth in private life as she made it up in "Letty Lynton" and "Rain." And, as you know, she has abandoned that over-painted mouth on the screen now, too. But, on the other hand, she has not returned to the pretty-pretty, Cupid's bow mouth she used to paint on herself in the old days. Joan's mouth isn't small and rosebud-like. It's big, sensuous and has a great deal of character. And she makes it up just that way. The lipstick goes clear to the corners. And she widens the lower lip just a tiny, tiny bit.

Her eyebrows are about the color of her hair—brown, with a reddish tinge. They need almost no plucking—just a few stray hairs from underneath to give them that beautiful clean sweep. For daytime, she uses the tiniest bit of brown pencil on them. In some photographs of Joan you will notice that her brows are carefully brushed into that sweeping line. In others, you will notice that the hairs at the center, nearest the nose, are not brushed—they are allowed to go anywhere they will. This I like. Without being in the least untidy or shaggy, it gives a very natural look.

Joan makes up her eyelashes with great care. They are very long. She darkens each hair with great precision, taking care that the lashes do not mat together. She uses brown mascara. Only on the upper lashes, however.

And these she always brushes outward, on a slant, rather than straight up. Gives a much more natural look.

Now, there's Joan. With a shiny nose, cheeks and forehead, ready for the street. Red-brown hair, enormous blue eyes, dark lashes, light red mouth, fair skin and freckles.

Oh yes, just one more point. She wears her nails very long and pointed (and says just the things you and I say when she breaks one) and she uses a very dark red polish—which she puts on herself—putting it entirely over the nail, right to the very end, leaving no white edge.

WHEN Norma Shearer gets made-up for the street she always looks perfectly stunning—so fresh and clean and well-groomed. Of course, Norma is a lovely woman but she's smart enough to know how important a careful make-up is—and you girls can learn a big lesson from Norma. Besides taking care and time with her face before she goes out she always carries with her enough extra rouge, powder and so on to keep herself looking well-groomed.

Norma's hair is light brown, her eyes are blue-grey, her skin fair. And, incidentally I believe I'm safe in saying her skin is the most delicate in all Hollywood. Fine-grained, smooth and altogether lovely. That's why she takes such good care of it. She could not, by the way, treat it in the healthy, vigorous way Joan treats her skin. And don't you, either, if you're one of those petal-skinned girls.

First of all she uses a good cleanser, astringent and powder base. Then she uses a little cream rouge on her cheeks. This, you know, gives a base for rouge that makes it stay on much longer. Now she pats the powder on with a puff, patting it in all over her face in large dabs and then with a tiny, soft baby's brush she brushes off the surplus powder. This distributes the powder evenly.

The dry rouge goes on next—subtly used and following the natural line of the natural color in her cheeks. (If your skin is seemingly colorless, you can ascertain where your natural color *would* be by gently pinching your cheeks.)

Norma's lips are not so full as many of the stars but you would never know it, would you? That's because she extends the lipstick—a fairly dark shade—beyond the natural outlines of her mouth. She uses a very clinging lipstick that stays on a long time, but the minute it shows signs of wear Norma puts on more.

Norma's eye make-up is a work of art. Although Norma's eyes are beautiful and expressive, several stars have larger eyes than she. Here's how she applies the make-up. She uses a little brown or blue eye shadow on the part of her eyelids nearest the temples. This extends a trifle farther than the lids. Then a tiny line underneath the eye, beginning at the middle and extending it toward the temple to follow out the shadow. Look at the two pictures of Norma and see the difference. On the upper lashes she uses mascara but none on the lower lashes.

A dark brown eyebrow pencil, following the natural shape of the eyebrows, completes the perfect picture.

NOW—there are two girls that the average girl could copy. And now for an individualist !

You may or may not approve of Clara Bow's make-up, but you've got to admit it's different. When you look at her it seems as if she is a study in orange color. Her hair is that flaming red with orange tints. Her cheeks are orange-tinted, her lipstick a dark orange and her eyebrows are orange, too. The eyes, heavily mascaraed in black, are the only accents. She uses a dark eye-shadow, too.

Those eyebrows give her a startling look and I heard that the English women were amazed at them, for Clara, instead of plucking her eyebrows, just shaves them right straight off—zut, like that—with a razor. "Saves a lot of time," says Clara.

Then she draws a thin, long (very long) line straight across her brow, with that reddish orange pencil. I must say I do not approve of it for ordinary purposes but because Clara is an actress and expected to do the spectacular, she can get away with it.

Her lips are full—almost too full, in fact—so she does not follow the line of her mouth with the lipstick on the lower lip. The upper lip she shapes into a cupid's bow.

Oh yes, and she makes her lashes curl up with one of those eyelash curlers. And there's Clara.

Constance Cummings is another girl with freckles, like Joan, but Connie uses an entirely different type of make-up. She has reddish brown hair, greenish-grey eyes and light brown, naturally curly eyelashes. Her skin is fair and she accents this fairness by using very little rouge.

Her powder base is an astringent and she puts the powder on right over that with no cream rouge because she looks better with very little rouge. She uses the dry rouge in a shade just going into the orange (but not Clara Bow's vivid color). On her eyelids she uses brown eyeshadow and her lashes take the light brown mascara. Eyebrows, too, have this same shade.

Her lipstick is light and follows the natural lip line. This style of make-up gives Connie a sort of neutral, monotone look that is decidedly interesting. There are no sharp accents about her face—all the cosmetics are brownish in color and she uses very little of any of them so she can keep the pale effect.

CLAUDETTE COLBERT—the vivid brunette—on the other hand plays up her type to the utmost. Dark powder, bright red rouge, dark red lipstick, dark brown eyeshadow and heavy mascara. She uses a good powder base, pats the powder in heavily, making sure that it soaks well into the pores and thereby stays on better.

Her brows are very heavy and so she must pluck them, but she is wise enough to know that a brunette looks

Continued on page 101

JEAN HARLOW'S WARDROBE

...and yours!

...How can Jean Harlow look so young and be so wise about clothes? You'll be amazed and delighted at the hints she gives. And don't forget our regular pattern page!

By VIRGINIA T. LANE

(Right) Jean calls this her cornstalk dress. It's a maize-tinted crinkly crêpe dance frock. It is slipper length, has bias lines and a short bolero. (Left and below) And here's a pattern for you to order—a pattern modelled after Jean's dance frock. The number is 5081 and the price is fifteen cents. Follow the instructions given on page 61.

S HE may be the completely charming vamp *de luxe* of the screen but somebody really ought to erect a statue in the hall of fashion fame to Jean Harlow as the Girl Who Made the Bias Line Famous.

Jean, believe it or not, was wearing what Robert Montgomery refers to as "those um-um slinky clothes" while Paris was still advocating loose, flour-sack dresses. She is the most independent-minded girl I have ever met, especially where style is concerned. She knows what looks well on Jean Harlow and she sticks to it—more power to her! She learned early that if she wanted to blossom out as an individual among the millions of women she had to *dress as an individual.* She was born with a flair for drama. She dresses more dramatically than any other star in Hollywood. Adrian, M-G-M's fashion creator, told me: "Even

(Left) Jean departed from her usual custom of wearing only black and white for evening and bought that devastating icy-green satin formal gown. The shirred bodice front is both very fashionable and very becoming. (Right) The back view. The wide shoulder straps (they're called bretelles) execute a loop-the-loop in the center of the Harlow back and fasten at the waistline with jewelled buckles. (Above) That small dark hat of Jean's is black stitched velvet.

Jean's clothes show emotions. They live and breathe with her." Which, after all, is the highest compliment a noted dress designer can pay a woman.

Now, mind you, I'm not intimating that all of us should follow the Harlow style. As a matter of fact, very few of us can. What looks outstandingly smart on her would make me, for instance, look as if I were striking a pose. Jean's favorite dinner dress is one she calls a "nun's frock." It's long and black with a white top having a boat-shaped neckline and she wears a large ebony cross with it. Fancy any rollicking sports girl or merry-eyed minx in an outfit like that!

BUT there are a great many things about Jean's wardrobe that will prove of benefit to every woman in choosing clothes. Notice the utter simplicity of these gowns in which she's pictured. Not a frill among them.

"I'd rather have a few dresses of very fine material than a whole closetfull of fussy, cheap-looking things." Jean summed up her style creed. "At the most, I buy but six costumes a season—usually two black crêpe street frocks, a dinner and a restaurant dress and two evening gowns. My wardrobe is never a large one. I didn't even buy a wedding trousseau. For one thing, I didn't have the time and for another I was satisfied with what I had. I find you don't tire of anything that is lovely in quality and line. It saves you money in the long run to get a good dress of which you're always proud and use it for two or three years. I'm not a bit ashamed to say that most of the things hanging here now are several years old." Which reminded me immediately of a very amusing incident that occurred at a première Jean attended last winter. She had on an exquisite satin gown, an original Vionnet model. Another movie celebrity, noted

(Above) Remember when hatter's plush was so popular a few years ago? Well, it's back in favor again. Jean has such a hat in white with the new inch and a half brim. She wears it at a decided tilt, no matter what fashion rules, because it's becoming that way. (Right) Jean's "everyday" fur coat. Jap ermine, edged with beaver clear down the front and at the ends of the full sleeves. Beaver forms the belt, too.

for never wearing the same dress twice, came barging up and exclaimed sweetly, "Oh, darling, I've adored you in that dress all the times I've seen you in it for the past two years!" And Jean just as sweetly replied, "Yes, I like it, too. That's why I keep on wearing it."

Now that the Vionnet model is showing definite signs of wear, she is having a duplicate made of it. She frequently does that with a well-liked dress. "I can do it because there's really only one type of evening dress I cling to," she remarked. A slight misstatement, if you'll pardon us. The evening dress clings to Jean. Clings beautifully, so that you don't wonder at long-legged, lithe young girls the world over going in for the present anatomical silhouette. When this vogue is followed to its source, it undoubtedly will be found that Miss Harlow had as much to do as anyone in freeing women from unnecessary folds and flounces. Even the great Garbo succumbed to the rage for spun-silver hair that Jean started. She has had an undeniably strong influence on fashions, this twenty-one-year-old platinum blonde with

(Left) Ah—there's Jean's best color combination—black and white! Ermine and seal are artfully combined to make this ultra-smart coat. (Above) Jean buys her clothes wisely, well—and sparingly. That large black antelope hat, you see, gives a dressed-up air to a black and white street costume. The little stitched velvet hat on page 97 can be worn with the same costume. Like the perky bow on this hat?

the lovely blue eyes. And this is what she has to say about the bias-cut gowns she popularized: "They require more poise than any other kind of formal dress. You can't slouch in them—or walk heavily in an ungainly manner. If you do they become a travesty of fashion. Something terribly un-smart. You have to hold yourself up and carry your head high to give them the right line. Sixty-inch satin is a favorite for these dresses because it lends itself to an unbroken line in cutting, doing away with seams, from bust to hemline."

THE white angelskin satin dinner dress you see Jean wearing on page 100 is one her delightful mother, Mrs. Bello, picked up for her in an exclusive shop not long ago at less than half its original price! It has the V-neckline she prefers above all others, that intriguing slinky look, and the short sleeves are banded with sable. And please notice, my dears—not a jewel anywhere! She never wears any with her gowns in the evening, believing that a dress of fine material should be permitted to stand

(Right) "How in the world," you ask, "can that Harlow girl get her gowns to fit so smoothly?" Well, one of the answers is sixty-inch wide material. It permits the gown to be cut almost all-of-a-piece, as that white angelskin satin one is—at least, down as far as the knees, where it begins to flare a bit. Very plain is this dinner dress, banded with sable just above the elbow. Nary an ornament does Jean wear with it. (Below) Jean favors simple negligées. She doesn't care for lace. The only trimming on that pale pink georgette wrap is the ruching on the wide sleeves.

Photographs in this feature by Clarence Sinclair Bull, courtesy of Metro-Goldwyn-Mayer

(Above) Jean wouldn't buy an ermine evening wrap for a long time because she thought them extravagant. But she can wear that three-quarter, blue-fox trimmed coat with so many gowns that she feels her purchase was justified. (Left) The very tricky little ostrich turban, bedecked with a black lace veil, and the little white kidskin military cape with the silver fox banding are two of the newest additions to Jean's wardrobe.

out by itself. The wrap she selects to go with it is white kidskin—a novel affair of rather military tendencies. (See above.) See the way the cape is swung from the shoulder in guardsman style. This effect is attained through the banding of silver fox which also creates the round collar. It's one of the latest models to catch the fancy of the fashion world. Kid, you know, is predominant among the flat furs for fall and of course fox is back on its pinnacle of glory. So bring out your old fox scarf, let the cleaner put it through a rejuvenation process, and wear it in a circular manner with a goodly air of dash.

Jean tops this costume with the cleverest little hat imaginable. It's a white ostrich turban—yes, indeed, *ostrich*—and there's a black cobwebby lace veil over it. One of the very few pieces of lace Jean has ever been known to wear. For some obscure reason she doesn't like it on herself, won't even have it on her French voile underwear. Personally, I think this is a left-over notion from her 'teens when she was deathly afraid that lace would make an ingenue out of her. Anyway, it supplies a softening touch to the hat—and can't you just see Jean attending a formal dinner in this outfit? A stunning picture.

For the first time since she was seventeen she departed from white or black for evening when she purchased the icy-green satin gown shown on *Continued on page 101*

Jean Harlow's Wardrobe

Continued from page 100

page 96. She makes you think of snow maidens and northern forests in it. The shirred front is very attractive, but it's the back that claims the spotlight. Bretelles cross, are looped, and terminate in rhinestone buckles at the waistline. The sandals are dyed to match.

HER three-quarter length ermine wrap has cape-sleeves which are trimmed with blue fox. (Page 100.) It has one of the newest collars—upstanding and small. "It was a long time before I persuaded myself that an ermine wrap would be a real economy," said Jean, the astute. "I had to pay quite a price for my velvet wraps and then they went with only one or two dresses. An ermine coat or any good fur coat goes with everything and it lasts for years. That's why I'd rather have fur coats instead of cloth ones. If I was buying another wrap, however, it would be black velvet with that deep plush pile that Adrian says is going to be so successful this winter. Black and white, you see, are almost invariably my choice.

"When I was five, mother took me to see Doris Keane in 'Romance' and it was from one of her costumes that I had the idea for this wrap," indicating the cutest, trickiest black velvet jacket you ever saw. "It made such an impression on me that I remembered every detail perfectly. As soon as I was old enough to wear evening clothes I had one made up exactly like it, although at the time peplums were not yet in style and neither were fitted waists nor stand-up collars." Jean wouldn't let us take a picture of it because it already had been photographed innumerable times—but it's still her best-beloved. She's taken such excellent care of it that there's not a worn-out spot on the wide ermine collar. Ermine also trims the peplum and sleeves. "I have two plain white satin gowns I wear with it. Sometimes I put on white satin pumps with black heels and other times black satin pumps with white heels. I change my belts around, too. And never once have I tired of the costume."

Black and white—the most dramatic of all color combinations. The supreme complement to Jean's sensational hair. And, incidentally, the very smartest of all color combinations for almost every woman.

However, shortly after she bought the icy-green gown she included in her wardrobe a dance frock of crinkly crêpe in a maize shade. (See page 96.) It's amazing how that shade tones with her bright head and brings out the warm color of her eyes. The frock fits to perfection—all of Jean's clothes do. She loves the small details of dress that make for smartness, such as hand-rolled edges and neatly finished seams. This frock is slipper length—the majority of the new dance dresses are—and it simply hasn't any back to speak of. The girdle that resembles nothing so much as an old-fashioned stomacher, ends in a bow that peeps out beneath the very short bolero accompanying it. Three diamond buttons fasten the jacket in front. Her sandals are the color of the dress. "My cornstalk costume," Jean calls it.

THE entire scale of browns is ideally suited to her. They're almost as charming a contrast on her as black. In her own home you'll frequently find her in brown shorts, a white polo shirt and tennis shoes. No stockings, even in the winter. An exceptionally chic outfit consists of a heavy crêpe dress in a dark chocolate brown, a Japanese ermine coat and a fascinating crêpe turban the color of the dress. (There's a picture of the coat on page 98.) Turbans are Jean's preference over all other hats. "I feel more at home in them, for I've worn them so long. They seem to be part of me." Yes, they're typical of her—sophisticated, urbane, svelte. "I know hats are supposed to be worn straight on the head this season but I believe I'll keep on tilting mine. I think they're more interesting that way." Strong-minded young woman! Keeping her weather eye open to fashion trends but letting her mirror decide whether she'll accept them.

That white plush sailor with the wisp of a brown bow and veil shown on page 98 is excellent with the outfit, too. It has the new inch and a half brim the fall hats are sponsoring.

The Japanese ermine coat is Jean's latest acquisition. I was with her when she bought it and it didn't take her five minutes to settle upon it. "I have my good mink coat that I've been wearing on all occasions. This is a semi-sport coat and it will save the other. I can wear it to the studio and around." The stand-up collar, belt and trim around the single lapel and down the side of the coat are beaver. It's long in the present fashion of coats. The sleeves are full at the bottom and caught at the wrists with tiny beaver cuffs.

Jean has a bright Kelly green dress she can also make good use of with this coat. There's always one dress of that shade in her wardrobe. Why? I don't quite know. But it's a very oh-be-joyful dress and when she tucks the turban of that color over her platinum curls and strolls down Hollywood Boulevard, even the newsboys gasp their admiration.

FOR afternoons Jean has a black crêpe coat dress. The skirt is gored (most of the skirts are gored or slightly circular this autumn; only a few pleats are shown for sports.) It comes to a V 'way up on the front bodice which gives you a feeling of a long, unbroken line—grand for you medium-sized and short girls. The yoke is white crêpe and crosses over in back to form the belt, and ties in front. There's a bolero that goes with it. The sleeves are small and puffed so that Jean's white gauntlets, trimmed with black, provide a very pleasant accent. Her slippers are black suede. The six skin sables are a gift from her mother. One of her new black hats that she wears with it and with her other black crêpe frocks is a large brimmed model of antelope (page 99) having a cut-out design on the crown and a clever small bow. Another is of stitched velvet with a tiny brim and it has a flower trim. (See page 97.)

Surprisingly enough, Jean's negligées are quite simple affairs. She abhors elaborate ones that are all be-laced and be-ribboned. The one you see her in on page 100 is pale pink georgette and it has ruches edging the sleeves. The only ornament is a flower of the material on the shoulder. Her mules are silver brocaded.

"Any woman of taste knows her life and the clothes that fit into it," she told me. "It's chiefly a matter of choosing the right thing to begin with and not allowing it to get out of shape or limp. *You have to have faith in your clothes, just as you have to have faith in yourself, to be successful in dressing.*"

Beauty Advice

Continued on page 94

very bald if her brows are just a tiny line so she keeps them fairly heavy, but neatly groomed.

Claudette doesn't need to use an eyebrow pencil, except right on the end of the eyebrows. Instead, she just brushes the brows free of powder with —of all things—a pipe cleaner. Yessir, she's found that a grand thing for generally cleaning up the face after the make-up has been applied. With it she takes off the surplus rouge around her mouth and also with it she draws an imaginary line vertically along the indentation above the upper lip from the tip of her nose to the middle of her mouth. Removing the powder from this part accents the natural indentation and enhances the beauty of the mouth.

Claudette uses mascara on both the upper and the lower lashes but she is extremely careful that it does not smear.

And when Claudette Colbert walks into a room her vividness draws every eye to her. Remember, though—while she uses all the make-up in the calendar, she still does it subtly and never looks theatrical.

So now you know exactly and in minute detail just how five of your favorites appear before their friends.

CAROLE LOMBARD'S WARDROBE

By VIRGINIA T. LANE

. . . It isn't only what Carole wears—it's the way she wears it! Study these pictures and read her advice about clothes

(Left) If you are slim and long-waisted, you can wear a suit like this one of Carole's. The material is steel-gray light-weight wool. The style is strictly tailored—notched lapels, cinched-in, one button closing, bound diagonal pockets and a single button to finish off the sleeves. But note the feminine touches Carole has added: the white satin waist, with its imitation-of-a-jabot collar, fastened with a diamond and sapphire brooch—present from husband Bill Powell. The gray suede pumps are bow trimmed. The gray felt hat has two bands and two bows in two tones of gray. (Above) Let's see how many fashion notes we can get from this evening gown of Carole's. Material, dull white crêpe roma. Very good—dull materials are best, you know. The circles of brilliants are very new. Observe how sparingly they're used on the bodice. No jewelry at all—it would be too much.

A flesh satin evening gown best described by the word classic. Those graceful sleeve-like affairs swing over the shoulders and keep right on going until they form a train in back. The lower skirt, too, which is a bit full, ends in a train. The V-neckline would have been spoiled by a necklace. A cluster of bracelets is good with this sort of gown.

Miss Lane calls this dinner gown a gem. Not only because the bodice is a solid mass of pearls, but because it is so unusual without being the least bit tricky. The skirt is black crêpe and floor length. Long ties of the beaded material fall from the surplice closing. This would be a good gown to copy. You could use dull white crêpe for the bodice.

TEN to one if you met Carole Lombard on a desert island, draped in fig leaves dashingly trimmed with red berries, you'd say: "Now *there's* chic for you! I must have a dress like it!" I know I would. Because this clever young Carole gives any costume she chooses to wear a style all its own. A style you want to copy. When I interviewed her I had to remind myself that steely-gray, the shade of the suit she had on, isn't my color and that I'm too short-waisted to have a cinched-in coat anyway. Otherwise I would have driven straight over to my dressmaker and gone into a deep, dark conference. The suit made that much of an impression. (You'll see it on the opposite page.)

It was strictly tailored. Narrow collar, single-buttoned coat and of a light-weight wool that was smooth and wonderfully cool looking. None of that wooden soldier effect our suits used to have. Now they're trim but softer in appearance.

Carole had added to it those feminine touches which are indispensable to modern suits. A white crêpe-satin waist with a fluttery imitation of a stock collar (it was half-way between that and a jabot) and she had fastened it with hubby Bill Powell's gift to her—an exquisite diamond baguette and star sapphire pin. Ordinarily such a pin would have been out of place, but this one was of so severe and heavy a design that it fitted in perfectly. Her gray pumps were bow-trimmed and her tilted hat was banded with a two-tone ribbon in gray. Grays, as a

(Left) Carole's pajamas are beige satin—beige is one of her favorite shades—and they're made in Russian style, with a high neckline and tiny stand-up collar. The trousers are just normal width, as most well bred pajamas are these days. Below you can see the detail of the top of the pajamas. The row of covered buttons with loop button-holes is nice. The hat is one of beige straw, with a brown bow in the back.

(Below) A very useful all-round suit of mottled gray tweed, banded with caracul around the capelet, sleeves and jacket edge. Note the novel little hat of the tweed and caracul. And the buttons on the front of the coat. You can see the detail in the small picture, below, left.

Write to Virginia T. Lane about your own wardrobe problems. She can help you a great deal, for she is in close contact with the head designers of the Hollywood studios. Address Virginia T. Lane, Modern Screen, 100 Fifth Avenue, New York, N. Y. Enclose a stamped, self-addressed envelope, please, for the reply.

rule, are difficult to blend well but she had succeeded beautifully.

"IT doesn't really matter," said Carole in that way she has of seeming to be tolerantly amused at herself and you and me for taking life seriously. "Where you live or where you shop has no bearing on whether you'll be smartly dressed or not. It limits the range of your wardrobe probably, but it doesn't effect the style of it. You can be quite as interestingly gowned in Podunk as you can in New York or Hollywood *if you want to be.* You've got to care! To care enough about your personal appearance to give plenty of thought to it and to work out the colors and lines that belong to you. To you personally—not just your type in general. It's easy enough to find out the latest trend of fashion from the various magazines. To apply it to yourself is a different matter. That requires concentration and study.

"We were passing through an isolated western town

(Below) Carole's favorite bathing suit is corsair blue and white ribbed silk. It has practically no back. The beach sandals are washable crêpe. (Right) This is probably the most useful garment in Carole's wardrobe. It's a three piece ensemble. A straight skirt and hip-length, double-breasted jacket. Large buttons trim the jacket which has a narrow belt of leopard skin to match the sleeves.

(Left) The detail of Carole's green and leopard skin top coat. Don't you like those sleeves, cut in one with the leopard skin yoke? A very new fashion note and very smart, this.

Photographs in this feature by Otto Dyar, courtesy of Paramount studios

on our way to location not long ago and it struck me how many of the girls were extraordinarily well dressed. There wasn't a hint of the 'grab-bag' dressing you so often see in larger cities where the stores display a wide variety of things to choose from. These girls wore nicely matched ensembles, neat sport clothes, hats at just the right angle. We stopped at a drug store for lemonade and I asked one of them about it. She was a vivid brunette and she looked charming all in blue and white.

" 'Fifty miles from nowhere like this, how do so many of you manage to keep up on fashions?' I inquired.

" 'Well, we're lucky, I guess,' she replied. 'We have a high school principal who is the most smartly dressed woman I know and she's made a point of teaching us the value of good clothes and how to combine colors. Of course, she gets all the latest style publications and some of us get them too, and then there's the radio. . . .'

"Which made me realize once and for all how little locality has to do with style sense. They ought to erect a statue or something to that school teacher—making girls happy that way. For if there's anything that brings peace of mind and contentment and a feeling of security to a woman it's the knowledge that her clothes are *right*.

IF I hadn't turned to acting I'd like to have been a dress designer. It opens up a tremendous field. A fascinating field. *You never can know too much about clothes!* And it *is* fun plotting and planning for your wardrobe. Discarding this trimming and that. Learning that two gardenias on a black dress are **Continued on page 106**

Continued on page 106

Carole Lombard's Wardrobe

Continued from page 105

much more effective *without* the foliage and fancy ribbon. That dangling earrings can—and often do!—ruin the loveliest gown. (I never wear them off the screen.) There are innumerable things that each one has to learn for herself. Sometimes a green feather in a hat takes away all the charm from a face . . . and then again it adds a cute piquancy.

"Now with me, for instance—there are colors which usually look well on blondes that simply don't suit me. Like brown. It gives me a washed-out look and an awfully uncomfortable sensation as if I'd been told to sit in a corner. Reds and orchid—ugh! Not for me! All bright, vivid shades (with the exception of emerald green and corsair blue) make me think that they're sweeping me before them. You know—Lombard lost in a tidal wave of color. I need soft, non-committal shades like gray and dead white and black. The champagne hues of tan are favorites of mine, too. And these new aquarelles, such as water-green.

"Do I design some of my costumes now? Of course! It's a grand pastime, and a kind of hobby with me. Last winter Travis Banton made up a gown from one of my sketches that Bill was especially fond of. It was formal; fashioned entirely of white bugle beads. It had very long lines and a trick back. The white velvet wrap that went with it was also very long and had leg-o'-mutton sleeves and trimming of silver fox. Another outfit that Bill liked immensely was a three-piece beige sport ensemble of broadcloth. The top coat was one of those big swanky affairs. Bill's tastes and mine are similar—fortunately. It's so satisfactory when your clothes please yourself and your husband at the same time!

"If they didn't," Carole added with a wise little look, "I'd dress the way *he* wanted me to at night and I'd dress to suit myself during the day. Men generally pay more attention to formal costumes anyway, I think."

HUSBAND BILL certainly ought to —and undoubtedly does—adore his wife in that angelskin satin evening gown shown on page 103. It is a pale flesh color and I can't imagine anything better adapted to bring out the charm that is Carole's own. The supple lines are reminiscent of the Grecian with those sheaths of material crossing in front and swinging low over the shoulders. They form a train in back and so does the skirt which achieves fullness below the knees. The simple classic cut is further accented by the simplicity of the Lombard headdress. A striking effect. And not a jewel or ornament in sight save the

diamond bracelets on her right arm. In accordance with the mode she wears them in a cluster. A single bracelet, as you know, is as passé as the Eugenie hat. To me, that modeled V neckline would be utterly spoiled had she worn a necklace. I've seen so many necklaces destroy the beauty of a lovely gown; they add a superfluous note or they are of a design at odds with that of the décolletage.

It takes more courage and discrimination to tone down a dress, to allow it to stand out by itself, than it does to decorate it!

Carole has another gown of the same satin which Banton has just completed for her. (He makes many things for her personal use as well as those you see her wear in pictures.) This gown is of a luscious pale corn-yellow. It swoops up the front in the spring mood of frocks everywhere—quite high up the front. The back it leaves without a stitch unless you count the narrow suspenders that cross at the waist. A yellow velvet waist-length jacket goes with it. The sleeves are the kind that swell above the elbow and end in long, slim forearms (a type of sleeve that's very much the vogue right at present). This pale yellow, by the way, is wonderfully becoming to Carole as it is to most girls with pale gold hair and gray-blue eyes.

But if you wish to cause a dazzling white glow, choose a gown like that crêpe roma of Carole's, shown on page 102. It's truly clever. The bodice does a rather disconcerting thing by having those shoulder straps go demurely down the back and fashion the belt. It's tied directly in front, handkerchief style. The circles of brilliants are something new and they're employed in a novel manner. No jewels of any kind here. They'd be a bit too much with the sparkle of all those brilliants. Her slippers are white crêpe.

I SUPPOSE," Carole said, "one needs most of all the ability to face facts in dressing. You can't wave away certain limitations of types. For example, can you fancy me in ruffles and tiers of flounces and bits of lace? I can go in for extreme lines, though. As a matter of fact, I like them. Those with snap and dash. My hats are always extreme. There's one I wear with a mottled gray tweed suit that goes on at an absurd tilt. It's a turban made of the same material and banded with the caracul fur of the suit and it has a gray silk bow in front to match the shirtwaist. The suit? It's the kind you jump into for all occasions—lunching, shopping, matinées. The small shoulder cape is bordered in the fur. So is the bottom of the jacket and the sleeves have flaring cuffs of it. The front is button-trimmed." (There's a picture of it on page 104.)

We fell to discussing suits, the sudden importance of them. Carole owns a black and white tweed that's very comfortable for the foggy days which are a part of every California spring. The tweed is of that new, loosely woven variety and it's trimmed with lynx. Lynx in generous quantities on the col-

lar, sleeves, and around the lower part of the jacket. There's a wide belt of black suede and the blouse that accompanies it is white crêpe with a soft neckline. Her pumps are black kid. The hat she wears with it is gray with a rolled brim of black and a black feather points heavenward up the back.

Carole hasn't a "faddish" article in her entire wardrobe. Some of these new suits might be classed as such. Those with tight-fitting mess jackets are for the moment only. They're cute, I grant you, but they belong to the very young, the very slim and long-legged. If you're a co-ed and you want something new to finish the last term, one of these bellhop flannel coats that have trig metal buttons, saddle shoulders and cap sleeves is excellent to go with a wool crêpe skirt. If you're a business girl I advise against it. It would be far more profitable to purchase a suit that can serve many purposes merely by changing the accessories and blouses. Smart women all over are doing that very thing.

CAROLE'S three-piece green suit (shown on page 105) lends itself admirably to this scheme. First of all, that top coat is the kind that may be worn with "dressy" frocks. Charming green silk prints with shirred organdie yokes, lustrous new crêpes in beige, parchment suede laces in yellow to blend with the leopard skin fur. The coat has a pleasing fullness, yet it's semi-fitting. Those sleeves in one with the yoke of leopard skin are fashion's last word. The suit that completes the ensemble is as swagger as any you'll find this season. The skirt straight and trim, the jacket hip length and double breasted. The buttons that march down it are very large and it has a narrow belt of the leopard skin. And wouldn't you know it would be topped with a rakish little hat having a slightly rolled brim on either side? The green kid slippers have a tan trim to match the heavy chamois gloves.

It's too bad heavy coats of tan will be taboo this summer. A nice even tan all over your back would be very easy to acquire in these latest bathing suits. Most of them are of such brilliant hues that you feel as if you'd walked right off a signboard. And one and all they reveal the spinal column in no uncertain way. The smartest are those that come in one piece and are made of wide-ribbed, heavy silk. Carole has this kind. (See page 105.) It combines corsair blue and white and there's an intriguing small bow at the end of the low décolletage in back. Her beach sandals are of washable crêpe. All beach wear has taken a new lease on life and it's determined to lend more color to the sad sea waves than ever before. With a red and white striped wool shirt you use blue flannel slacks. Then the bright bloomer suits with ribbed knees, cross-over straps and square neck, dot the landscape. The bandana handkerchief has come to the front, too—you tie it around your neck and wear it for a waist. Carole chooses an all-white jacket for the beach. A startling jacket that gives her a "powder puff" silhouette. It's made up of yards and yards of jersey trimmed with balls of white yarn. With this, of course, she wears a white jersey bathing suit.

AT Malibu, beach pajamas still hold sway for all hours, but they're of an altogether different mode than those worn last summer. When Carole was invited to the beach home of a famous writer recently she appeared in delightful beige satin pajamas patterned in the Russian style. (They're pictured on page 104.) The blouse, with its small stand-up collar and buttoned closing, was loosely tied with a sash. The flowing sleeves and wide trousers found a complement in the positively enormous hat. This hat was a beige straw that sported a brown bow in back to give it character. A highly decorative costume. Ideal for Malibu and it established a new vogue there.

Beige satin, incidentally, is stressed in Carole's wardrobe. Her "best" negligée is fashioned of it, and trimmed all the way around with sable. Her everyday negligées and house pajamas are of washable crêpe in the pastel shades she loves.

"It's a good idea," announced Carole, "to save your fine frocks by having house garments of some kind to slip into. They're inexpensive—easy to put together—and they certainly keep the dry cleaning bills from climbing up."

She's a practical person. Most well-dressed women are. She plays the part of a model in this picture she's just finishing—"Sinners in the Sun." And she wears *one hundred and fifty* different costumes in it. "The only time I ever tired of clothes was when I was being fitted for all of them!" she confessed.

Carole has a black and white dinner gown that's a gem. Literally. The waist is a solid mass of pearls. The sleeves are slightly puffed above the elbows and then are tight to where they extend over the wrist. Long ties of the beaded material fall from the surplice closing. The black crêpe skirt is floor length and matched by the black slippers. A flawless gown that enhances the Lombard beauty. (Look at the picture of it on page 103.)

But if your mind is occupied with weddings and graduations and such things, here's an idea for a frock that is synonymous with June: White organdie embroidered in silver! Now if *that* doesn't make you think of moonlight and roses, my dears, nothing will! A crushed silver girdle indicates the high waistline and a diminutive peplum, four inches wide, is edged with the silver. The dress is worn over a slip of dull crêpe and white crêpe sandals complete it. Silver sandals would have given it a garish aspect—made it seem overdone. It's by being attentive to such little things as this that one arrives at chic. As Carole says—*you've got to care.* That's the important thing.

Norma Shearer's New Home

Continued from page 75

recognize it as being the bedroom of an exceptionally smart woman with very good taste. There are the side chairs, for example, of indelible blue with white antique satin backs and seats. The lamps of white glass shaded by white taffeta that rest on the magnolia wood bed-end tables. The crystal floor lamp having crystal discs on the foot, and a shade of white duroid.

Each of the three master bedrooms has its own dressing room and bath. Double doors connect Mr. Thalberg's room with Norma's. His room is strictly modern—a typical man's room done in blue and beige. The furniture is sycamore and walnut with a brown onyx trim. Tôle lamps are on the very modernistic night tables. In front of the windows, which are draped in a blue and beige heavy woven material, are a blue couch and chair.

The guest room adheres more to the French Provincial style than does any other room in the house. The tête-de-nègre carpet affords an interesting contrast to the flame and honey color of the glazed chintz curtains. The same tones are used for the upholstery of the chairs and stool. An antique French mirror is placed immediately above the carved walnut chest of drawers. The quilted spreads on the twin beds are honey colored taffeta and above the head of each bed is a French plaque.

And now we come to the domain of master Thalberg; who expects to celebrate his second birthday before long, thank you. His nursery is the brightest nursery you ever saw. It's all pink and white and blue and there's nothing missing from blocks to a miniature victrola to provide entertainment.

The upper hall has a high pitched beamed ceiling and as we crossed it I stopped to admire the most beautiful antique French commode I've ever seen. It's of burled fruit wood, carved by hand in so delicate a manner that you wonder how on earth it was done. Near it are a glazed chintz settee and chair in bright blue, yellow and green.

what really happened to doris day

Continued from page 61

She sang with Les Brown and Bob Crosby and Barney Rapp. The singing was an economic necessity. She was both mother and father to her Terry and there were long periods of time when she saw neither her son nor her mother. As recently as six or seven years ago, I remember watching her shuffle into the lobby of the Plaza Hotel in Hollywood, (after she had been divorced from George Weidler,) a lonely, weary, tired girl, disillusion on her face.

I've seen Doris Day smile. I've heard Bob Hope call her jutt-butt. I've watched her give out with that gay, deceiving, flip air of enjoyment. But to me, her blue eyes have always been sad eyes. This girl has never hungered for fame or money or adoration. All she has ever wanted is to leave the rat race, to get away from it, to settle down with her husband and family in a nice, middle-class neighborhood.

You may well ask—"Well, why doesn't she do it?"

If she quits tomorrow, if she renounces the whole crazy world of show business, can she retain the love and admiration of her friends, her husband, and her mother?

Doris Day is probably the best-loved actress in Hollywood. She has never harmed anyone. She has never climbed the ladder of success, lad by lad. She has never engaged in subterfuge or underhand politics. She has achieved success through her own effort and talent.

The success she has achieved, however, has brought her fame, money, and position. It has brought her practically everything but the one thing she has always needed most—peace of mind.

In the weeks to come, let's all hope she finds it. A better, kinder, sweeter, more unselfish girl was never born. **END**

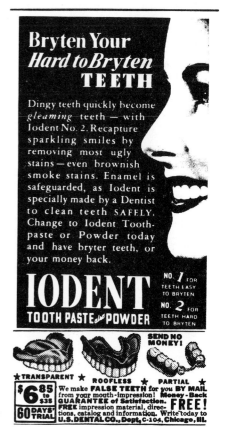

MODERN

5160

We have chosen Bette Davis for our model this month. And we have a pattern cut for you, modelled after the dress Bette is wearing at the left. A grand dress to wear for daytime—under a coat, while the weather is still cold, and, very soon, without a coat. It would be perfect made in a dark blue, one of the smart dark browns or good old reliable black of a light weight wool and trimmed with a very bright striped silk scarf and bow. It has raglan sleeves with those new wide armholes and a sectional skirt. The hat, of course, should match the color of the dress. Bette's hat is French felt, with a braided trim and a bow of self material in the front. The pattern, cut after Bette's dress, is shown in its front and back views, above. The number of it is 5160. It comes in sizes 12 to 42 and costs fifteen cents. (In ordering, follow carefully the instructions given on the next page.)

SCREEN'S PATTERNS
FOR EARLY SPRING

5151—The flattering deep yoke extending in points front and back gives smart shoulder width. Yoke can be in contrasting or self fabric. The sleeves, wide above the elbow and narrow below, are another important detail. Sizes 14 to 42.

5145—Different—but not difficult to make. The tucked sleeves with their wide armholes would be smart in contrasting color. The skirt has slenderizing diagonal lines. The buttoned closing and little bow are chic details. Sizes 14 to 42.

5139—Right for almost any daytime occasion. The dropped shoulder line yoke can be in contrasting or self fabric. It can be made with the youthful round collar and matching cuffs on the long sleeves or with a collarless neckline. Sizes 14 to 42.

5159—This may be made in either evening or afternoon length. The neckline may be oval or square. The puff sleeves are made in two sections to permit the use of contrasting fabric if desired. They may be long or short. Sizes 12 to 42.

5147—The cape sleeves are smartly pointed at the edges. The applied front has cowl drapery, which extends to the back where it is finished with tie ends. The skirt may be made shorter if you like. Sizes 14 to 42.

5145

5151

5139

5159

5147

To order patterns: enclose fifteen cents in stamps or coin for each pattern ordered. Be very sure to state the size or sizes wanted. Write your full name and full address plainly on the letter. Mail to MODERN SCREEN Pattern Service, 100 Fifth Avenue, New York, N. Y. For Canadian and foreign orders send twenty cents in coin—Canadian and foreign stamps will not be accepted

GRAND ILLUSIONS

During Hollywood's golden years, the city was a virtual dream factory of idol worship. Movie stars in the 1920's, 1930's, and 1940's were bigger than life on the silver screen, so their private lives and their family trees had to become grander than reality to perpetuate the myth.

In order to facilitate this elaborate facade, the movie studios twisted the facts about actor's backgrounds to create a manufactured delusion of grandeur. Often these screen gods and goddesses were in real life quite the opposite of the personalities they seemed to be in press releases or up on the cinema screen.

The misconceptions started as far back as the 1920's. Exotic vamp Theda Bara was the screen's first Cleopatra, and if one believed the hype, you'd have thought that she was related to King Tut himself. In actuality she was just plain Teodosia Goodman from Chillicothe, Ohio. Handsome leading man William Haines was one of the decade's major heart-throbs, but in reality he was not only gay, but was having an affair with his screen stand-in, Jimmy Shields. When he was given a choice between his film career and his lover, he chose Jimmy. Once out of his studio contract, Haines became an interior decorator. Cute-as-a-button flapper Clara Bow had her career cut short when it was discovered that she had not only slept with half of the leading men in Hollywood but one night took on the entire University of Southern California football team!

Movie fan magazines were prime outlets for the studios to plant their version of the truth. Some of Hollywood's grandest illusions have appeared in *Modern Screen*'s pages, like Rock Hudson and Tyrone Power's widow planning to marry, or how Judy Garland does *not* have a drug dependency problem, and of course the biggest one of all: what a great mom Joan Crawford is!

In 1932 Cary Grant appeared in seven films. In one of them, entitled *Hot Saturday*, Cary co-starred with Nancy Carroll and another young actor named Randolph Scott. That same year, Cary and Randolph took an apartment together, and they were to remain roommates for nearly ten years. They eventually found a house on West Live Oak Drive which they shared. During this same period, Cary married and eight months later divorced Virginia Cherrill, and Randolph Scott married chemical heiress Mariana DuPont.

Although the marriage between Scott and DuPont lasted for two years, Mariana lived across the country in Virginia, while Randolph continued to reside in California with Cary Grant. Eventually Cary and Randy moved to a house on the beach in Santa Monica, at 1018 Ocean Front Avenue.

In the September 1937 issue of *Modern Screen*, Cary and Randy showed off their Santa Monica beachhouse in a photo spread entitled "Batching It" (page 112). When they had shared their first Hollywood house, it was Carole Lombard who nicknamed it "Bachelors' Hall." In this article *Modern Screen* appropriately dubbed their sand-and-surf abode "Bachelors' Paradise!" As the copy reads, here we see Grant and Scott going "down to the sea in shorts"!

Naturally, the Hollywood rumor mill has been speculating for years that Cary and Randy were really "Playing house." However, all that we can see for sure is that Cary and Randy were living proof that "boys just wanna have fun" too! Draw your own conclusions.

On the other side of the fence we have Marlene Dietrich. A big star in Germany before she ever came to Hollywood, Dietrich was beautiful in a cat-like way, and in spite of her femininity she was always a bit on the butch side. Americans were startled in 1932 when gorgeous Marlene began showing up in public attired entirely in

> "I refuse to have my children's emotional lives crippled by some fantastic idea—like their mother's having fangs or being a secret drinker."
> —Joan Crawford
> *Modern Screen*
> July 1951

men's clothes. When she arrived with Maurice Chevalier for the premiere of the film *The Sign of the Cross* (1932) in full male drag, wearing a tuxedo and a felt hat, flashbulbs flared!

One of the resulting stories appeared in the April 1933 issue of *Modern Screen,* entitled "Why Dietrich Wears Trousers" (page 114). "I wear trousers for the reason that they are more comfortable!" proclaimed Marlene. "The men's shirts and coats that I wear are also more comfortable than most any dress I have ever worn." Of course, Josephine Baker had already appeared on stage in Paris in a tuxedo, but America wasn't Europe, and unfortunately was not quite ready for this.

Dietrich touched off rumors that she loved behaving mannishly and had several close women friends whose company she preferred. Here she candidly discusses her penchant for men's clothes by explaining, "In my present wardrobe, though, I have ten suits—a few pairs of extra trousers—a sweater or two—some shirts and a polo coat."

Jean Cummings, who wrote the article, concluded it with the multiple-choice question: "Are women jealous of Dietrich in pants? Or do they hold the idea in contempt? What do you think?" Shocking!

Make-up, lighting, and camera angles are very important to a star's on-screen image, but every once in a while a bit of plastic surgery is the only answer! "Made Over Faces," from the September 1932 issue of *Modern Screen* (page 116), gives readers the lowdown on three male celebrities who decided to improve on what nature had given them. The article is complete with "before" and "after" shots of actors Johnny Weissmuller and George Raft, and boxer Jack Dempsey. Here the public first found out that although Weissmuller was perfect to star in the movie *Tarzan, the Ape Man* (1932)—where he is raised by a family of apes and swings through the jungle on a vine—it was impossible for him to do so with his own nose!

The planned deception in January 1939's "Meet Aunt Judy" (page 119) is that young Judy Garland is a normal, healthy teenager at the age of fifteen. In reality, MGM was pumping her full of pep pills to keep her thin and working on the set non-stop, the sleeping pills at night.

Look at the two photos on the right, and then look at the two photos on the left, and you will see Judy's incredible weight loss, due to the Benzedrine that she was being given to look the part of Dorothy in *The Wizard of Oz* (1939). After her nervous breakdown, in the September 1950 issue of *Modern Screen* the studio was still trying to deny that Judy even had a problem. The article was called "The Brutal Truth about Judy," and in it the following piece of fiction was manufactured and planted: "a Hollywood scandal sheet began running a series of sensation columns on Judy and Seconal pills, the implication being that Judy was addicted to them. This was sheer nonsense. The only thing Judy's ever been addicted to has been her career." Unfortunately, Judy too believed that her problem was not a problem at all. Years later her "sheer nonsense" problem finally killed her.

And now we come to Hollywood's grandest illusion, Joan Crawford, a/k/a "Mommie Dearest"—the beast of Brentwood. For Christina and Christopher Crawford, the "wicked witch of the West" wasn't a character whom Margaret Hamilton portrayed on the screen, she was in fact their very own Mommie severest!

After her first two marriages were dissolved, in 1939 Joan decided that she needed to portray a new role in life—that of "bachelor mother." Over the next couple of years she adopted four children: Christina, Christopher, Cathy, and Cynthia.

From the July 1951 issue of *Modern Screen* is a classic article on Crawford as the ideal mom, "No More Husbands for Joan" (page 120). The beatings, the severe discipline, and the performance of various tasks of obedience before appalled guests are now public legend, due to Christina Crawford's searing 1978 best-selling memoir of an abused child, *Mommie Dearest.* Who can forget those damned wire hangers?

In "No More Husbands for Joan," we find Crawford gushing to her friend Helen Hayes: "I think I envy my children their childhood. Because what I really want is for someone to plan an Easter egg hunt for me. I want someone to bring me a glass of warm milk before I go to sleep." Poor confused Joannie!

Helen Hayes has since been quoted as saying, "Joan tried to be all things to all people. I just wish she hadn't tried to be a mother."

From August 1942 issue of *Modern Screen* (page 132) is a portrait of Joan about to "center all that Crawford talent on two lucky kids." Those poor children!

ROCK HUDSON
June 1959

BATCHING IT

Santa Monica's sands provide a bachelor's Paradise for Randolph Scott and Cary Grant

3. The boys sprawl out for a snooze, while Old King Sol sheds his ultra-violet glamor on them.

4. Down to the sea in shorts. Cary and Randy indulge in their morning aperitif of suds. There's quite a wallop to these suds of Neptune, and all on the house, too. No hangovers, either!

1. The first dip being the hardest, Cary and Randy spar for time. They experiment with various racing dives, knowing darned well that the only thing they'll race for is a towel and a cozy place in the sun.

2. Randy's only regret is that overhead chandeliers went out with Douglas Fairbanks. "I used to be a ninety-seven pound weakling—something like Grant over there," he confides, "until I took to answering fan mail." Cary won't talk until Scott puts down that grisly double-headed sledge hammer of his.

5. At the rate the boys are loping along, Billie Robinson could beat them running backwards. "It's a dog trot," explains Cary, but it must be a pretty small dog he has in mind.

6. The end of a perfect spray. Exuberant, but not too exuberant to remember his etiquette, Cary radiates good health and cheer from the safe vantage of a bath sheet.

7. Bolder than Grant, Randy displays a physique that should answer maidens' prayers from the rock-bound coast of Maine to the sunny shores of California.

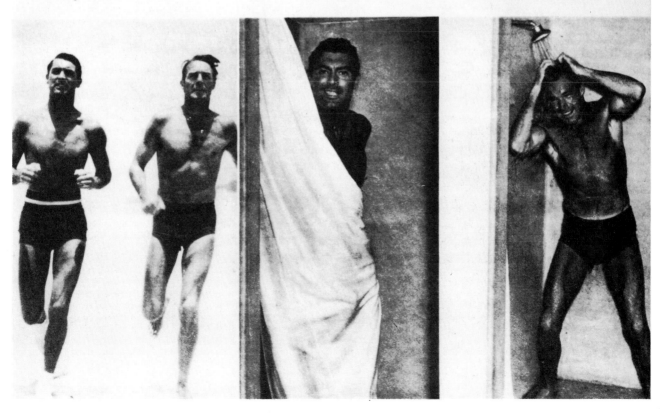

International

WHY DIETRICH WEARS TROUSERS

... Marlene's reasons as to why she has been appearing in public in trousers tailored in regular masculine style

By JEAN CUMMINGS

Here is the famous beauty in smart tuxedo and trousers and felt hat—all made in the most masculine fashion. As a matter of fact, a man's tailor did them for Marlene. Maurice Chevalier was highly appreciative of Marlene's appearance. We can't blame him.

SEEN at the opening of "The Sign of the Cross" in a man's tuxedo, Marlene Dietrich topped the entire evening! Maurice Chevalier, who spent the intermission with the German star, seemed positively envious of the perfect cut of Marlene's mannish coat!"

The above item, in a Hollywood paper, brings Marlene Dietrich's "trouser season" to a climax. Besides Chevalier, most of the men at the theater cast longing glances at the beautiful, blond gal who stood, hands in pockets of the most perfectly fitting tuxedo in town!

True, trousers are nothing new to Dietrich! She has been wearing them for months around Hollywood. Worn them so *often*, in fact, that there is grave doubt in the minds of many onlookers that she even *owns* a dress now! Worn them in spite of the fact that almost every writer in Hollywood has twitted her. Hollywood doesn't like it! Says so—and means it! Still, Dietrich goes on wearing her trousers.

Why?

Almost everyone in the colony has put forth at least one answer to the question . . . but until now, no one has thought to ask the lady herself! Here is Marlene's own answer—told quite matter-of-actly and without pose:

"I WEAR trousers for the reason that they are more comfortable!" smiled Dietrich (who at the moment was wearing gray flannels). "One can slip into a pair of trousers in two minutes, even without the aid of a mirror, and lounge around in perfect ease. The men's shirts and coats that I wear are also more comfortable than most any dress I have ever worn. I wouldn't advise *every* woman to wear trousers, however, because they don't fit every figure . . . my shoulders are wide like a pair of masculine shoulders!"

Before Marlene continued, I noticed that while she was wearing a suit, she wore no vest! A striped shirt with a broad, black four-in-hand tie. Silk sox and low-heeled shoes! A small beret, worn over one eye, completed the ensemble.

"Trousers and masculine clothes make me appear *more* feminine than dresses do!" Marlene went on, crossing her feet as she leaned against the door of her dressing room while lighting a cigarette. "I think you will agree, that certain types of women look well in masculine clothes . . . even better than they do in frills and laces! I always wear plenty of flowing gowns in my pictures, but in real life a man's suit makes me feel *Continued on page 118*

Continued on page 118

PORTRAITS

Photograph by Eugene Robert Richee

Marlene Dietrich, wearing her best poker-face expression, is probably sternly suppressing a desire to beam happily over the fact that people have practically stopped comparing her with Garbo. Fans are anxiously awaiting her next picture, "Shanghai Express." Clive Brook is her leading man in that film. Following its completion, Marlene will go to Germany to do a screen version of Cleopatra's life, Josef von Sternberg directing, of course. Marlene lives in a Beverly Hills home formerly owned by Charles Mack and employs Bebe Daniels' former chauffeur. She numbers Joan Crawford and young Doug among her few friends.

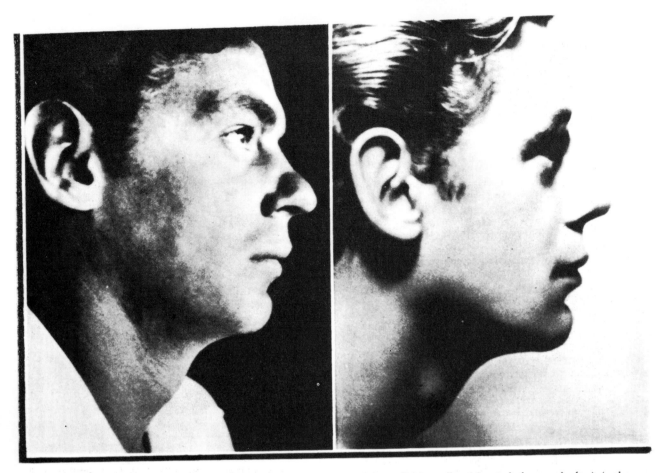

MADE-OVER FACES

Johnny Weissmuller (above, before and after) is the classic example of what remodeling can do. (Below left) Dr. Balsinger. (Below, right) Dr. Ginsburg.

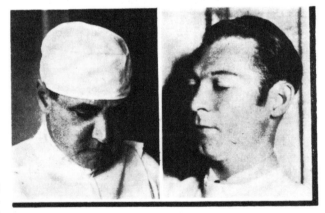

I'D give you the part in a minute, young man, if your nose were all right, but you can see for yourself how wrong it is," the director told a young applicant for an important screen rôle recently.

Ten years ago, such a statement would have meant the end of the world for an ambitious young actor. But not now. In Hollywood today, features are subject to change without notice. For there is a group of reputable and skilled surgeons, who are able to and do perform miracles for the benefit of camera.

A few months ago, the above remark was made to Johnny Weissmuller after his first test for the rôle of Tarzan was run off in the projection room. He was physically perfect for the rôle and passed one hundred per cent in that portion of the test where he was required to swing gracefully from one limb of a tree to another. But when the close-up of his face was shown, the defective hump in the end of his nose stood out grotesquely and

ruined all that his previous efforts had accomplished.

But did he give up in despair when he heard the director's verdict? He did not. He went home instead and talked the thing out with his young wife, Bobbé Arnst, and they decided to leave the matter in the hands of capable Dr. Josif Ginsburg, who has performed over a thousand successful facial operations on the film famous in the last two years.

The operation itself was trifling, according to the surgeon. Local anaesthetics were administered in much the same way as when a dentist deadens a nerve in a tooth he is about to extract. Dr. Ginsburg began by injecting the anaesthetic into the tip of the nose and then worked upward until the entire center of the face was

George Raft had an ear operation for the sake of the camera. Jack Dempsey had an operation on his nose. Here are their "before and after" pictures.

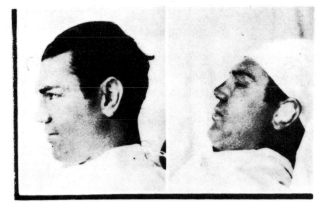

. . . You'll be amazed at the number of Hollywood stars who have had remodelling done to their faces. And why not? It's part of their job to make themselves look as attractive as possible

By MARY SHARON

devoid of feeling. Then, with the patient wholly conscious, the work of slicing and repairing was accomplished. It sounds gruesome, but it wasn't half as bad as it sounds, if we may take Johnny's word for it. And look at the result. He walked away with the coveted rôle. When you saw him as Tarzan did you look at his nice, new nose? There is no evidence remaining to show that it was once broken and badly shaped.

I VISITED the consultation and operating-rooms of several of Hollywood's best known beauty surgeons. While I was sitting in the reception room waiting to see Dr. Ginsburg, an actress whom you all know by reputation came in. She was heavily veiled, but when she picked up a magazine I recognized a priceless ring upon her hand. She had shown it to me about two months previously, and had told me that it was unique—the only one of its kind in the world.

We were alone in the room, so I spoke to her, calling her by name. She was upset by the fact that I had recognized her.

"Please don't mention to anyone that you have seen me here," she begged. "I will be ruined if this gets out. You won't tell, will you?"

I quieted her fears and asked why she did not wish her visits to Dr. Ginsburg to become known.

She raised her veil, since it had proven a useless disguise.

"I will tell you. I am really only thirty-one years of age but there was an ugly little line coming under my chin that was quite evident in close-ups. I had to do something. A friend, who had *Continued on page 118*

Continued on page 118

Made-Over Faces

Continued from page 117

undergone an operation for the same thing, advised me to have Dr. Ginsburg work on me. But—if the fans knew that my face had been operated upon, there would be a million different stories broadcast about it, and everyone would be saying that I am forty or fifty years old. It would sound as if age had me down. You know Hollywood. I couldn't bear it, if this leaked out."

I promised I would forget all about it. Just then, Dr. Ginsburg invited me into his holy of holies. I learned a lot about the beauty business in the hour that followed. I learned, too, that practically every actress in Hollywood, who has passed the twenty-five-year-old mark has had work of one sort or another done upon her features. And quite a few of the men. You might call it a concession to their vanity, but it is nearer the mark to call it a concession to business. The public applauds and pays to see youth. And when a favorite begins to age, their fans turn to a newer, fresher idol. Small wonder then, that there are those who are willing to risk everything to retain their place in the sun. For not every beauty operation is a success.

There is one woman in Hollywood, the wife of a noted actor, who is doomed to go through life wearing a veil, because a quack doctor attempted to correct a small defect on the tip of her nose, and bungled.

Thais Valdemar, one-time fiancée of big Karl Dane had her mouth operated upon to make her lips into a cupid's bow. It looked all right but she went to court because she said she lost the sense of feeling in her lips, that she could not feel even kisses. So what good was her mouth to her, anyway?

In justice to the surgeons who have given years to the study and practise of plastic surgery, it must be said that for every failure there are hundreds of successful operations performed. Dr. Ginsburg and Dr. Balsinger, two of Hollywood's most popular beauty surgeons, both served in European hospitals during the war, restoring the features of wounded soldiers. This experience has since proved invaluable, especially in cases where grafting is resorted to. Dr. Ginsburg successfully grafted the fourth toe of an actress upon the stub of her little finger, which had been amputated in an accident. After the operation, the synthetic finger was placed in a cast and after three months it could easily pass for a normal finger.

Georges Carpentier was one of Dr. Ginsburg's first Hollywood patients. He had his nose straightened.

BEBE DANIELS had the end of her nose remodeled and her later pictures show that there has been a decided improvement in it. Carmel Myers and Vivienne Segal both underwent nose operations that improved their beauty considerably. In fact, when Vivienne had hers operated upon, she was about to be let out by Warner Brothers on account of the imperfection in her profile. After the operation, they signed her for five more pictures. So she was amply repaid for the risk she ran.

When he first came to this country, Paul Lukas was told that he was an impossible camera subject on account of the bulbous shape of his nose. He placed himself in Dr. Ginsburg's hands and now wears a perfect nose.

George Raft is the newest big cinema name who has had a facial operation in the interests of business. George's ears weren't all they might have been in the way of beauty so he had them made over by Ginsburg with splendid results.

One of Dr. Balsinger's most famous patients is Jack Dempsey, who submitted to an operation on his nose back in 1924. He was working in pictures at the time and each day the make-up man had to build his nose up with putty, to disguise the place where it had been broken in one of his early fights. This worked all right until summer came and whenever he started to perspire the putty would melt and run down on his face. Jack decided it would be less grief to have his nose remade than to keep having it made-up. After the operation, a number of friends feared and predicted that the nose would be ruined during his next pugilistic encounter. They were wrong. The new nose is stronger than the original one, since it has twice as much cartilage in it as it originally had. Jack has been in three major fights since the operation and his new nose is none the worse for it.

Three weeks before his sudden death, Louis Wolheim arranged for Dr. Balsinger to remodel his nose, which was broken in a football game in his youth. Much of Wolheim's appeal as a character actor was based upon this very feature and when the studio learned what he was planning to do they got the district court to issue a restraining order. He was upon the operating table when the document was handed him, and was much disappointed at being prevented from going through with the operation.

Dr. Balsinger has performed a number of operations upon the knees of dancers to give them dimples. And has also corrected hair lips. This is the most delicate form of facial surgery, since it is a natural defect and the tissues grow in opposite directions.

A number of well known actors and actresses are consulting with various beauty surgeons regarding operations upon their noses and other facial repairs. Walter Byron, who suffered a broken nose in an automobile accident, is planning on having a new nose soon.

Much publicity was given the report that Clark Gable had been operated upon to improve his ears. This is not true. When Clark was still in the extra ranks, he consulted with Dr. Ginsburg regarding an ear operation, but the cost was too prohibitive for his purse at the time. He was only making five dollars a day and not every day at that. After fame came, he decided that an operation was unnecessary. Now, for close-ups, the make-up man places adhesive behind his ears and in this way pulls them close to his head. Douglas Fairbanks is reported also to have made use of this method of restraining his ears.

Dietrich's Trousers

Continued from page 114

(and, I hope *look*) more feminine than the most beautiful dress in the world!

"Also, it takes too much time, trouble and MONEY to be a well-dressed woman in Hollywood. Motion picture stars are always buying some terrifically expensive gown, wearing it once or twice and then discarding it because they 'can't afford' to be seen in the same dress more often! As for me, wearing a dress more than twice is easy. If it weren't for the fact that the style changes before one has the opportunity to get the gown on the third or fourth time! Isn't it silly to spend all that money . . . just for a whim? It really isn't worth it!

"In my present wardrobe, though, I have ten suits—a few pairs of extra trousers—a sweater or two—some shirts and a polo coat! That is all I need— the style will be good two years from now! I tried to figure out, the other night, what it would cost me to wear dresses during those two years . . . I quit before I reached the astounding total!

The other day, we overheard several women talking about Dietrich's costume at a recent party. They seemed unanimous in their shocking reaction. The group of *men* at the party had eyes for no other woman! Are women jealous of Dietrich in pants? Or do they hold the idea in contempt? What do you think?

"Hey, have you any blue notes I haven't? 'Cause I'll be worried if you have," Judy Garland asks her little niece, Judith Sherwood.

MEET AUNT JUDY

Remind me I'm fifteen now. It's so hard to remember!

Judy's one star who admits the pool she swims in is not her own. Right, this ping-pong game takes concentration, what we mean!

no more husbands

■ "I've made three mistakes. I'm not proud of any of them. Three pretty wonderful guys have loaned me their last names. Four is a lot of husbands," said Joan Crawford.

The reporter, startled by her frankness, sat back and stared at the beautiful star. She hadn't dropped a stitch in her knitting. She had told cook the lamb chops were to be broiled. A silence followed, but suddenly Joan's laughter broke it.

"Funny thing about truth," she said. "You can't hide it. I'm tired of having to simper and duck whenever the subject of husbands comes up. I'm weary of trying to apologize for living alone. And I refuse to have my children's emotional lives crippled by some fantastic idea—like their mother's having fangs or being a secret drinker—and thus not being able to get them a father to complete the family."

Dusk had crept around the house unnoticed as she spoke. Joan rose and turned up a few lamps. Soft lights revealed warm coral cushions, deep comfortable furniture, and generous spreads of green plants.

The room fairly danced with life. In the center, a pot-luck table told the story of this house. It bore a one-armed doll, a pile of movie scripts, a half finished chocolate bar, a hair ribbon and a jar with a grasshopper inside.

It seemed too warm and gracious to be the room of a woman who "lived alone and liked it."

As if reading the reporter's thoughts, Joan said, "Do you find it so hard to believe I can be content without a husband?"

There could be no answer. Just, "thank you," and "goodbye."

A few nights later Joan gave a small party. Among her guests was Joan's very dear friend Helen Hayes.

Helen and Joan retired to a corner after a while. They exchanged compliments on dramatic roles, clothes and then settled down to their real love—gossip.

"Joan, this is the first time I have ever seen you without powder on your nose," Helen exclaimed.

"Good heavens, I forgot!" Joan gasped.

"I didn't say you had spots, just no powder," Miss Hayes soothed.

But Joan refused to be soothed. "You don't understand. Two days ago I was interviewed. I talked big, emancipated words. Now I'm not so sure I told the truth.

"Helen, have you ever felt two opposite ways at the same time?" Joan asked, almost pleading. *Continued on page 122*

Vacations with her children are the high spots in Joan's life. Here Christina, Cynthia, Joan, Cathy and Christopher present a solid Crawford front as they cross the lawn of Alisal Ranch. Christopher is the man of the family.

All of Joan's children are adopted: Christina and Christopher know this. She is as frank and honest with them about the possibility and problems of her remarriage when they ask, "Why don't we have a daddy?"

for joan

Is she too independent to remarry? Has she lost her faith in love? Joan answers these questions in the frankest story we've ever printed.

BY LADDIE MARSHACK

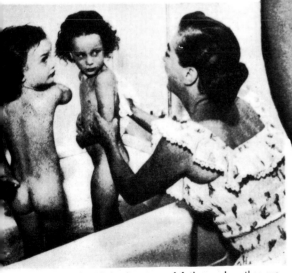

Joan has combined the functions of father and mother successfully as far as the children are concerned. But she feels this dual role may be a hindrance to her appeal as a woman.

no more husbands for joan

Continued from page 120 "Yes!" Miss Helen Hayes said, simply.

This was all the reassurance Joan needed. She repeated her remarks of the interview and then told Helen Hayes, "But I do yearn for someone who makes me want to keep powder on my nose, too."

And the two great actresses giggled like school girls. Joan had started confessing and couldn't stop.

"Helen, I think I envy my children their childhood. Because what I really want is for someone to plan an Easter egg hunt for *me*. I want someone to bring *me* a glass of warm milk before I go to sleep. I want someone to kiss my finger to make it well. Does that make me an awful heel?"

Miss Hayes didn't have to answer. Mrs. Van Johnson, whose children number three, had overheard.

"Joan, that makes you just about the best kind of a mother—human," Evie said.

After her guests had left, Joan made the usual rounds—covered Christopher, who is a blanket-loser; looked in on Christina, and made sure that Cathy and Cynthia, the twins, weren't still clutching their teddy bears.

The night's conversation recalled itself. Something was inconsistent. She'd flatly denied any dissatisfaction to the reporter. Yet to Helen she had admitted a longing for "someone to watch over her." Was she lying? Was she showing one face in print and another in private? Back and forth the thoughts shuttled. "I feel like the net on a badminton court," Joan indecisively concluded.

THE next day Joan had lunch at the studio commissary. Mel Dinelli, the director, met her and they began their usual heated discussion about everything. Joan's opinions are rarely tepid. The axe Joan had decided to grind that lunch hour was movie stars—women stars.

"Mel, don't you think every woman who becomes a star begins to develop some masculine know-how? She learns to deal with men in a man's world. She catches on about quarreling for her rights. Pretty soon, even if she is basically timid and cautious, she observes men and starts to take chances—gambles for her beliefs. And pretty soon, she gets the feeling that her femininity is gone, vanished, not there. A hundred doubts start gnawing at her.

"Her gestures become self-conscious. She withdraws more and more, until she becomes a hundred times more sensitive than the ordinary housewife. A man says 'hello,' and she feels herself blushing like a sophomore. At a party a not-too-bright, not-too-handsome, not-too-original fellow pays her a soupçon of attention and right away, he's Galahad, Cary Grant and William Shakespeare."

Mel was having a hard time catching up with her. "Joan, what are you trying to say?"

"I don't know myself, Mel," Joan admitted. "I've had to become the executive of my own small world. In a way I *am* capable of thinking like a man, and I do when the need arises."

Mr. Dinelli was gentle with his next words. "Honey, are you afraid you aren't making the grade being both mother and father to the kids?"

Joan didn't answer him. That was only a part of her fears. What she was really thinking about were her marriages . . . how she very often anticipated some masculine want because she'd trained herself to understand men. Perhaps that wasn't good. Or anyway didn't make for a happy marriage. Because of this trait she often saw holes in a man where other women

saw solid brick.

By the time dessert came around Joan was beginning to detect the cracks in her own armor, but she had as yet reached no final decision.

When she got home that evening there was an invitation to a party. "Formal," the invitation read. Joan was pleased. It had been a long time since she'd dressed to the teeth and sallied out to a ball. She would have to buy a gown.

But first she called Caesar Romero. "Butch, want to take me to a party?" That's how secure and relaxed their friendship is.

The night of the party Butch picked her up in *his* car. "Joan, none of this 'I can go home alone if you're having a good time and don't want to leave' stuff. I'm taking you and I'm bringing you. And if you insist on driving your own car I'll let the air out of your tires," said Caesar.

Joan loved him for insisting on *his* way, and went gaily with him to the Van Johnson house.

Even though she has made innumerable grand entrances in movies and faced battalions of fans, Joan still has to prod herself through a door at a party. But she had scarcely entered this one when she found her arm held tightly in the paw of a guest. "Can I get you a drink, Miss Crawford? Or how about a hors d'oeuvre, or some coffee and cake. I know I should

be offering you the Taj Mahal, ho, ho, ho. Boy, it sure is hard to believe *I* am talking to the fabulous Joan Crawford."

Those were the last words Mr. Let-Me-Drink-You-All-In uttered to Miss Joan Crawford. Politely, Joan unwound his fingers from her arm and excused herself. Her next encounter was with the genus, Let-Me-Take-You-Out-Of-All-This. He said, "You really don't belong here, Joan. I see you in a field of corn flowers, gay and child-like. These people don't really understand you." Joan decided to put an end to this line. "On the contrary," she said, clearly. "These people understand me very well. You see, *they're* my friends."

By the time she was introduced to a plain-looking sandy-haired man her eyes were blazing with indignation. "How do you do, Miss Crawford? Won't you sit down?" he said, and Joan fell in love with him. Only his disclosure that he was happily married with three children restrained her from proposing on the spot.

Not one of the men she'd met that night interested her. Not one had been direct and simple (except "Sandy") or had waited for her to indicate what pleased or displeased her.

Worse than that—not one would have been a solution to something Chris had asked a long time ago. It was the inevitable question—"Mother, why don't we have a daddy?"

And even though Joan had prepared herself and her words for the occasion, it was still very difficult to answer.

"Chris, what if I brought home someone who didn't like you?"

Christopher Crawford decided that was a silly question. "You wouldn't do that, Mommy."

"Well, what if I brought home someone who liked you and didn't like Christina or Cathy and Cynthia?"

He dismissed that one as easily as he

had the first. "You'd just *have* to bring home someone who liked all four of us."

"Darling, what if I brought home a daddy that liked all of you, but didn't like my work?"

Chris Crawford recognized he was out of his depth. A little subdued, he finally said, "Mommy, it's kind of hard to find a good daddy."

Joan hugged her son for his wisp of understanding. "Yes, darling, very hard. But I'm trying."

THE party broke up soon after Joan returned from Evie's dressing room where Chris' memory had sent her. On the way home Butch asked, "Have a good time?"

Joan couldn't sham. Her resentment burst forth unchecked. "Butch, what's the matter with men? Do they really believe that girls are so gullible?"

Butch parried her question with one of his own. "Joan, are *you* gullible?"

Her answer was "No. And what I dislike most is that practically every man I've met recently acts as if I were the last woman on earth. The date he is asking for is the last date he'll have on earth. And tomorrow the earth is going to stop spinning on its axis.

"What I'm looking for is old-fashioned courting. An introduction, flowers, dinner and eventually, but not that night, a good night kiss."

Butch nodded understandingly, and the conversation, the evening were over. Alone in her room Joan mulled over the whole disquieting problem. Once again, was she a liar? She glared at herself in the mirror.

"Well, Miss Joan Crawford," she challenged. "Do you want a man or don't you want a man?"

"Yes, I do," was the answer. "But not at any price!

"Not at the price of my self-respect. Not at the price of my children's happiness. And most of all, not at the price I have paid in the past."

Sleep came easily and sweetly that night.

IN the morning, refreshed and sure of herself, Joan arranged for another interview with the press. When the reporter arrived she was knitting, as before.

"I asked you something the other day that was unfair," she said. "I couldn't even answer it myself. I think I can now.

"Let me tell you a bit about my marriages," she went on. "I blame myself for their failure. I overwhelmed my husbands. If they asked for a pillow I ordered swan feathers from France, linen from Ireland and personally hand-stitched the puff, with tender, loving care.

"The way I feel about it is that I spoiled them. I gave and gave and gave . . . But I don't presume to intrepret for them. Maybe they felt I didn't give enough. I don't know. But I do pride myself on their friendship to this day.

"Maybe my fear that I wasn't feminine, because I am a career woman and love it, made me too anxious. When I fell in love I *had* to be all kinds of woman—mother, wife, sister, favorite cousin from Omaha. And I still don't know how to right this 'me.'

"Because every minute I'm in love I'm on Cloud Number 7.

"My palms are out to any man who can accept the kind of woman that I am. For, to be truthful, I don't think I will ever stop giving."

The reporter didn't have to take notes this time. He shook Joan Crawford's hand, thanked her and headed for his typewriter.

He'd never felt more certain of his story in his life. Or more certain that he had just encountered a truly courageous and honest woman. THE END
(Joan Crawford can be seen in the Warner Bros. picture, Goodbye, My Fancy.)

A. L. Whitey Schafer

JOAN CRAWFORD

You'd never dream she harbored the soul of a homebody to watch her jive through Col.'s new "They All Kissed the Bride"! Hoofed for the first time in 10 years, went at it so vigorously she sprained her back. Passed her huge $112,500 salary check on to charity. Despite Glenn Ford's constant calls on the set, she insists, "I won't marry any man until the war ends." Plans to settle down, anyway, with two adopted kids, Christina, 3, and Christopher, 15 mos. Is marketing for a 400-acre Pa. farm to replace N. Y. as her getting-away-from-it-all haven, seeing no one, going nowhere, devoting her entire time to reading, resting, writing up her life and times for publication, centering all that Crawford talent on 2 lucky kids!

HOLLYWOOD REBELS

ollywood was filled with temperamental stars, and many of them fought bitter battles with the studios that made them into household names. But nobody in film history bucked the system like the legendary rebel Frances Farmer. Whatever demons she battled within her own mind drove her to a fate worse than any of the "B" movies she was cast in. When *Modern Screen* published "Nobody's Yes-Girl" in its February 1938 issue (page 126), she was well on her way to becoming Tinsel town's most obnoxiously opinionated star. At a time when young starlets were dying to become famous so that they could wear chic clothes and drive a big, expensive car, Frances was seen around town in worn-out slacks and tennis shoes, still driving her tired old green car. It went further than merely normal disregard for convention; her unhappiness was from somewhere deep inside.

Although she had been a smash in *Come and Get It* (1936), *Ebb Tide* (1937), and *The Toast of New York* (1937) with Cary Grant, she considered herself too serious to bother with all of that glamour nonsense. When she was picked up by the police for drunk driving without a license on October 19, 1942, the real nightmare began. She could have politely gotten out of the whole mess, but she was dying for a fight with someone—and the Los Angeles Police Department seemed like a great choice. Her spicy brand of foul language won her a 180-day jail sentence, from which she was released on probation. This was followed by a fight with the movie studio's hairdresser, in which Frances dislocated the hairdresser's jaw. She was seen running down Sunset Boulevard topless after a drunken brawl at a bar. On a rapid descent, she next found herself behind bars for neglecting to report her whereabouts to her

> " If you're independent and speak your own mind, you're described as a fantastically rebellious person."
> —Frances Farmer
> *Modern Screen,*
> February 1938

parole officer. She was dragged kicking and screaming from a room in Hollywood's Knickerbocker Hotel. She punched a police matron and knocked a policeman to the floor.

Once she had been seen on the screen in beautiful gowns; her next outfit was a straightjacket! Her mother had her committed to a mental institution for a "rest," but fiery Frances just did not want to "chill out." Her road back to the outside world took the path of insulin shock treatments, and eventually a frontal lobotomy. She was raped and sexually abused several times, and her story was later captured on the silver screen in *Frances* (1982) and in the TV film *Will There Really Be a Morning?* (1983).

"That Complainin' Roz," from *Modern Screen*'s April 1937 issue, finds Rosalind Russel not getting her man on screen or off. Reported by Dorothy Kilgallen, the article tells the tale of how Roz had to fight for attention early in her screen career. Many of her best battles were still ahead of her. One of her most famous rebellions came in the film that was going to change her career, *The Women* (1939).

The Women was a huge hit on Broadway, and when MGM bought the film rights to it and announced that it was going to be done with an all-star cast, Roz was determined to be a part of it. Recalled Roz, "MGM tested everybody but Lassie and Mrs. Roosevelt for *The Women*. Even the maids' roles were being fought over." She desperately wanted to play the part of gossipy Sylvia Fowler, so she convinced producer Hunt Stromberg that she deserved a test with director George Cukor. She played the part three ways: direct, drawing-room comedic, and outlandishly exaggerated. It was the later interpretation that won her the role, which immediately made her into a screen comedienne.

The two top stars of *The Women* were Norma Shearer and Joan Crawford. At that time, Norma had a clause in her contract stipulating that no woman's name could appear with hers above the title of any of her pictures. She made an exception for this movie with Crawford. Roz, however, was stealing scenes right and left during the filming, and she was not about to be billed after the title. She had already been the star of her most recent films, and was not about to take a demotion. She had an idea: she'd call in sick and refuse to return to work until Norma Shearer relented. She had cleverly waited until too much of the film had been shot to replace her, and she won her battle. That complainin' Roz was learnin' to become a rebel!

"*Modern Screen* is the first magazine to reveal the explanation as to why the Hepburn girl loves to shock and amaze Hollywood," proclaimed the May 1933 issue of the magazine, when it published "The Real Reason for Hepburn's Amazing Behavior" (page 130). When this was written, Katharine Hepburn was one of the new breed of independent women in Hollywood who cast convention to the wind.

The photos are from Hepburn's second movie, *Christopher Strong* (1933), which was followed by *Morning Glory* (1933)—for which she won her first of four Academy Awards. "Katharine of Arrogance" is what they dubbed her. Her 1934 return to the New York state in *The Lake* was a disaster. After seeing Hepburn in *The Lake,* acid-tongued Dorothy Parker made the famous comment, "She ran the gamut of emotions from A to B."

Hepburn returned to Hollywood to film *The Little Minister* (1934), *Break of Hearts* (1935), and the delightful *Alice Adams* (1935). *Stage Door* (1937), *Bringing Up Baby* (1938), and *Holiday* (1938) were all critical smashes, but were doing poorly at the box office. In 1938, in the *Independent Film Journal,* an article ran entitled "Box Office Poison." It proclaimed, "Among these players whose box-office draw is nil can be numbered Mae West, Edward Arnold, Greta Garbo, Joan Crawford, Katharine Hepburn, and many, many others." Hepburn had the last laugh by enduring as a star through the next five decades on the screen, and in the pages of *Modern Screen!*

Tallulah Bankhead was one of those movie stars whose personal lives are more famous than any of their films. The one shining exception to that rule was the suspenseful *Lifeboat* (1944), which is an Alfred Hitchcock masterpiece.

Tallulah had been a big hit in London as the star of several stage plays, *The Dancers* (1923), *Conchita* (1924), and *The Green Door* (1925) among them. Paramount signed her for five films, beginning with *Tarnished Lady, My Sin* and *The Cheat,*

all in 1931. *Modern Screen* published "Tallulah Bankhead—Gambler" in its November 1931 issue (page 133), after her first two films had been released to a decidedly cool reception. After completing *Thunder Below, The Devil and the Deep,* and *Faithless* in 1932, Tallulah passed on both Paramount's and MGM's offer to sign subsequent contracts—for far less money. She opted to return to the theater. The one movie that she really wanted to do was the screen version of *The Little Foxes* (1941). Tallulah had originated it on Broadway, where she was a huge success, but the film version starred Bette Davis.

Like Bankhead and Hepburn, Mae West was a huge draw in the theater before films, which was why all three women were brought to Hollywood in the early 1930's. With the instant popularity of talkies, the movies desperately needed actresses who could deliver dialogue.

Mae was pegged as a Hollywood rebel from the very first day of production on her first film, *Night After Night* (1932). After reading the script that had been submitted for her screen debut, West snapped, "This part ain't big enough for Mae West; you could get anybody to play this." Indeed, it was George Raft's first film, and Mae had been offered the film to boost the prestige of the production. She insisted upon rewriting all of her own dialogue, and to placate her the studio allowed her to do anything she wanted. She was such a sensation in the film that her performance turned an average gangster film into a special event. George Raft admitted, "In this picture, Mae West stole everything but the cameras." Paramount begged her to sign for two more pictures in 1933: *She Done Him Wrong* and *I'm No Angel.* Her first three films literally saved Paramount from bankruptcy, and made Mae West one of the most successful actresses of the thirties. Of course, Mae's reputation for delivering some of the most suggestive lines of the decade was established early in her career. From the May 1933 issue of *Modern Screen* comes "Bad, Bad Woman" (page 134). Reading it is certainly good for a thrill, and as Mae used to say, "A thrill a day keeps the chill away!"

In the late 1940's, Montgomery Clift represented a new breed of Hollywood star. Monty scandalously showed up on the set in worn blue jeans and a tee shirt, although he was already an established star! Hollywood was shocked in the article "Barefoot Boy with Shows On" from *Modern Screen*'s February 1950 issue (page 136). The next year would find him in one of his most successful starring roles, opposite Elizabeth Taylor and Shelley Winters in *A Place in the Sun.*

KATHARINE HEPBURN
May 1933

Frances Farmer is one star
who refused to be glamorous,
which decision didn't hurt her
a bit for, after a brief career as
an ingenue, she was soon in
the star class.

NOBODY'S YES-GIRL

BY DORA ALBERT

When Frances Farmer speaks
her piece, things begin to happen

The Hollywood men didn't appeal to Frances either. But Leif Erickson fixed that.

"Ebb-Tide," in color, is Miss Farmer's latest, and Ray Milland her leading man.

HOLLYWOOD always tries to fabricate a super-personality for you," Frances Farmer said. "If you're the sweet type, it presents you as being a hundred times sweeter than any human could be. If you're independent and speak your own mind, you're described as a fantastically rebellious person."

We were sitting in her dressing-room at the Belasco Theatre in New York. Just a few moments before, Frances Farmer had seemed glamorous on the stage in "Golden Boy." Now as she stripped off the dress she'd worn on the stage, as she brushed back her shining hair, she seemed to be stripping from herself all the habiliments of glamor and emerging as a human being.

Looking at her, you knew that her features were beautiful; that no miracle of makeup had supplied the glow on her cheek, the strange, almost fascinating directness of her hazel eyes; that no fake glamorizing process had anything to do with the intelligent forehead, the wide, sweet mouth.

Few Hollywood women would have dared to face an interviewer as Frances Farmer was facing me, wearing just scanties; but her figure is lithe and lovely, and she has nothing to fear from the most critical eyes. She stood up for a moment and then began to pull a pair of gray slacks over her legs; she slipped on a beige jacket and a blue neckerchief and slipped her feet into low-heeled tennis shoes.

SHE SAID, "Hollywood makes such a fuss over the things you naturally take as a matter of course. Then, if it runs out of stories, the studio publicists and the writers get busy and invent them. I used to feel chagrined when I read things about myself that were not true, but now I don't mind. I was annoyed, I'll confess, when an interviewer said that I ate raw vegetables exclusively and stood on my head to get thin. Anybody'd be annoyed at

a statement like that, I think. It sounds ridiculous.

"In Hollywood, any number of methods of conduct were outlined to me, but the most frequent advice I got—both from people in Hollywood and from people who'd never even seen the town—was to keep up a front. Well, I can't do that. No matter how much advice I got, the only thing I could do was to be myself. I'd feel like an ass trying to be glamorous. I'm not the type."

Suddenly, I remembered why I had come. I had heard so many rumors about Frances Farmer, that she was a poseur, a fake, a rebel; that she had been a thorn in the side to interviewers and a pain in the neck to her own publicity department; that she had put plenty of do-re-mi into "Golden Boy"—just for the privilege of appearing on Broadway. I decided to investigate those rumors.

Frankly, I was prejudiced against Miss Farmer. I thought of the slacks she wore and the faded green car she drove and the fact that she had only one evening gown. All these antics seemed to be part of a carefully calculated pose.

When Frances sprang that old line on me about wanting to be herself, I couldn't resist asking, "Why do you keep on driving around Hollywood in a dinky, second-hand car? Isn't that keeping up a front—in reverse?"

"I was broke when I got to Hollywood, so it was the only kind of car that I could afford," she answered. "Now I wouldn't dream of getting rid of it because it suits my needs; it still runs and it has room enough. When it stops running, I'll get a new one, but not before that. I don't think there's any affectation there. I'd be uncomfortable if I had to sit in a long, shiny car. Besides, I'm trying to save money."

Checking up later, I found that there was a reason for her modest way of living. In spite of the fact that she has played in two of the very biggest *Continued on page 128*

Nobody's Yes-Girl

Continued from page 127

pictures of the year, "Come and Get It" and "Ebb-Tide," her salary, with bonuses, still hovers around the four-hundred-dollar-a-week mark. And that doesn't go far in Hollywood toward keeping up a front.

VERY early in her picture career, Frances' Hollywood bosses became alarmed at the unpretentious way in which she was living. One day Phyllis Laughton, who was training talented newcomers at Paramount, called Frances into her private office, and said to her, "Frances, there's something I've got to tell you. It's . . . it's . . ." Miss Laughton seemed to find it hard to go on.

"Why are you afraid to tell me?" Frances asked. "You know I've never minded when you criticized my work."

"It's not that," Miss Laughton said. "It's the way you dress on the street. Never wearing a hat and the horrible slacks and that faded jacket. You're being groomed for stardom, and the fans expect stars to be glamorous-looking when they see them on the street."

"So that's it," said Frances, smiling. "You know, Phyllis, you don't give a darn about the way I dress, so obviously someone from the front office has been talking to you. Who was it?"

Phyllis Laughton looked uncomfortable.

"Phyllis," Frances said, "do something for me, will you? Go to him and give him this message from me. Tell him if the executives at the studio paid as much attention to the parts they give their actresses as they do to the clothes they wear off the screen, we'd all make a lot more money."

Not for a moment did Frances stop to think that she was being impudent, and that she might imperil her brand-new career by being so frank. But if she had stopped to think of it, it wouldn't have checked her. For it isn't in the girl to bow and scrape and "yes" people to death.

There was the time, for instance, when a very powerful columnist asked her to appear on his program, so that he could introduce her to his listeners as the most promising newcomer of the year. Into the script he had put some pretty telling lines against Katharine Hepburn, which Frances Farmer was expected to deliver.

Now Frances likes and admires Katharine, and she didn't want to deliver those lines. At rehearsals, she tried to have them changed, but failed.

When the time came for her to broadcast, she didn't know what to do. Never in her life had she said something she didn't believe. On the other hand, she knew that if she antagonized this columnist, she might make a very dangerous enemy for herself, for his broadcasts were heard and his newspaper columns were read throughout the country, and it was said that he had a million fans.

When she got to the mike, the words she was really thinking about Hepburn tumbled from her lips in a flood; instead of condemning her, she praised her. All her life, Frances has been accustomed to saying exactly what she thought, and when she was put to a test, she couldn't do otherwise.

When she played with veterans in "Come and Get It," in a scenario written by a man who had had seventeen years' experience, directed by Howard Hawks, who had been directing box-office hits while she was going to college, she never hesitated to challenge the things these veterans said. At first they wondered at the gall of this young upstart who dared to say to the director, "What you suggested

isn't right. I don't feel it. The line should be changed."

As they discovered that there was intelligence behind that wide brow of Frances, the attitude of these men changed gradually from resentment to respect.

"Did you once say in an interview, 'I have been a rebel all my life'?" I asked Frances.

"Hell, no," she answered.

"Didn't you say once that a lot of people dislike you?"

"Of course not. Even if those things were true, I wouldn't say them. You, of all people, oughtn't to believe the things you read. You're supposed to write them, not to read and believe them."

Nevertheless, she has been a rebel, ever since that day in grammar school, when she penned an essay called "God Dies," in which she tried to prove that the individual ought to fight his own battles and not depend upon a beneficent Providence for aid. Because of the sensational title of her essay, she was condemned by both students and faculty, and considered a dangerous firebrand.

IN college, she majored in drama and appeared whenever she could in the shows given at the Studio Theatre of the University of Washington. Since her parents had very little money, Frances had to earn her way through college by working at such odd jobs as typing, appearing in radio skits, assisting in a dye factory, acting as camp counsellor to campfire girls, and doubling as a waitress and a singer of Indian love songs for the guests at a Mt. Rainier resort.

More than anything else, she wanted to get stage experience, and she realized that New York was the center of the theatrical world. But the money she had earned had been just enough to see her through college. How was she going to get there?

Opportunity appeared in a strange guise. The *Voice of Action,* a radical newspaper, offered a trip to Russia to the person getting the most subscriptions for it. Frances hustled around and persuaded as many people as she could to subscribe; not because she was interested in going to Russia, but because she wanted to go to New York.

When she won, her friends in Seattle were horrified. She was considered a menace by most of the people there, and held up as a horrible example of the inroads Communism was making upon our American colleges. But it didn't matter. What did anything matter, so long as she got to New York? Now she could bombard the offices of all the theatrical producers.

That was what she thought. But she hadn't stopped to realize that it was midsummer, and that most producers were out of town and wouldn't be back till September or October. In the meanwhile, on what was she going to live?

A man she had met on the boat going to Russia introduced her to Shepard Traube, who knew Oscar Serlin, at that time head of the talent scout department at Paramount. Amazed at finding an inexperienced actress, who was as beautiful and intelligent as Frances, Serlin suggested that she take a test.

"At the time I took the test I didn't take movies seriously," she said. "I didn't think I had a chance."

When Paramount offered her a contract, she realized that she would be a fool to turn it down, since such an opportunity might never come her way again.

During her first three months in Hollywood no one paid any attention to her, and she was restless. She made an average of two tests a day with unknown young men, and told the publicity department, "I prefer my own company to that of most of

the men in this town. If they want to pass me by, that's all right with me. I think all the boys in Hollywood are terrific bores. If I couldn't stand my own company, I'd be the unhappiest girl in the world, because I'm alone morning, noon and night."

If there were nights of desperate loneliness and days when even the career on which she had staked all her happiness didn't seem sufficient compensation for the emptiness of her personal life, no one knew about it. She held that proud head of hers high, and said that the only thing in the world she wanted was to become a fine actress.

Matched with her in some of the tests she made and at rehearsals in the dramatic classes was a handsome, tall young actor named Leif Erikson, who was as ambitious as she was. After meeting him, it was no longer possible for her to feel that all the young men in Hollywood were bores.

WHEN they first began to slip over to Frances' apartment for additional rehearsals, it never occurred to her that anything else motivated them save the fierce desire both had to get ahead with their careers. But the other newcomers noticed that when they were teamed together in a scene, their work took on new fire, as though each caught inspiration from the other.

One day they eloped to Yuma and were married very quietly.

She and her husband stayed away from night clubs, gaudy premieres and the usual Hollywood social gatherings and spent most of their spare time practising their roles in the old-fashioned living-room of their home.

At first Frances was put into distinctly sappy roles, in pictures like "Too Many Parents" and "Border Flight," which were Grade B or worse. Just when Frances was beginning to feel she'd never get a break, Howard Hawks saw the test she'd made and asked if he could borrow her for the role of Evvie Glasgow in "Come and Get It."

Had Frances played that role she might never have gotten anywhere in pictures, but she prevailed upon Hawks to test her instead for the dual role of Lotta and Lotta's daughter. Given a silent test as Lotta, she registered a vital, unforgettable personality. Andrea Leeds was then given the bit role originally planned for Frances.

"Weren't you frightened playing such an important part after having done just bits and ingenues?" I asked Frances.

"No," she said. "It was too much of a relief to get something I could work at. I found it twice as difficult to do the dumb ingenue in 'Rhythm on the Range' as to play the dual role in 'Come And Get It.' It takes an awful lot to be a good ingenue. I guess I'm not the type, for it drives me crazy when I'm supposed to stand around looking pretty. I feel like such a chump doing it."

Frances is intensely loyal and when she heard that a woman who had been very kind to her had been fired from her job at the studio because of politics, she went straight to the executives and said, "I think that's a very dirty trick you've just pulled."

But when I asked her about it, she said, "I'd rather you didn't use the incident. She has a job with another company now, and the story couldn't possibly do her any good."

The idea that the story might do Frances Farmer some good, that it might help to clear up some of the fog of misunderstanding that has been built round her personality, never seemed to occur to her.

That simplicity of hers—the old clothes, the second-hand car, going around hatless, all that—is not an act. Frances Farmer can't pretend about anything.

Roz Russell is one of the smartest girls in Hollywood. She designs her own clothes, has a grand sense of humor and likes Hollywood—although there's one thing about the place that she doesn't understand.

You will agree that Rosalind Russell is almost justified in raising a rumpus

— by Dorothy Kilgallen

That Complainin' Roz

ROSALIND RUSSELL would like, just once, to "get her man." On the screen, of course.

Off-screen the situation presents no difficulties. She is a merry, witty person, slender, urbane and assured, friendly and beautiful. It is not hard to picture a flock of young men ringing her doorbell, sending her orchids and taking her to dance at the glittering places.

But in the minds of the celluloid moguls, Rosalind is royalty. She is always the haughty duchess or the unsympathetic princess. She is the intellectual fiancée who loses her man, or she is the hateful wife who does ditto. Oh, maybe once in history Rosalind wound up with the hero in a final close-up, but it is such a faraway instance that she has forgotten the name of the picture. Usually the blonde with the smile wins. And Rosalind is getting a little weary of it.

"I'm awfully tired of being royalty," she says with amusement.

"Where does it get you? No matter how good you are in an unsympathetic part, it doesn't win you an audience. I think I'd almost rather be bad in a sympathetic part. The way it is, no one cares what happens to the kind of girls I play!

"How I'd like to get my man!" she said. "Just once. Then I could go back to playing royalty."

It is because her film career has been a succession of cool, chilly, or downright icy roles that Rosalind was terrified to play "Craig's Wife." At first she flatly refused. She felt she needed a gentle and human part to balance the frigid ones. It was Irving Thalberg who persuaded her to do it.

"He was right, of course," she says now. "The audiences hated me on the screen, but they noticed me. Why, I sat in one theatre shivering. I heard them hiss me. How they hated that woman! But the fan mail was marvelous. They liked me. However,

I still think I deserve a gay and romantic role."

Rosalind is one of the smartest girls in Hollywood. Smart and smart-looking. Sitting in the Brown Derby at tea time, or sitting anywhere else anytime, she is a portrait of a chic New Yorker. I haven't seen a better dressed woman in Hollywood, and I have been looking at a lot of stars. Rosalind is beautifully dressed without beads, fringe, white fox or silver lamé. She is beautifully dressed in a black wool dress and twisted pearls around her throat and a conservatively made black hat with a narrow red band on it.

SHE DESIGNS all her own clothes, but they are by no means "homey." You could run across Rosalind in Tulsa or Detroit or San Antonio and you would know she and her wardrobe came from Manhattan. She has never taken up the Hollywood fad *Continued on page 132*

THE REAL REASON FOR HEPBURN'S AMAZING BEHAVIOR

(Left) As she appears in her newest film, called, at the moment, "Christopher Strong." (Further left) Another pose from the same film. It's the story of a woman aviator.

By NINA WILCOX PUTNAM

KATHARINE HEPBURN'S eccentric behavior has been amazing Hollywood ever since she became a cinema sensation with the release of "Bill of Divorcement." Any number of tales have been going around concerning the amazing and unusual things she has done. Each one more surprising than the previous one.

And a number of reasons have been advanced for Katharine's goings-on, from the obvious one that she's doing it for publicity to the laughable one that she's not all there mentally.

But I don't think any of the reasons are right. I think that the reason for the Hepburn's present behavior lies in the past. I think so because meeting Katharine in Hollywood has made me remember certain happenings of years ago—

It was years ago—yes, and outside the Woman's Suffrage Organization Offices in New York! An excited little girl of about nine years of age was selling balloons—balloons with "Votes for Women" written on them in white letters. Her mother was praising the child—not scolding her, mind you, but *praising her* for the fact that she'd been lost for nearly four hours on the New York Streets! Lost, yes, but she'd sold a dozen balloons for "the cause!" And who was it? That little girl was Katharine Hepburn.

Another picture flashed across my memory: Twelve grave, intellectual ladies seated at a luncheon table discussing matters of social revolution, while the same little girl screamed at her play, snatched dainties from the women's plates and acted as "natural" as a young savage—all unreproved.

"I want her to express her true self, fully!" Mrs. Hepburn told the members. "We never suppress her."

The Club was "The Heterodoxy Club" and beside myself and members were Katharine's mother, Crystal East-

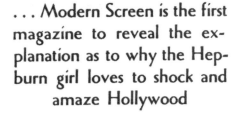

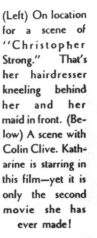

(Left) On location for a scene of "Christopher Strong." That's her hairdresser kneeling behind her and her maid in front. (Below) A scene with Colin Clive. Katharine is starring in this film—yet it is only the second movie she has ever made!

... Modern Screen is the first magazine to reveal the explanation as to why the Hepburn girl loves to shock and amaze Hollywood

man, Mrs. Will Irwin, Emma Goldman, the Anarchist, Charlotte Perkins Gilman, the great suffragist, Fannie Hurst, Margaret Sanger, the birth-control propagandist, Isadora Duncan and many other liberal thinkers. Little Katharine not only sat and listened to these women's talk, sometimes on Emma Goldman's knees, but was encouraged to join in the talk—an extraordinarily intelligent, precocious child, given to the use of long words and not only expressing astounding ideas but doing so with a semblance of knowing what she said.

A LATER picture next came to mind—a household up in Hartford, Connecticut, where the house was run to suit the Hepburn children. They got up when they pleased, ate when they pleased, came and went as they pleased, unquestioned. Katharine played golf, I recall, on a course which adjoined the home, but it never even occurred to her to regulate her golfing hours to the household routine. Instead, her meals were served when she got ready to eat them. The usual rules of home discipline

were reversed and the household routine (if such it could be called) was made to fit the self-expression of its younger members. Indeed, with the exception of Doctor Hepburn, the father of the family, nobody gave heed to any set hours or habits.

Oh dear, oh dearie me! I feel that I myself am partially responsible for Katharine's oddities! You may recall that when she first came out to the RKO lot, Miss Hepburn's clothes were a source of much concern to those who had to put her best foot forward for her. The truth of the matter was that Katharine would not, or could not, dress properly.

She wore old slacks, or any old housedress, when she should have been looking her snappiest. The studio even went so far as to send to New York for an expert to dress the wild woman, whether she liked it or not. And as I looked at Katharine's rebelliously worn blue costume (and it was chic enough, goodness knows) I recalled still another early portrait of the girl, seated with dangling legs, on my desk at the Woman's *Continued on page 132*

Hepburn's Behavior

Peace Party Headquarters, while the girlish, half-grown Katharine asked me about reform (yes, I was also a Dress Reformer then!) and listened attentively while I expounded the evils of conforming to basically ugly and swiftly changing fashions.

I recall well how her eyes widened as I enlarged on the freedom of the body, the beauty of Greek costumes and the cult of the classic dance.

"Well! My body is *always* going to be free!" she declared in solemn agreement with me.

And then, I remember, we both turned to criticize the costumes of the women passing on Fifth Avenue below the office window. The tight, uncomfortable costumes of early, pre-war days, mixed with the uniforms of all nations. I wore a Greek robe, myself, and Katharine was as interested in it, if not more so, than in the anti-war propaganda our office was putting out. In that day I little dreamed that, in two short weeks, President Wilson would have declared war in spite of our puny efforts, and that I would have changed my tunic for a military tunic, and my desk for the driver's seat of an ambulance, but such was the case— While Katharine—well, Katharine, with all of the indelibly printed radicalism of her childhood background fresh in her young mind, was to be plunged during her most formative years, into the flaming youth set which was such a notable by-product of the World war!

That was all years and years ago. My world moved—as did the Hepburns'. We drifted apart. Even the name came to mean little to me. And so, when Katharine Hepburn started startling Hollywood—where I have been living for some years—I did not realize it was the same little girl who had been taught to always express herself.

I finally met the wild young lady. I looked at her with a puzzled expression in my eyes. Then the past came back.

"WHY, I remember you from the old days," I said. "And your mother—"

"Oh," Katharine burst out. "Oh, I was afraid you would. And if you do, you know altogether too much. I hoped you'd forgotten!"

I had forgotten, but now I remembered plenty. Her family far from opposing the girl's stage career, had been delighted at her choosing the theater as a profession. They would have been equally pleased if she'd decided upon big game hunting in Africa, provided Katharine was "expressing her true self fully."

I noticed that the aftermath of the war has left a mark of change upon her, so that the little lines about her mouth and eyes tell a tale of deep experiences and fierce emotional battles. But the girl was no longer a puzzle to me—knowing these intimate details of her hitherto secret youth, I understood—her fierce rebellions—her impatience—her superior attitude—for it is a fact that, whatever else may be said of her, Katharine Hepburn is not as other women. And you know the reasons.

132

That Complainin' Roz

Continued from page 129

of wearing slacks and beach pajamas on the street or to night clubs and premieres. You feel she would smile if you suggested it.

She doesn't keep a pet tiger or even a tame racoon. She's never dyed her hair red or painted her toenails green. She doesn't throw champagne bottles in night clubs. She never has quarreled because her dressing-room was too small or her leading man too dull. She has a sense of humor.

Rosalind is a Connecticut girl, daughter of a criminal lawyer. She was educated in New England and never has done anything but act. She has been in stock and on Broadway, and good in both. When she first came to Hollywood she was the girl nobody wanted, in spite of the fact that they had begged her to come out.

"It was terrible," she confesses, dimpling. "My feelings were horribly wounded. I made up my mind that after the way they treated me, I'd never act in the movies—well, not for a long time, anyway.

"I came out on a vacation, under contract to a major studio," she said. "I really intended to go back to do a play, but I was curious to see what I'd be like in pictures. They said they wanted me to make a test every day for two weeks at a hundred dollars a test. It sounded like fun, and what could I lose? So I came."

She came and they met her at the train and took her to the studio in a speeding car. She was led into the office of the casting director. The casting director was sitting behind a desk. He didn't get up. He didn't ask Rosalind to sit down. He didn't look up.

"This," said the man who had brought her to the studio, "is Miss Russell from New York."

The casting director gave Miss Russell the quick onceover.

"Hi, sweetheart," he said.

"How do you do?" she said, a little startled. She was yet to learn the Hollywood habit of calling a girl "darling" before learning her name.

HE told her to come back the next day and make some tests. A little puzzled, she left his office figuring he wasn't very excited about her. The general attitude bewildered her no little. When she was in New York they had sent her telegrams, written her letters, begged her to please fly moviewards. They had pleaded that productions were being held up until she came to play the parts nobody else could play.

So Rosalind couldn't understand why, when she finally stepped on a Hollywood lot, nobody seemed to know who she was. Nobody paid any attention to her. But she reported to the make-up department next day.

The make-up man was reading a trade paper. He didn't look up when she came in.

"I've come to be made up," she said cheerfully.

"Sorry, sister," he said, equally cheerfully. "Can't takeyah."

"But I'm to have a test this afternoon," she said.

He went on reading the trade paper.

"Can't takeyah," he said.

Rosalind shrugged. "Perhaps later," she suggested, and went to the studio hairdresser.

"Will you fix my hair?" she asked politely.

The girl looked at her blankly.

"Sorry, dearie," she said. "I can't takeyah. I've got to take Gloria Stuart in a little while."

"Oh," said Rosalind.

So this is Hollywood, she thought. She was a babe on the sound stages. She didn't know which way to turn. At two o'clock, the time set, she was on the appointed stage ready for the test. John M. Stahl was directing it.

"Where's that girl?" he asked impatiently.

Rosalind came out of the shadows with the script in her hand.

"Here I am," she said.

Stahl took a look at her, without her make-up and wearing her own knitted dress. He flew into one of the famous Stahl rages. Rosalind waited. Then she flew into one of the rare Russell rages.

"Listen to me," she said. "I was hired to act. I was hired to do a part. If you'll tell me what you want me to do, I'll learn the lines and I'll act. I don't know anything about screen make-up and that's why I'm not made up. But I can act, and I will."

STAHL'S rage subsided slightly. But that didn't get Rosalind in front of a camera. She just sat in a chair and read lines, while a succession of leading men were tested for a part in a new picture. She tested with ten men, on ten different days, but she never appeared in a foot of film. She was just a voice.

That was enough for Rosalind. She was ready to shake the dust of Hollywood off her feet and call it a day with glad huzzahs, when up popped Metro-Goldwyn-Mayer with an offer.

"Not I," said Rosalind. "I've been insulted enough. I've had plenty of Hollywood, thank you very much."

She turned up her pretty nose at all pleas. Hollywood had done a grand job of ignoring her, and she was returning the compliment in case anyone cared. Finally they persuaded her to "visit" M-G-M, just to talk things over. She went.

Take a test, they coaxed. No one will ever see it but yourself if you don't like it. Even if you don't want to go into the movies just now, you may some other time, and the test always will be here. They flattered her and treated her gently and Rosalind warmed a little under all the sweetness and light. She took the test.

It was a very good test. The producers liked it and persuaded Rosalind to stay. She's been there ever since.

And with a forthrightness that is characteristic of her, Rosalind holds no high-hat attitude toward pictures. She is a motion picture actress now and she has forgotten the stage and devoted herself to films. She has decided to stay in the movies and she thinks an actress can be just as good in one medium as the other.

She is twenty-seven years old, has never been divorced or even married. Her hair is black and naturally curly, her eyes brown. She rides horseback beautifully. She smokes too many cigarettes, and wears platinum nail polish because it screens well. She calls John Boles "Oatmeal" because she's sure he eats it every morning. She has been temperamental only once in her life; that was when they wanted her to wear clothes she thought were ridiculous. She just refused to wear them, took a few sheets of paper and a pencil and sketched her own. She designed all the clothes she wore in "Craig's Wife."

. . . Tallulah Bankhead has made a brilliant success of the "take no thought for tomorrow" theory. She gambles on today—and wins!

Says Miss Fletcher: "Tallulah is a born gambler. She dares go out and get whatever it is she wants." The smaller picture is a scene from "My Sin," Tallulah's second American movie. With her is Fredric March.

TALLULAH BANKHEAD— GAMBLER

By ADELE WHITELY FLETCHER

WHAT about this Tallulah Bankhead? If you have seen her in her first picture, "Tarnished Lady," you may or may not like her. Everybody won't like Tallulah, that's sure. She's much too decided a personality for that. But whatever your reaction it's altogether likely that you are curious about her.

If you've heard any of the conflicting stories going the rounds about Tallulah, then, of course, you're intrigued. There is, for instance, the story of the woman who came over to Tallulah when she was lunching in a London restaurant and slapped her face. That seems to be a fairly well authenticated story. Tallulah, you know, proved her *savoir faire* on this occasion by nonchalantly picking up her hat which had fallen off in the excitement, slapping it back on her head, and calmly lighting a cigarette. Then, as if to contradict evidence of such poise, there is the rumor that Tallulah is a fury, that she ordered Adolph Zukor off her set. Adolph Zukor, no less. The truth of this is that while she was making her first picture she was, naturally enough, nervous. And when Mr. Zukor visited the stage she asked him if he would leave, because of her

nervousness. She did it graciously. I have that on the best authority. And Mr. Zukor quite understood and that was all there was to it.

Undoubtedly you're aware that Tallulah is a southern girl, the granddaughter of Senator John H. Bankhead and the daughter of Representative William B. Bankhead, and that she had a sensational stage success in England.

However, whatever you've heard the chances are you haven't heard the half of it and that half of what you have heard is wrong. Because Tallulah is the type certain to be talked about. And no wonder, for she is, without a doubt, one of the most colorful figures on the screen today. And I don't mean the sort of colorful figure that is built up by a hard-working press *Continued on page 139*

Continued on page 139

BAD, BAD WOMAN

Harold Seton

(Above) This is as she appeared when she was first successful in vaudeville. And this (right) is as she appears in "She Done Him Wrong."

By CAROLINE SOMERS HOYT

. . . Mae West, the famous exponent of sex in the theater, makes her Hollywood début. What's she like? Well, she's different, and startling, and amazing—see for yourself

WHEN Mae West first swayed across hundreds of American screens with one hand on hip and shoulders hunched forward, folks in the audience turned to each other and said, "Oh boy, I'll bet that baby has had a past!"

And, oh boy, that baby has had one, too!

Let's start right at the very beginning and find out how Mae West got that way—where she got that whiskey voice, that Bowery walk, those smart come-backs. What, in other "woids" (that's the way Mae would say it on the stage) makes Mae West tick and how was she able to give dignified magistrates a laugh when the people of New York preferred charges against her?

It all begins back in Brooklyn when Mae West was a kid. A dignified aunt used to watch Mae bullying the boys in the street and say to her mother, "Tcht, tcht, that child is too wilful. She'll come to no good end. Why don't you make her act more like a lady? Why do you let her have her own way? Why don't you correct her?"

Modern Screen's exclusive cameraman for the Eastern territory—J. Culver—got this swell picture of Mae in New York.

If that same dignified aunt could see her, now that she has become famous playing bad, bad women for the edification of thousands of audiences! If that aunt could see her jewels and her spangled gowns and could hear her say—as she said to me a few weeks ago, in that husky voice:

"Listen, there's some bad in all women. I work off my energies—and I've got plenty of energy—by being that sort of woman on the stage and screen. If I didn't have that outlet I might have been one of 'em myself. I couldn't make any prophecies. I've always been interested in women like that. Maybe it was the theatre that saved me. Anyhow, I've made a lot more money in the theatre."

MAE was a wilful kid. Once she and her mother were invited to a friend's house for tea. It was one of those dignified gatherings. But immediately after the wraps were "laid off" Mae espied one of those living-room atrocities—waxed flowers underneath a cylinder of glass. She thought it was the most beautiful thing she had ever seen and because it was so beautiful she wanted to touch it. So, wanting to touch it, she did—running her little hands over the smooth, rounded glass.

The hostess—a fluttery woman—ran to her. "No, no, dear, you mustn't touch that. That isn't for little girls to play with."

Without a word Mae walked into the bedroom, got her own coat and hat and her mother's. She carried her mother's wraps to her and said, "Here put these on. We're going home."

The hostess begged them to stay. She lured Mae with promises of the lovely cakes that would arrive with the tea. She told her that there would be piano playing later on. She begged Mae to forgive her.

"She even," said the West in telling the story, "offered to let me play with the damn thing."

But all this cajolery was no use. Mae had been insulted. Mae was going home. And because her mother adored the child and was later to sit in a theatre watching that same daughter play in "Sex," "Diamond Lil," etc., and see nothing bad about the plays, she put on her hat and coat and went home with the little girl.

Some months later the mother promised Mae a doll. She could have any one she chose and together mother and daughter journeyed to the store. There were hundreds of dolls in great piles. All of them were lovely but right at the very top was a doll dressed in a lavender frock. This doll was perched precariously at the top of the pile—almost touching the ceiling. Mae pointed upwards.

"I want that one," she said.

The salesman smiled and began to look for a doll like it on one of the lower shelves, but found none. He begged her to chose another, pointing out the merits of the more easily reached ones.

But Mae stood there, pointing. "I want that one."

They explained how inaccessible was the toy. They offered her bigger dolls, more *Continued on page 139*

Barefoot boy with shows on

■ "You'd think the guy was a
derelict. I've seen sharecroppers dressed
better than he. And the places he lives in! That
sixth-floor walk-up apartment he lives in in
New York, a soda-jerk would want to
move out of. And over at Paramount, you
know, they were so embarrassed by that 1939
junk heap he drives around they begged him to
get a new one—but he's still driving the
wreck. What a barefoot boy!"

The speaker was a Hollywood starlet. She was
referring to a young actor who, after being
seen by the public in three pictures, has become a major
star, with a major star's income—Montgomery Clift.

Gus Goetz, who, with his wife, wrote the screenplay
for *The Heiress*, was stunned the first time Clift
walked on the set.

"He was wearing," Gus says, "a pair of tattered
blue jeans, a T-shirt and a jacket full of holes.
He looked like a bum. 'Good Lord,' I
said to myself, 'is this the fellow who's going
to play the suave, elegant character of Morris
Townsend? This will be ridiculous.' But
when Monty got into costume, the transformation
was really startling—he seemed the most fastidious
youth you ever saw. Still, it took me a couple
of days to get over my first impression of him."

Why does Montgomery Clift seem to choose
deliberately to appear a vagabond? The answer
is simple. In a sense, he *is* a vagabond.

"I like to travel," he says. "I like to keep going.
People who have lots of possessions—big houses,
Cadillacs, swimming pools, lots of clothes—usually
are tied down. Without a huge clutter of
worldly goods, and wearing old clothes, I feel the
way I want to be—comfortable and free."

Aside from his trip to Germany to make *Two
Corridors East*, Clift has in recent months
been on the move from Los Angeles to Paris to
Switzerland to Italy to Israel to London to New York
to Los Angeles to New York and to numerous
way-stations. "Why does he travel so much?"
people ask. "Is he *Continued on page 138*

He just won't live

his life the way a movie

star's supposed to—

yet Hollywood accepts

Monty Clift's individualism

It's the only way

they can have him.

BY ARTHUR L. CHARLES

just restless, or is he trying to find out something?"

He's trying to find out something. He has a deep curiosity about the whys and wherefores of human relationships. By nature, he's a lone wolf. But, while primarily he's a self-contained individualist, devoting his life to his profession with the ardor of the true artist, there's nothing anti-social about him.

"To be convincing," he explains, "an actor must share, or at least be aware of, experiences familiar to the audience. Otherwise, he's making faces in an emotional vacuum and nobody knows what on earth he's trying to express. He must get around and meet the people—people everywhere. Any young actor with the fare should visit Israel. There's one of the few really new nations established since the American Revolution. Everything there is dramatic and challenging—and wonderfully stimulating and broadening.

"I can't stand being in the hothouse atmosphere of Hollywood for more than a few months at a time. People there live such an artificial existence that they lose contact with ordinary people. . . . But please don't misunderstand me! I owe Hollywood a lot, and I know it. I hope I never turn out to be one of those jerks who reap the rewards of Hollywood and then blast the place for ruining their 'artistic integrity.' Guys like that didn't have integrity in the first place if they let that happen to them."

Clift's insistence on maintaining his integrity has been the despair of publicity men. He simply doesn't believe in leading his private life in public nor will he lend himself to the exhibitionistic projects dreamed up by publicists. He's been that way from the beginning of his career.

Several years ago, he was playing on Broadway in *Foxhole in the Parlor*. The press agent in charge of exploiting the play hired 50 bobby-soxers to lie in wait for the young actor outside the stage entrance of the theater. It was planned that, as Clift came out, the 50 were to "mob" him, camera shutters were to click and, it was fondly hoped, pictures of New York's new "matinee idol" were to be plastered over the drama pages of the newspapers.

Clift was told about the scheme. He was, to put it mildly, lukewarm. The press agent argued earnestly—and Clift reluctantly agreed.

Then, at the last minute, Clift's honesty prevailed. He turned up his coat collar and sneaked out of the theater by a side entrance.

When writers ask him for permission to interview his mother or father or older brother or twin sister for background material, Clift always politely but firmly refuses. "Look," he says, "what could you find out, anyway? What can my mother say to strangers? That I was a cute baby, that I cried at night, that she's proud of me? Nuts! Who cares? Such things don't mean anything. And besides, if I didn't keep my family out of my public life, it would be a terrific nuisance to them. Why should they be bothered?"

To date, Clift's feelings about his family have been honored—largely because, when he does grant interviews, he's quite cooperative in telling all about himself. All, that is, except about something his family probably wouldn't know about anyway: his love life.

"I like girls," he says flatly. "All kinds of girls. But I just won't drag any particular girl I like into the spotlight by talking about her to reporters. And I can't describe what type of girl I like bet-

ter than another—I just don't know. If I meet a girl I like, then I ask her for a date. That's all there is to it."

In the past year, Clift has been "linked romantically" in the gossip columns with a number of girls. But what male star—with the exception of Lassie, and he's supposed to be a girl—hasn't? Here are the ladies the news-hungry columnists have recently mentioned in connection with Clift: Actresses Peggy Knudsen, Ann Lincoln and Myra Letts; writer Tricia Hurst, and WAC Lieutenant Mary Carter. At this writing, his engagement to none of those ladies has been announced. Any more than it has to Elizabeth Taylor who, through studio arrangement, he escorted not long ago to the Hollywood première of *The Heiress*.

At the beginning of 1946, Clift was completely unknown to movie-goers. Today, his fan mail is second to none in volume (and probably intensity) and exhibitors everywhere will tell you he's an actor who attracts more profit than even their popcorn machines.

Clift is modest indeed about his phenomenal screen success. "I've been very lucky," he says, "to have had fine directors for all my pictures. I've always felt that a good director is the most important factor in a good picture."

When he signed with Paramount to make three pictures for a minimum of $100,000 apiece, he insisted, besides the right to approve the final script, on having a stipulation in the contract that each film would be directed by one of four top-notchers—Frank Capra, William Wyler, George Stevens and William Wilder. He has already finished two of the three pictures, *The Heiress* and *A Place in the Sun*. What his third will be, he doesn't know. But he does know that when he makes it, he will be in the masterful hands of a first-rate director.

money isn't everything . . .

Now, this is definitely an unusual arrangement. One may well wonder why other actors don't make the same sort of deal. Actors like Gary Cooper, for instance. Cooper has been around for years, he's got great prestige, he's a tremendous box-office draw. Why doesn't Cooper, like Clift, battle and argue over scripts and directors?

The answer is that Cooper's main reason for making movies is to make money—$200,000 a picture, with frequently a percentage of the profits. To Clift, making money is strictly secondary to helping achieve an artistic creation.

In 1946, Howard Hawks phoned Clift in New York from Hollywood and offered him a job in *Red River*. He described the role and the story. Clift turned him down. "I don't think the part's right for me," he said. And at that moment of superb refusal, Clift was broke and living on unemployment compensation.

But Hawks persisted. "It's impossible for me to give you a fair idea of this picture over the phone," he said. "Tell you what: I'll wire you expense money and you come out here and let me talk to you. If you still don't like the part, you can fly back. Fair enough?"

Clift agreed and went to Hollywood. "I was very much afraid of the part," he says. "I didn't think I was physically right for it. I didn't believe I could stand up to a man as big as John Wayne. But I liked the story and Hawks gave me a good deal, so I signed."

In Clift's second picture, *The Search*, he refused to play the role of the GI unless he could do it as he thought it should be done

—in a natural, realistic manner. "And the way the part was written," he says, "the character was a Boy Scout type spreading nobility and virtue all over the lot. I was supposed to be so darned saintly a special prop man would've been needed to polish my halo. I felt the soldier had to get mad at the kid and yell at him when the situation was established, just as any normal adult does with a difficult kid."

When Clift was told the characterization couldn't be changed, he said he'd bow out of the picture. He was reminded that he'd signed for six weeks and couldn't bow out. "O.K.," he said. "Suppose the picture isn't finished after six weeks. Is there anything to prevent me from bowing out then?"

The script was changed and Clift was permitted to play the role as he saw it. The picture was a success, Clift's artistic conscience was satisfied, and demands for his services arose in every Hollywood studio.

Montgomery Clift may often give a first impression that he's a sort of barefoot boy. If he is, he's a barefoot boy with his feet planted firmly on a path going up—a path very definitely of his own choosing.

THE END

THE MARCH ISSUE OF MODERN SCREEN IS OUR ELIZABETH TAYLOR BIRTHDAY BOOK

why rock walked out
Continued from page 91

An hour later Rock was on the trans-atlantic phone, his mouth set.

"Phyllis. It's me. Now, look, Phyl—what is this, you renting a house without even consulting me?"

"Honey, wait a minute. I would have written you and asked, only I had to take it in a hurry or not at all. Someone else wanted it too. And it's so perfect, Rock. Besides, this way it can be all painted by the time we get home, we can move right in—"

Rock's voice was grim. "I'm not moving into any house I haven't ever seen. I don't know that I want to move at all. We didn't decide definitely, Phyllis. And I have a right to be consulted. I'm the man in this family."

Phyl's voice rose, tense. "And I'm a grown woman. I'm not a child, going to her father for permission. I have a right to make decisions in this family, too. A—house is a woman's business. Everyone knows that. All I did was—"

"All you did was sneak around behind my back! All you did was try to take over my life! A house is my business and you've got no right—"

They hung up on each other. And a few days later Rock had word that Phyllis was in the hospital with acute hepatitis.

Maybe this will work

And then Rock went to Europe to make *Farewell To Arms*. In a few weeks Phyllis was to join him. They both looked forward to it immensely. It would be a second honeymoon—better than the first. A time to relax and take stock of their lives—a time away from home to make plans for a better life.

And then, three weeks or so before Phyllis was due to leave for Europe, a letter arrived from her. "Rock, I've just rented the most lovely house in Malibu

Continued on page 155

Bad, Bad Woman

Continued from page 135

easily reached. Much prettier dolls. Mae wasn't interested. "I want that one." And turning to her mother, "You said I could have any doll I wanted."

THEY finally saw it was no use trying to dissuade her and at last two ladders were brought from the back of the store and Mae—the gal who always gets what she wants—proudly bore home the lavender-dressed doll.

It was this same stubborn and precocious child who, at the age of six, panicked a Brooklyn audience on amateur night by doing imitations of Eva Tanguay and other famous stars. That began her theatrical career—a career that was to lead her through stock, through vaudeville into musical shows and at last to make her author, producer and star of the sensational "Sex" and "Diamond Lil" and eventually to lead her to the screen in "Night After Night" and "She Done Him Wrong."

Mae West was the first person—according to Mae West—to do the shimmie on any stage!

That was way back when she was in musical shows.

Another story goes that Mae West was a member of an acrobatic act in vaudeville and also lifted what was supposed to be a 500-pound weight.

When she got her chance to get out of the lowbrow end of theatrical life and be a producer and star in her own right she figured—and she figured smart:

"Every Broadway actress has her own line," Mae said. "I'll give 'em something different." And the sensational play "Sex," which she wrote herself and in which she played a harlot, was the result.

Mae gets her material in strange ways. One night she was coming into her hotel when another guest at the hotel—a man who had had a bit of a past himself—said to her, "You know, when you wear all those diamonds (the ones, incidentally, that were stolen in Hollywood) you remind me of an old sweetheart of mine who had more rocks than any gal I ever knew. Come to think of it—you look like her when you put your head down and sort of look up through your eyelashes with that hot look."

"Yeah?" said Mae, "Who was your friend?"

"They called her 'Diamond Lil.' "

AND that's how Mae got the idea for her greatest success. Diamond Lil was a real character of the 'nineties—as beautiful as Lillian Russell and much more spectacular. Mae didn't know whether she could play a 'nineties belle or not. Her mother told her she'd have to put on a lot more weight. At the time she tipped the scales at just 110.

"So I ate my head off," said Mae, "and opened in 'Diamond Lil' weighing 130."

"Sex" had been running on Broadway for some time before the law decided that it was offensive. So Mae was summoned to appear in court. Also

there was the little matter of a play called "The Drag" which she had authored but in which she did not star. Later she wrote and produced "Pleasure Man" and the city of New York wanted to see her about that, too.

She appeared in court smiling and swapped wisecrack for wisecrack with the city fathers.

All during the time of her extremely spectacular Broadway success don't imagine that there weren't men in her life. Mae knows plenty about men. And then along came a lad whose last name is Timony. He's a brunette gentleman who wears a derby hat, smokes big black cigars and doesn't mind getting hard-boiled when the occasion demands. You'll see him around back stage or wherever Mae is. He gives her plenty of good advice and Mae has liked him in a big way for a couple of years now. Timony is what is known as a character.

Yessir, it's men that Mae knows best—and men who like her best, in Hollywood she found she got on much better with the men than the women. Women sort of resent Mae. They know her reputation. They know what kind of roles she has played and when Mae comes into the room all the nice little Hollywood girls cast anxious glances at their boy friends and decide it's about time to go home.

For Mae speaks a man's language. She loves prizefights and things like that. Hollywood had never seen anything quite like her. She's so doggone honest and sincere and real and—well—just what she is, Mae West.

I asked her if the roles she played didn't make people misunderstand her—make them think she, herself, was that sort of woman.

"Certainly!" said Mae.

And then I asked her what she did to counteract that impression.

"Well, I'll tell you," she said. "I don't try to change anybody's opinion. A person who is interested in the sort of woman I characterize likes it a lot better if he thinks I'm that sort, too. And people who are not interested in women like that—well, they're just not interested at all. So I just don't bother.

"People can get any sort of impression about me they want to have. And I'm still not doing so bad!"

Tallulah Bankhead, Gambler

Continued from page 133

department. I knew Tallulah several years ago before she went to England to become the toast of Mayfair, before she had the benefit of any press-agent. And she was quite as colorful then as now.

TALLULAH is a born gambler. She dares go out and get whatever it is

she wants. She always has. She always will. She's built that way. In her veins flows the adventuresome blood of adventuresome southern families. Her mother's family staked all they had on cotton. And lost. Her father's family staked all they had on the support of their constituents. And won—seats in the Senate and the House of Representatives.

And years ago Tallulah dared leave the security of the little town of Huntsville to make her way to London and a glamorous stardom.

Now she is back in New York making pictures. She hopes she'll be good in them. She says, quite frankly, that she certainly needs to make good in them. She admits, without any parley, that she is broke.

Tallulah was the darling of London. In stage plays like "Let Us Be Gay" and "Her Cardboard Lover" she took the lovely old city so by storm that often it was necessary for a cordon of police to guard her progress from the stage door to her car. Shopgirls crowded the gallery to applaud her. The most sophisticated sophisticates crowded the orchestra. Peers and their ladies gave box parties not so much to see the play itself as to see the young American girl who had become the rage.

Tallulah's openings were events. Florists counted them red letter days. Cards engraved with famous names accompanied the baskets of gardenias and camellias. Cards engraved with illustrious names, proud names, came with the boxes in which lay the exciting crimson of American Beauties and the calm sophistication of waxy callas. Sometimes a memento would come with the flowers. Once the blue fire of a sapphire in the ivory velvet of a jeweler's box. Once a speck of a milky white Pekinese, Maxmillian by name, raised his head from the heart of a basket or orchids.

All of which gives you some idea of the handsome salary the London managers did well to pay Tallulah.

"But I couldn't save," Tallulah says. "The English tax takes one third of all you make. That means four months out of every year you work for the government. And I had my house in Mayfair to maintain. A staff of servants. A car."

OF course there is no law that compels a star to have a house in Mayfair or enough servants to constitute a staff. Or the kind of a car in which Tallulah undoubtedly rode about. But true to her gambler instincts, Tallulah always has felt that she had just as much to spend as her bank balance showed. It is typical of her to have such a house. That many servants. Such a car.

However, it is my opinion that if Tallulah wasn't this kind of a person we never would have heard of her. Certainly she never would have gotten to England when she did.

After years in convents and a select girls' school in Washington, Tallulah came to New York and enjoyed some measure of success on the Broadway stage. She always looked very smart. She always maintained at least an adequate address. An English agent, visiting America in search of talent, saw Tallulah and felt she would be exactly right for the part of an American girl in a play soon to be cast. He asked her if she would come over for a try-out if they payed her way across and back

Continued on page 160

HOLLYWOOD AT PLAY

As exciting as the movies that they appeared in, the public's fascination with where the stars went for a glamorous night on the town, was just as great. There were all sorts of famous restaurants and nightclubs that were favorite spots for star gazing. Amongst these were Ciro's, Romanoff's, The Brown Derby, The Coconut Grove, and La Bohème. *Modern Screen* always featured on its pages, photos of the movie kings and queens "holding court" on a dancefloor, a day at the races, or just relaxing with their friends and co-stars.

From the September 1933 issue is the photo page "Come to the Coconut Grove" (page 142). In the thirties the magazine's favorite cameraman, Scotty, often contributed glamour spreads depicting the nightlife of the stars. While the rest of America was in the grip of the Depression, the stars were busily sipping champagne and living the exciting lives they were expected to lead. Among the revelers depicted here are Jean Harlow and her third husband, cameraman Harold Rosson. They met during the filming of *Red Dust* (1932).

The most elaborate and exciting private parties held in Hollywood were usually thrown by Marion Davies, the famed mistress of newspaper czar William Randolph Hearst. Although she was beautiful and was a gifted comedienne, Hearst insisted that she play roles unsuited to her talents in lavish, heavily publicized films that he financed. In the Hollywood inner circle, Marion's nervous stuttering and her drinking problem were as famous as her

> "You don't have the right attitude. Take a look at this boy."
> —Rock Hudson
> *Modern Screen*
> October 1950

secure position in films.

Unfortunately, the one thing that Marion really wanted to become was Mrs. W. R. Hearst, a role she was never to play, as it had already been cast, and divorce was out of the question. In "Masquerade at Marion's" (page 143), from *Modern Screen*'s August 1931 issue, you'll find Mr. and Mrs. Douglas Fairbanks, Jr., Robert Montgomery, and Marie Dressler, and of course Marion. Because Hearst would not condone Marion's drinking, at parties like this one, often one of her friends would go into the bathroom ahead of her, and hide a cocktail for the hostess!

"Modern Screen Goes on a Date," from the August 1942 issue (page 146), is typical of the exclusive "concept" photo spreads that the magazine was always famous for. Here we find Betty Grable getting ready for a date with George Raft at The Palladium. Notice Betty's "sumptuous gown" that cost $25, and dashing Raft in a suit and an apron back at Grable's house. Betty always claimed to suffer from an inferiority complex—but check out those gams!

In the January 1939 article "Everybody's Doin' it" (page 150) we find Joan Crawford "cutting a rug" on the dance floor. In her first films, including *Our Dancing Daughters* (1928) and *Our Modern Maidens* (1929), Joan was best known as a dancing flapper.

Rock Hudson headlines the list of Hollywood stars wrapped up in a towel for *Modern Screen*'s October 1950 feature "Stag Night at the Steam Room" (page 152). With Rock's private life now exposed, his nights out with the boys, have taken on new connotations!

140

OVER 200 INTIMATE PICTURES

ModernScreen

ARCH
RKO
ENTS

THE LARGEST
CIRCULATION
OF ANY | SCREEN
MAGAZINE

WHOM WILL
Tyrone Power
MARRY?

TYRONE POWER
AND
SONJA HENIE

TYRONE POWER & SONJA HENIE   **March 1938**   141

All these pictures are by Scotty, MODERN SCREEN'S exclusive cameraman. He took them on the opening night of orchestra leader Abe Lyman's return to Cocoanut Grove. (Above) The crowd, dancing to Lyman's music. (Left) Eddie Cantor with Lyman. (Right) Harold Rosson, Jean Harlow, Irene Jones and Johnnie Weissmuller. What, no romances? (Below, left) Harold Lloyd and the missus, greeting Lyman. (Below, right) Franchot Tone, Joan Crawford, Bob Abbott of the Boston textile Abbotts (he's Joan's Boston boy friend) and Helen Hayes.

MASQUERADE
AT MARION'S

When Marion Davies gives a costume party, Hollywood's most famous people come arrayed in the finest of the fine. A gorgeous display of movie stars for your delight

These pictures especially posed for MODERN SCREEN and photographed by William Grimes.

What ho for Douglas Fairbanks, Jr., as a dashing Austrian officer with medals and braid and everything. Yes, even to the neat milit'ry moustache. And wife Joan Crawford in the Empire ensemble is quite something to wire home about. And isn't her new shade of hair becoming?

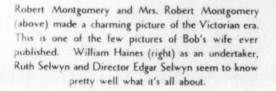

Robert Montgomery and Mrs. Robert Montgomery
(above) made a charming picture of the Victorian era.
This is one of the few pictures of Bob's wife ever
published. William Haines (right) as an undertaker,
Ruth Selwyn and Director Edgar Selwyn seem to know
pretty well what it's all about.

(Above) Harpo Marx won the prize for the best disguise as Kaiser Bill. Marie Dressler's costume looks familiar. Remember her in that outfit in "Anna Christie?" (Left) Kent Douglass, Leslie Howard, Marion Davies, a non-professional, Buster Collier, George K. Arthur, Ramon Novarro and Eileen Percy.

MODERN SCREEN GOES ON A *Date!*

A Saturday night spree with Betty Grable and George Raft at the Palladium, Hollywood's swing rendezvous!

1. "Nice out? What'll I wear?" Ever since they started going steady a year ago last Feb., Betty hasn't dated or even danced with anyone else!

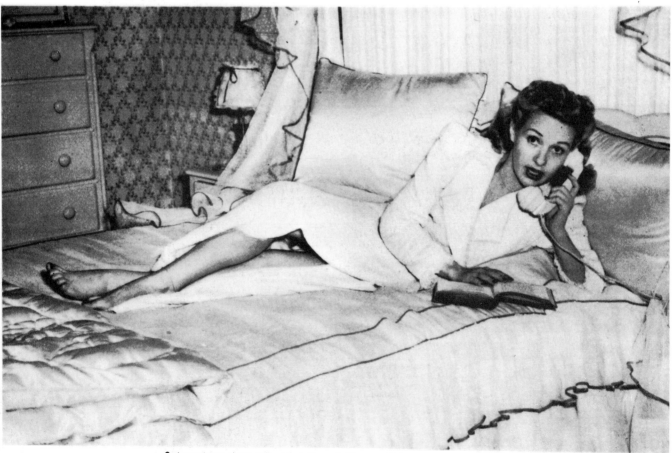

2. Last-minute phone call. Mack Grey, Raft's man Friday, daily buzzes to make final arrangements for their dates. Both hate phoning, and call's over in an even 2 mins. Her photo of George on bureau is inscribed, "To Betty, the most wonderful girl I've ever known."

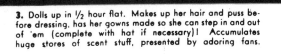

3. Dolls up in ½ hour flat. Makes up her hair and puss before dressing, has her gowns made so she can step in and out of 'em (complete with hat if necessary)! Accumulates huge stores of scent stuff, presented by adoring fans.

4. Raft lives only 10 mins. away in Beverly Hills, came early and sat outside till the appointed time, then dashed in at 8:45 on the dot. Makes her nervous if he comes too soon. He's currently appearing in "Broadway."

CONTINUED ON FOLLOWING PAGE

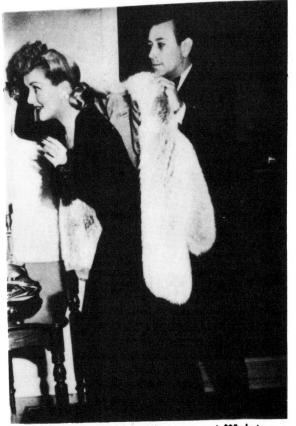

5. She's here! A love match, they find each other sufficient company, rarely double-date except with the Jack Bennys for Sat. night cards. Both are shy and self-conscious. On the "Footlight Serenade" set, Betty was tongue-tied when George appeared!

6. That last-minute pat. Scrumptious gown cost $25, but most of her 10 evening togs hover near 350 mark, hail from N. Y. Fox coat's one of 7 fur jobs. Geo. prefers her in tailored togs. She thinks he's sleek in each of his 40 suits.

9. After-dinner discussion. He'd like to break her 1½-pack-o'-spuds-a-day habit. She wants to sub vegetables for that steak-French-fries-apple pie dinner he gobbles 365 days a year! They're both convinced teetotalers!

8. Ordering at the Palladium. They dine together nightly followed by dancing or baseball week-ends; gin rummy till her 9 p.m. bedtime workdays. Both love "Frenesi" (popular when they met) own tremendous platter collections.

7. Betty's mom was too modest to pose, waved from the front door as they whipped off in Geo.'s chauffeur-driven Cadillac. Betty calls him "Old Boy" (in a broad English accent) in reciprocation for his "Honeys" and "Babys."

10. Midnight snacking at Grable's. Geo. never drinks coffee, even at his apple pie and milk breakfasts at 2 p.m! A fuss budget, he cleans up after guests leave, putters around his house straightening shades, smoothing slipcovers!

11. That good-night kiss! Betty says he's the kindest person she's ever known, sometimes wishes he'd do something wrong just once! He thinks she's perfection itself. Bribed her into dentist's appointment with gifts of aquamarine!

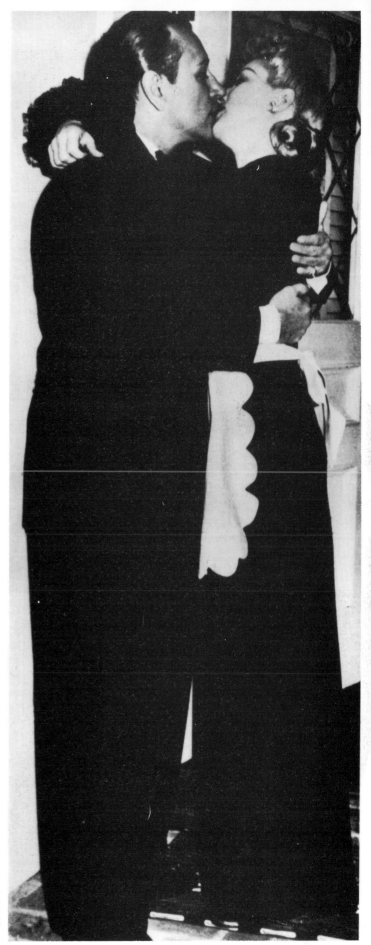

Everybody's DOIN' IT

So Joan, too, climbs on the dance wagon and does a little rug-cutting

Never let it be said that a Crawford can't swing it with the best of 'em. Mind you, nothing as simple as the Yam, Big Apple or Suzy-Q for la belle, but a tango, waltz, two-step, rhumba and tap all rolled into one! "Joan of all dances" is she, and she's out to prove it—or else!—in "The Shining Hour."

It's been years since the lady collected an array of loving cups for doing the Charleston in night spots around Hollywood, but with all that experience and silverware behind her, she certainly oughta click!

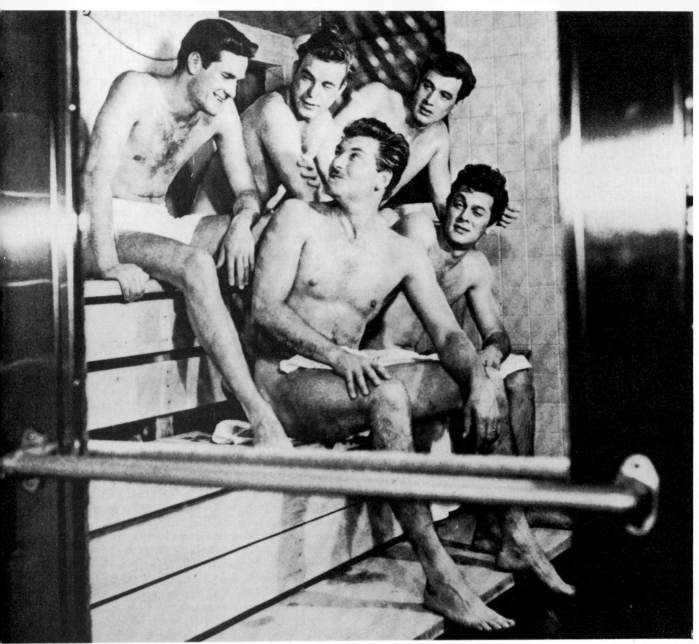

Hugh O'Brian, Scott Brady, John Bromfield, Rock Hudson and Tony Curtis sit on hot shelves of various temperatures at the Finlandia Baths.

Rock takes a close shave as Tony and John relax.

stag night at the steam room

by Jim Burton

■ Women have the monopoly on beauty treatments. Men generally take the faces that God gave them and do the best they can. Mud packs, permanent waves, facials—they're for the girls. Probably the biggest disadvantage of all this is that there are no beauty parlors where men can get together and gossip.

Imagine the male delight when 13 years ago a fellow name of Sam Amundsen opened a Finnish bathhouse—for men only. Here at last was a place where the boys could let off steam, and improve their physiques at the same time. It was a natural. Before long every Hollywood he-man worth his weight had made a habit of Finlandia, which is located in the basement of the Bing Crosby building. The Crosby brothers, Kirk Douglas, Humphrey Bogart, Cornel Wilde, Zachary Scott, Paul Douglas—they all drop in for the treatment, and the talk.

On this particular afternoon, MODERN SCREEN got a call from Scott Brady.

"How about joining us for a quick bake?" he said. Since it was only 90 degrees in the shade, photographers Bert Parry, Bob Beerman, and I were only too happy to go somewhere nice and warm. We hustled over to Finlandia and there found Scott, John Bromfield, Rock Hudson, Tony Curtis and Hugh O'Brian in various stages of undress.

The body-building equipment at Finlandia consists first of a hot room (temperature between 120 and 170 degrees). You go into the room, climb on a shelf, and let your pores relax. The higher the shelf, the higher the temperature, and the more relaxed you become. Sit there twenty minutes and you're so relaxed you can pass out. Finnish bathing, though, is not without a purpose. It's supposed to rid the body of poisons through perspiration. We all grabbed towels and took the bodies into the steam room.

"Well," said Scott, "I've had enough."

"You've only been here two minutes," said John Bromfield.

"Clock-watcher," sneered Scott, and sank back.

Bromfield looked very happy up there on the shelf. Every once in a while he'd yank a cord which dropped water on some steaming rocks in the corner. Every yank raised the heat 20 degrees. *(Continued on next page)*

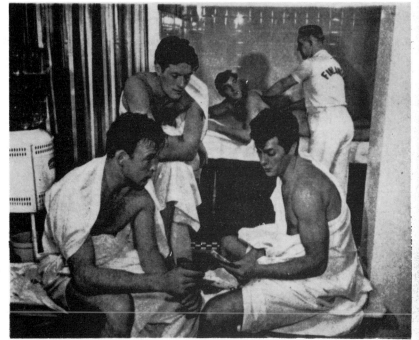

"You should be in the gambling racket, son," Scott tells Tony, who is beating him soundly at gin rummy. Hugh kibitzes while Rock gets a salt rubdown in the next room, so he can go back to the steam room and sweat some more.

Chowtime at Finlandia is a special privilege. Sam Amundsen, owner of the Finnish baths, provides such a spread only for men who make a party of coming down to his establishment. The hungry mob wastes no times digging in.

MORE ➤

153

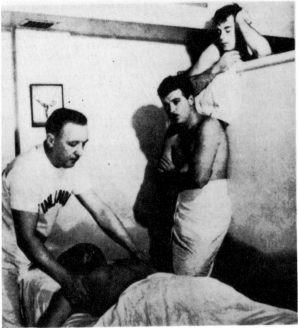

"Ah, this is wonderful!" sighs Hugh, as masseur Kaarlo gives him a vigorous alcohol rub, to close up his pores. John and Scott watch skeptically.

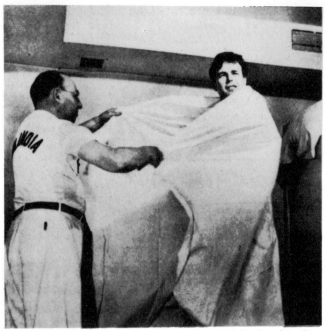

Scott shivers as Richard Wolfs, head masseur at Finlandia, dries him off after his alcohol rub by fanning him with a sheet. This helps the pore-closing process, but it's a shock right after a 170-degree bath.

Tony's getting an icy shower, whether he likes it or not. "Good for you," says Scott, holding him there—Brady's way of making up for the gin game.

Weighing-in time proves interesting—and slightly disconcerting. The boys are supposed to have lost weight after their steam baths, but Hugh claims he's gained! He doesn't see Scott's hand on the scales.

stag night at the steam room

contd.

"Hey, cut that out!" said Tony Curtis, after the second yank.

"Can't take it, uh?" said John.

"Me? I love it," said Tony. "But the other guys—they're evaporating."

"It's not the heat," groaned Rock Hudson. "It's the humidity."

"I think I got rid of enough poison," said Scott, getting up. "The Red Cross could use me now—as a bandage."

Everyone followed Scott out of the room—except John. "He-men!" he laughed, and energetically yanked the cord.

"Listen, character," said Scott. "I hope you melt."

As he left the room, Tony jammed the door with a wet towel, and blithely stepped into a cold shower. Two minutes later, Bromfield was banging on the door. "Let me out of here!" he yelled. "For Pete's sake, boys, let me out!"

Continued on page 155

stag night in the steam room

Continued from page 154 "Temper, John," said Scott sweetly. "Temper."

"Aw, let him out," said Tony. "Maybe he can play gin-rummy."

"With you?" said Scott. "He's better off where he is."

"Hey, fellas!" screamed John, and they let him out.

Draped in sheets, the boys sat around and played cards. Scott lost a quick round of gin rummy to Tony, and gave up his hand to Hugh O'Brian.

"I've had enough of this guy," said Scott. "Played with him for 16 weeks while we were making *Shoplifter*, and didn't win a hand."

"One thing's sure," said Hugh. "In this joint, at least, he won't have any cards up his sleeves."

"Gin," said Tony.

"Why don't you go back to Brooklyn?" Scott asked Tony. "With your brains you could make a million running a card parlor."

"Naw," said Tony. "I'll stick with you. Couple more pictures together and I'll be wearing mink."

"Okay, sweetheart," said John Bromfield. "Deal me in."

WHILE John was being shellacked by Tony, everyone else was getting alcohol rubdowns. (Alcohol closes the bather's pores and prevents him from catching cold when he goes out into the normal temperature of the street.) Finlandia's two masseurs, Kaarlo and Richard, who've been there so long they're practically water-proof, worked over us.

"I believe I'd rather catch my death," said Scott, as Richard wrapped him up in a sheet and started to fan him dry.

"You don't have the right attitude," Rock Hudson yelled from the next rubbing room, where Kaarlo was massaging Hugh O'Brian's back. "Take a look at this boy."

Scott peered over the partition, and said, "He looks like he's dead."

"Superior ability to relax," Hugh mumbled, as the masseur pushed his nose into the pillow. "Mind over matter."

"Like I said," Scott replied, "you look dead."

"Treat him with respect," said Tony coming in on the tail-end of Scott's remark. "Know what this guy does for a hobby?"

"Yeah," said Scott. "He makes pictures. *Rocketship X-M*, starring Hugh O'Brian. I can get you tickets."

"Listen, dope. He's the athletic instructor for 17 of the most beautiful dolls in Hollywood. Works out with them three times a week."

"My old pal, Hugh," said Scott. "Why didn't you tell me, Hugh?"

Hugh shrugged his free shoulder, and smiled.

"Up at the 'House of the Seven Garbos,'" said Tony. "You know, the boarding house for models. The girls wanted to exercise. So Hugh was kind enough to donate his time and effort. Would you be kind enough?"

"Smart enough, you mean," said Scott. "I get my exercise boxing with my brother."

JUST then Sam Amundsen came in to announce that lunch was ready. One of the reasons Finlandia is so popular is proprietor Sam. He likes to please his customers. He'll not only have them steamed, rubbed down, and wrapped up, but if they come in parties, he'll order a snack from the Scandia restaurant across the street. The snack for us turned out to be huge cuts of roast beef, turkey, ham, Scandinavian cheese and plenty of potato salad. Along with this went fruit juice, soda and beer.

For a little while everyone was silent. Then, after the last few slices of meat were polished off we went back to the dressingroom for a nap.

"The steam will get rid of the poisons in your body," Sam tells his guests. "And a rub down will loosen up your muscles. But there's nothing more refreshing on earth than a half-hour's sound sleep. At least, it never *hurt* anyone."

Everybody dropped off except John Bromfield and Tony Curtis.

"Going on a fishing trip," said John. "Me and Corinne. You know Corinne."

"I'm crazy for Corinne," said Tony.

"My wife!"

"Calm down," pleaded Tony. "It's hopeless."

"Better be," said John threateningly. "Anyway, we'll both be free from work for the first time in six months. When I finished *The Furies*, Corinne started *Irma Goes West*. Now we're keeping our fingers crossed about sudden assignments. Going up to Lake Mead. You know, the bass up there are more than a foot long—practically jump into your boat."

"I'll believe that when I see the pictures," laughed Tony.

"Wise guy," John said grimly.

"Okay," Scott called, "Pipe down."

"Get that guy," said John, crawling onto a cot. "Fifteen minutes in a steam room and he can't keep his head above the water. Fifteen measly minutes. . . ." And the sandman swooped down over Finlandia.

THE END

---

why rock walked out

Continued from page 138
Beach for us. Once you've lived there a while, you'll love it. It's near the beach so you can be in and out of the water all day while I'm fixing it up—"

Did I do this?

On the phone again, frantic with worry, accusing himself, he spoke to her doctor. When he hung up, his face was grey with pain. A friend standing by said, "Well? Listen, you could take off from here on Saturday night, and be home Sunday night and then leave again on Monday. It's rough traveling and you'd miss a day and a half of shooting, but you could see her for an hour."

In a dead voice, Rock said, "No. I'm not going." He walked past his friend to the car, got in, started the motor. Then he said: "They tell me hepatitis is always serious. But they can lick it. But in Phyl's case—there's a complication." He turned anguished eyes on the other man. "Phyl—Phyl doesn't want to live. She isn't trying. She doesn't care." One hand gripped the steering wheel, turning the knuckles white. "She used to be so full of—energy and fight and craziness and now—" With his head bent forward, Rock Hudson wept and hardly knew it. "I did that to her," he said. "I did that to her—"

And knew for the first time, that love was not enough.

And knew, too, that when a husband could bring not comfort and healing but only more pain, more danger to the bedside of his sick wife—that marriage was over.

He planned to tell her in Hawaii. He went there directly from Italy, to work on *Twilight For the Gods*. When Phyllis was well enough, he had arranged, she would join him there, to bask in the sun and regain her strength. And he would tell her.

The truth is out

But as it happened, there was no need. For Phyllis had had the long weeks of illness and recovery to think. Weeks away from Rock, away from the sudden bursts of love that had given her hope before. And when she came to Hawaii, she too already knew.

They waited just long enough to go home together, settle a few things, tell a few close friends. They had no fights in those last quiet days together. They hardly spoke lest one of them slip and say suddenly—"We can't do this. I love you—" They were very careful. And on a sunny October day, Rock Hudson closed the door of his home behind him and moved into the Beverly Hills Hotel.

And now he lay on his back, staring at the ceiling, remembering his mother's words—and searching.

In the darkened room, the telephone rang. Rock reached out a long arm and picked it up. He had registered in the hotel as Roy Fitzgerald, but he knew it wouldn't work for long.

"Hello?"

"Hello, Mr. Hudson. Sorry to bother you, but I'm calling for the NEWS. Could you tell me, sir, just very briefly—why you and Mrs. Hudson are calling it quits?"

Rock let the receiver slip down to his shoulder. Now was the time. Now was the time to say: *Because we never should have gotten married. Because it isn't enough to love somebody—there must be other things, other loves and wants and a way of life to share. Because if there are not, two people who love each other can destroy each other.* Now was the time to say that, for the reporter, for his mother, for everyone who would ask *why?*

"Hello?" the voice said. "Hello—er, Mr. Hudson? Excuse me sir. I asked why you broke up. I wanted to know—is there any chance of your getting together again?"

"No," he answered, "no, there's no chance." He took a firmer grip on the phone. "As to your last question," he said, feeling what no man expects to feel—the slow warmth of tears forming behind his eyes—"as to why we broke up—I'm sorry, I don't really know the answer to that. I just—don't know."

END

Rock will appear in A FAREWELL TO ARMS *for 20th Century-Fox, and in* TWILIGHT FOR THE GODS *and* THE TARNISHED ANGELS *for U-I.*

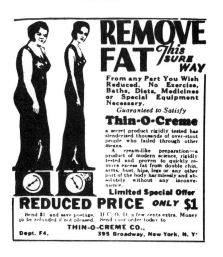

MARRIAGE-GO-ROUND

Weddings and divorces have always been one of *Modern Screen*'s favorite topics. Articles like these have become the magazine's forte: "Bette Davis' Marital Vacation" (January 1939), "Can the Gable-Lombard Love Last?" (May 1939), "Jean Harlow's Trousseau" (January 1934), "Tyrone Power Plans a Marriage" (June 1939), "Marilyn Monroe in Agony—Marriage Ending" (December 1960), to name a few. Unsurprisingly, Elizabeth Taylor, for that very reason, has been one of the magazine's most written-about brides.

The most frank and outspoken star in Hollywood has always been Bette Davis, and she's captured at her best in "Friendly Divorces are the Bunk," from *Modern Screen*'s August 1936 issue (page 158). The marriage discussed in the article is her first, and it was to Harmon O. Nelson, whom she fondly refers to as "Ham." They were married on Agusut 18, 1932, and were divorced three years after this article appeared.

In the pages of *Modern Screen,* Bette had previously recounted the calamity of her wedding in a wilted dress in 107-degree weather in Yuma, Arizona. Said Davis "We were married in the house of a Methodist minister. The two poodles washed themselves all through the ceremony. I wore a two-piece beige street dress that resembled the sands of the Arizona desert after the rain it never gets, brown accessories, and two limp gardenias. I kept thinking of the picture I'd always had of myself as a bride—dewy and divine in white satin and orange blossoms, coming up a white-ribboned aisle to the strains of Mendelssohn."

One of the most famous articles to appear in *Modern Screen* was "The Exclusive Inside Story of: The Separation of Joan and Doug," in the May 1933 issue (page 162). When Lucille LeSueur moved to

> **"A divorce is a public admission of defeat.... Kidding about it is like tying a pink ribbon on a machine gun."**
> **—Bette Davis**
> ***Modern Screen,*** **August 1936**

Hollywood in 1925 as a dance competition-winning flapper, the thought of changing her name to Joan Crawford and marrying Douglas Fairbanks, Jr., was but a shopgirl's dream. But that's exactly what happened. Joan had wed into Hollywood royalty on June 3, 1929, having acquired Douglas Fairbanks, Sr., and Mary Pickford (doyenne of Beverly Hills society) as her father-in-law and step-mother-in-law. Not bad for a Charleston dancer from Kansas City!

By the spring of 1933 the romance between Joan and Doug was over; however, they had never formally discussed divorce. But it was Joan, who at that time made the decision to call it quits. Katherine Albert had been one of Joan's first friends at MGM's publicity department when Joan came to California. Katherine had since gone to New York City to become a writer. During a Hollywood visit, Katherine asked Joan about her marriage, and Joan confessed to her friend, "Katherine, I'm going to divorce Douglas."

Shocked, Katherine asked, "Are you sure that's what you want to do?"

"I'm sure," replied Joan. "And I want you to have the story exclusively."

"But you know I work for *Modern Screen,* Joan. I couldn't get it in print for thirty days. You can't keep a secret that long. Not in this town."

"I think I can." Crawford insisted. "You know how well I keep secrets."

"Yes, I do. Tell me, does Doug know?"

"No," Joan answered. "Only you. And that's how it will remain until *Modern Screen* prints your story."

Indeed, *Modern Screen* was the first publication to print the whole story, even before Doug found out that his marriage was on the rocks!

However, only five days before the magazine hit the stands, nosy

156

gossip columnist Louella Parsons phoned Crawford for some quotes about how smashing Joan and Doug's marriage was. Joan calmly implored Parsons, "I wish you would not print anything like that right now." Parsons pried the news out of Crawford and frantically cranked out a piece for that evening's newspaper. Thanks to Louella's news leak, days later the May 1933 issue of *Modern Screen,* with it in-depth article by Katherine Albert, sold like hotcakes!

Parsons was never one to forget a slight, and eighteen years later the old gossip was still mad that Katherine Albert knew the facts first. You'll find Louella still complaining about the story in "The Truth about My Feuds," from *Modern Screen*'s May 1951 issue (page 184).

In 1919, after becoming a big star at Triangle Pictures, Gloria Swanson made her first Cecil B. De Mille film, entitled *Don't Change Your Husband.* The movie was a smash, but Gloria never followed the advice that the title suggested. In 1916, at the age of seventeen, she married Wallace Beery, but it was a disaster. Gloria found he was an abusive lout. When she went to Paris in 1925 to film *Madame Sans-Gêne,* she returned with husband number two: the Marquis de la Falaise de la Coudraye. She was living the life of royalty—why not have a regal title to match her lifestyle? And so, she became the first Hollywood star to actually become royalty, years before Grace Kelly became a princess.

Like changing partners at a Cotillion Ball, La Swanson dumped the Marquis and married husband number three (of her six!). Constance Bennett had always longed to become royalty too, so Swanson simply passed her used Marquis on to Connie. That Gloria was always such a generous gal!

From the January 1932 issue of *Modern Screen* we have a glimpse of Connie and the Marquis, and ex-Marquise Gloria with her latest conquest (page 173). The page was from a spread entitled "Modern Screen Film Gossip of the Month." Indeed it was!

In the 1940's and 1950's there was Hedda, and Louella, and not far behind, there was Sheilah Graham. Sheilah has written several books on the Hollywood scene that she was so much a part of, and of course she is also known for her affair with F. Scott Fitzgerald. The Fitzgerald/Graham love story was made into a movie, *Beloved Infidel* (1959), with Gregory Peck and Deborah Kerr.

Anyway, in the November 1950 issue of *Modern Screen,* Sheilah penned the amusing "They Were Brides Too Soon" (page 170). In it she discusses all of the starlets who had gone to the altar in their teenage years, only to end up with a fast divorce. Among the teen brides dis-

cussed by Graham are Janet Leigh, Jane Wyman, Doris Day, Esther Williams, and Rhonda Fleming.

Graham's observations are sharp and witty: "Here and in other big cities of course the marriage plan seems to be 'I'll have one husband while I'm a teenager, another for my twenties, one more for the thirties, etc.' Anyway that's exactly what Bette Davis has been doing all these years." Continues Sheilah: "Some girls like to live happily ever after, every few years. They shed husbands like snakes shed skins!" What a line!

When aspiring young actress Nancy Davis took Ronald Reagan to the premiere of her film *The Next Voice You Hear* (1950), she had no idea that he was going to end up as the President of the United States and that she would be cast in the role of First Lady! "The Next Mrs. Reagan?" comes from the December 1951 issue of *Modern Screen* (Page 174). It observes, "To put it bluntly: the current conception of Nancy Davis around town is that she's a decorous, unexciting and glamourless mouse, built for convention not speed." But, boy could she pick out a mean china pattern!

Someone who was clearly built for speed was Elizabeth Taylor Hilton Wilding Todd Fisher Burton Burton Warner. From the May 1950 issue of *Modern Screen* comes "I'm Yours!" (page 178). That same spring, almost as a trial run, Liz walked down the aisle, and Spencer Tracy gave her away, but that was on the set of the movie *Father of the Bride* (1950) (see page 181). On May 6, 1950, it was the real thing, and she became Mrs. Conrad Nicholson Hilton. At the time she exclaimed, "There is no doubt that Nicky is the one I want to spend my life with." Less than two years later, Hedda Hopper wrote the March 1952 cover story for *Modern Screen,* entitled "Liz Does It Again." Reported Hedda in that story, "Liz to me has been the Helen of Troy of Hollywood....At nineteen she has two broken engagements, one divorce, an interrupted near-engagement to her credit. Now comes Wilding." If at the time Hedda had even envisioned what lay ahead in the future in terms of Elizabeth Taylor's weddings, she'd have dropped her hat!

By far *Modern Screen*'s most covered marital triangle was the Debbie Reynolds/Eddie Fisher/Liz Taylor story. When Eddie left Debbie for Liz, *Modern Screen* followed—with cover stories like "Liz Taylor's Pledge: 'I Will Be Faithful'" (July 1959), "The Tragic Facts About Liz' and Debbie's Fatherless Children" (November 1959), and "Eddie to Return to His Own Children" (August 1960).

And so, in the pages of *Modern Screen,* the marriage-go-round goes round and round and round!

DEBBIE REYNOLDS
August 1960

Bette with her husband, Harmon Nelson.

Bette Davis tells why she has contempt for the modern viewpoint that two divorced people should pretend compatibility

By Ruth Rankin

FRIENDLY DIVORCES ARE THE BUNK

A DIVORCE is a public admission of defeat," said the girl in green, twisting a Daiquiri cocktail, "so why put on an act about it?"

We, who are about to interview, have come to anticipate a round with Bette Davis as a rare delight. She is regarded, fearfully, by her sister actresses as the family problem-child who is apt to break out any minute with the most shockingly frank revelations about their sacred-cows. . . .

She treads where angels fear, looking like an angelic school-miss with a "Cause" and possibly a dainty pearl revolver in her stocking.

"What I mean is," Bette flashed her eyes at us like a landing-field beacon, "this business about 'we're still friends.' A divorce implies conclusively: two persons, married, can no longer bear each other's company. The two say, in effect, 'We are sick and tired and disgusted and *through*. We hate each other. Give us, we pray and beseech, a decree of divorce that we may be free to begin our adult lives again, to seek solace and contentment elsewhere.'

"That last part of it is in the lap of the gods. Maybe they are so washed up with the whole business they don't want to seek. But the primary motive is freedom from a bond no longer endurable. If it is at all endurable, then they have no business asking for the divorce.

"But look what happens now in this, our Hollywood. After they have made their public declaration, what occurs? This. They go to the Trocadero that night and in a dim corner you find them all wrapped up like a pretzel, avec photographers. A columnist, the next day, declares it is the dawn of a new understanding, the 'birth

of a beautiful friendship'!

"Sure, I know. It's all supposed to be very new and modern—twentieth century sophistication. They are being civilized. And it is not indigenous to Hollywood, it goes on all over the country—the world. In a lesser way.

BUT YOU can't tell me that any woman who has ever loved a man, really loved him, or any man who has loved a woman, can be friends again after a divorce. No two persons who have had that can be friends, ever again, whether they were married or not. It isn't in the cards. There are too many visions of the past to haunt them, too many wounds that can be healed only by years and then leave scars.

"They can't be casual, and mean it, if they have honest human emotions. The whole thing is a forced, unnatural attitude and many a woman is dying a little inside while hundreds of morbidly curious eyes are trained on her to see how she is taking it.

"There is a wide-open spot for some woman with the courage and the confidence to be simply honest. Some one who refuses to compromise with this syrupy ridiculous sophistication. Divorce is a serious business which wrecks innumerable lives—look at the suicide and homicide statistics.

"Kidding about it is like tying a pink ribbon on a machine gun.

"You can't tell me people wouldn't respect the woman who said, 'I hate the guy. He made my life miserable. I don't want anything further to do with him, any more than I would with any other *Continued on page 160*

158   August 1936

Bette Davis, who has the courage of her convictions, will be seen next in "Mountain Justice."

Tallulah Bankhead, Gambler

Continued from page 139

person who failed me. I refuse to go through with this ironic pretense for the sake of appearances. Whose appearances, for heaven's sake? I've put him out of my life, and I want him to stay put!' And the same applies for the men."

Bette pushed her hat off her forehead and warmed to her subject.

"Fine talk, fine theories!" we declared, fanning the flame. "But would you carry through, in a similiar spot?"

"Would I! Look—I never had a divorce and I never intend to get one, with any luck and the wind on our side. Barring an act of God or the public enemy, Ham is my husband for life. That was our intention when we married, and it remains so. But if anything happened to us—a long if—I would hate him doubly for having once been fond of him. He would have to let me down terribly, which I cannot imagine him doing, and it would disappont me so bitterly, I wouldn't even want to hear his name again, as long as I lived.

"A divorce is no disgrace nor is a broken heart. But putting up a lying front to honest emotions, is.

"Why all the smoke screen? What is there to cover up? Two people have appeared in an open court for all the world to see, hear, and know that they wish to be rid of a hateful tie. The reasons advanced are devious and mainly puerile, but easily penetrated. So the public knows, beyond any question of doubt, exactly what again, agreeing that her salary would be so and so if she was engaged for the part. Tallulah agreed. The agent sailed for home. And three weeks later Tallulah had a cable to come.

Her father came up from Washington to arrange for her passport. She bought the smartest clothes she could find. And the smartest clothes Tallulah can find are the smartest clothes to be found. Count on that. She staked everything on the British manager liking her. I'm reasonably sure it never even occurred to her that he might not. Tallulah still is young enough to believe in the miracle of tomorrow. She went around in a seventh heaven of bliss. She remembered how Estelle Winwood, an English actress, had insisted that she go to England, saying she was the very type the English would adore.

Then, just a day or two before Tallulah was to sail, another cable came.

"So sorry," it read. "Another actress engaged for part. Don't sail. Letter follows."

TALLULAH didn't know what to do. Or rather she didn't know how to manage what she was determined to do. For even while she read that cable that would have struck despair to almost anyone's heart she knew she was going to England anyway—cable or no cable.

"That same day," she said, "I secured an appointment with Evangeline Adams. I told her how things stood," Tallulah went on. "She cast my horoscope. *And she told me to go to England if I had to swim.*"

Tallulah knew her father never would allow her to go if he was told the offer was recalled. He was none too pleased about her going, anyhow. So Tallulah did something that she found extremely difficult. She telephoned General Dupont, a friend of her grandfather's

Continued on page 177

Friendly Divorces Are the Bunk

Continued from page 158

they think of each other.

"So then, why the glad greeting when they meet? Whom are they impressing? The publicity is over—they couldn't escape it with the divorce, if they wanted to. I say *if*. They have taken a stand about each other—why not stick to it? What are they being brave about? The time to be brave was before the divorce—brave enough not to get it.

"Another thing. I do wish somebody would take a week off and define 'mental cruelty' for me. The other day I saw where a woman said it was mental cruelty because her husband called her 'a little squirt!' I thought to myself, 'Baby, you should hear some of the things *I've* been called. And for good and sufficient reason, too. Then that old jealousy line is one that never fails to get me down. The little woman lisps, 'Judge, he wouldn't even let me dance with other men.' The time for complaint, lady, is when he doesn't give a continental.

IN order to apply for a divorce, it seems only logical that you should have a real reason in the first place. In England, where they take these things a mitē more seriously and give them some time and thought, you have to go into the English courts and tell all. It makes absolutely no difference whether you are Duchess, Lord, or bar-maid. You present reason and show proof, and go to it hammer and tongs, while a lot of profound gentlemen in long black robes and curled wigs sit in judgment—and tolerate no nonsense on the subject.

"Probably it makes the English deliberate a while before they get around to it, and so a lot of them never do divorce. The persons who want to be divorced badly enough to go through this ordeal seem to go right on living afterwards even though most of their private linen has been aired. There is a place where gallantry ceases to be gallant, and it strikes me that when a person whom you have taken in sacred matrimony is messing up your life sufficiently to make you wish to cancel your vows, gallantry is as superfluous as a third leg.

"It is definitely sadistic to expect a new wife or husband to accept the old one as a member of the family. At least it is decadent and contrary to the laws of Nature, and an awful strain on somebody, no matter how noble a front they may put up.

"Of course, in a small town like Hollywood, ex's are always running into each other. And no matter how horrible the divorce was, at the time, no doubt they have to adopt some protective measure or coloration or whatever. Nobody wants public scenes or a frantic scrambling of one out of the back door as the other enters the front. They can be civil, if necessary, but this new intimacy is nauseating!

"It is really terrible when there are children. I feel so strongly about divorce because my mother and father were divorced when I was ten; they hated each other then and they still do. If they had striven to keep up a pretty-pretty front for my sister and me, I couldn't have had the least respect for them. My reasoning would be: if you can do that much, then why did you have to go to the extreme length of breaking up our family and getting divorced at all?

"Out here in Hollywood a lot of angles enter, which do not apply to the rest of the world. Two persons with screen careers, married, wish to part. They feel, or are persuaded, that they must 'keep it clean' for the sake of the other person's career. But you find careers beginning to slip just as often after a 'clean' divorce, a frank divorce—or any divorce at all. Especially among those who have been married over five years. People grow to be dependent upon each other in ways they do not realize until they are separated." Bette paused, and we thought of a dozen illustrations to this point, but silently.

"You know, honestly, I used to have the weirdest ideas about marriage. I thought in order to be a good wife you were expected to be dull. That antagonized me, so I tried going to the other extreme. The first two years I was married, Ham was away in the East most of the time. So I dashed about merrily and threw the challenge in their teeth. I, a dull, stodgy, stay-at-home Frau? Never! I thought it was terribly smart to show up some place with four men, to give the gossips a good run for their money.

"Then Ham came out, and one day he remarked in that slow, sensible New England way of his, 'If you ever stop to realize marriage is marriage, you'll be a lot happier.'

"You see, I thought marriage was giving up your rights. Now I know it isn't. It's getting 'em!

"Of course, no woman on earth is so difficult to live with as an actress—or any independent woman. Men have developed almost an entirely new approach to cope with them. Personally, I think the old one is still the best: the one who assumes man is the head of the household and woman is a weak, helpless creature who is better off with her neck under the conquering foot. She is, too, a darn sight.

WE are brought up to be self-sufficient and independent—then we have to do an about-face and let a man run us. And believe me, any woman who doesn't is a fool. No woman with any brains at all allows her man to think he is other than complete master of his household.

"When I get uppity, Ham calls me 'Queen Bess.' That fixes that.

"The other night I overheard Ham and his sister, who is visiting us, in a discussion of marriage and divorce. Ham said, 'Marriage is completely up to a woman. She is never a success at it unless she has lots of give-inny.'

"And after you've put in eight years of give-inny with one man, will you please tell me how you can go into a public court-room admitting you were a failure, or he was a failure—then turn around and go to a theatre opening with him that same night?

"But you can never tell. Maybe I'll turn yellow and do the same thing, should I ever be faced with it." Bette thought it over. "But I don't think so."

She pushed down her hat, pulled on her coat, of some nondescript fur, and started home.

"What, no mink?" said I.

"Nope, no mink," said Bette. "My idea of a failure is a woman whose idea of success is a mink coat—even if she has to buy it for herself. My husband can't afford one."

It gave me added pleasure to state that the best young actress in Hollywood does not own a mink coat, but did win the Academy Award.

Which has nothing to do with the story except to give you a further idea of the one actress in Hollywood who does not play run-sheep-run. The only one who has the courage and confidence of her convictions to come right out and say what none of the pseudo-sophisticates have had the intestinal fortitude to say that she is bored with the absurd "We're Still Friends" pretenders, sees through them with disarming clarity and feels terribly sorry for them.

THERE'S *Glamour* ON THE SCREEN AGAIN

BECAUSE

Gloria's Back!

Star news of the year for every movie fan who's over seven!...You'll see what you've missed when you see what she does to you in this hilariously amorous story of two love-birds who eloped without his children's consent!

You'll Suh-woon Over Her Trunkfuls of Stunning Fashions!

Adolphe
MENJOU

Gloria
SWANSON

In A Screaming Comedy

Of Life Among The In-Laws—With Reverse English

"Father Takes A Wife"

with John Howard

Desi Arnaz · Helen Broderick · Florence Rice

RKO Radio Picture

Produced by Lee Marcus · Directed by Jack Hively

Original Screen Play by Dorothy and Herbert Fields

THE
EXCLUSIVE
INSIDE
STORY OF

THE SEPARATION

By KATHERINE ALBERT

IT has happened!
And for the next few months you will be seeing dozens of stories about Joan's and Doug's separation. Each writer will have his own opinion. But here— the first magazine story to mention the separation as an actuality—you will find the complete and absolute truth; the real reason for the parting of these two people.

I have been wanting to write this story for months. I, as one of Joan Crawford's best friends, have known things which my loyalty to her prevented my telling. But they can all be told—now that it has happened!

First of all—the cold, hard facts!

Doug has moved away from their Brentwood home. Joan remains at that house. There will be no divorce at present, because neither of them wants to remarry. It is a legal separation. They have talked the matter over like the lady and gentleman that they are and have come to the agreement as the only way out.

And now for the story behind these vital statistics—what is it?

The trouble has been brewing for months. Remember when Joan and Doug went to Europe in July, before there was even a hint of discontent? That trip was made for a purpose. It was a last fling—an attempt to revive the thing that they saw going—their happiness. Before their European trip they were on the verge of separation. They thought perhaps if they could get away from Hollywood, have a swell time together, be free of the work that drives them both so hard—the nervous, exciting work—they might be happy again.

They came back rested. They had had a grand time.

"IT'S NOT FAIR TO YOU NOR TO ME. WE HAVE GIVEN IT EVERY TRIAL."

...A thousand conjectures have been told and written concerning the separation of these two people. Modern Screen gives you the inner truth —by someone who knows them well

OF JOAN AND DOUG

They thought that they could once more make a go of it. Joan had developed a sense of humor. She could look at it more calmly. But the trip to Europe was only a drug that deadened pain. It did not remove the cause of the trouble and back in Hollywood it all began all over again.

IT has come so slowly—their drifting apart—that it is impossible to put your finger on any one set of circumstances to blame for it. They had simply gotten on each other's nerves. Remember how young they were when they married. Remember how much each has changed. And don't forget that they both give much of themselves to the camera they serve.

Joan likes to be alone when she has finished a day's intensive work. She has one of the most remarkable minds I have ever known and she likes to think—by herself.

Doug is a gregarious person. He enjoys people—

spritely, amusing people, it is true—but he does want people around. Doug can throw off the day's work in a way that Joan never can. When she has done a terrifically emotional scene in the afternoon she is devastated for the rest of the day. Doug can come home and chat. Who can say which way is best? They are merely different ways, but I do know that this tremendous difference in temperament has caused much of their unhappiness.

Once, while they were still making that valiant effort to revive the love that they saw slipping away from them daily, Joan suggested that they go away together for a week-end—just the two of them—to talk things over. Doug agreed. But by the time the week-end arrived three or four other people had been invited to go along. Doug had asked them. Joan and Doug did not go away on that week-end trip.

They have, during the last two years, grown apart temperamentally. When they (Continued on page 169)

They met first in 1932 working in "No Man of Her Own." It was distinctly not a case of love at first sight, for Carole was Mrs. William Powell and Clark, the husband of Rhea Langham.

Meet Josephine Dillon. Clark did in 1924 when she gave him diction lessons and he presented her with a wedding ring.

With his second and present wife, Rhea Gable. She is that surprised that he wants a divorce! Can you imagine?

In 1931, when Carole and Bill Powell were one, they kept a great many night spots flourishing. Their marriage lasted but two years. The clubs are still going strong.

THE MARITAL *Mix-up*

OF CAROLE AND CLARK

There's a woman in their cards who, they say, is blocking out the altar

The most glamorous friendship on the Coast. She's free to become Mrs. Gable and they say he'd like to be free.

MARRIAGE À LA COLBERT

"When Norman is coming over for the evening," says Claudette Colbert, Norman's wife, "it's quite as exciting as if we were engaged." (Right) The two of them aboard the freighter on which they spent their vacation.

Claudette Colbert—and her amazing plan for happiness in her marriage

By ADELE WHITELY FLETCHER

CLAUDETTE COLBERT and Norman Foster have been married three years. Throughout that time Claudette has lived in a small apartment and Norman has stopped at the Lambs' Club. Not because they don't love each other enough to live in the conventional way, sharing the same home. Rather because they love each other too much; too much to risk glamor being dulled by monotony; too much to permit Claudette's good-by kisses to become habit, offered in a perfunctory way, while she telephones the grocer.

It would be a girl like Claudette, dark and vital, like a Goya painting, who would fling traditions and conventions to the wind and live as she wanted to live.

But let us go back to the beginning for Claudette and Norman, to the time when they met during rehearsals of that successful stage play, "The Barker." It's really necessary to do this if we're going to understand the exciting, modern plan by which they live their lives.

It was three years ago, perhaps a little more, that "The Barker" was ready to go into production and the cast called for a first reading. The company was almost entirely assembled on the stage, seated in a semi-circle in the usual variety of decrepit chairs and stools available in an empty theater. Straddling an old ladder chair, his arms resting on the back, was Walter Huston, the star. Squatted on an ottoman that was rapidly oozing its stuffing was Norman Foster, the juvenile. The best seat of the lot, an upholstered and half-way respectable chair, remained empty. It was for Claudette Colbert, the leading lady.

THE call had been for two o'clock. It was twenty minutes past two before Claudette arrived, flushed from hurrying and from her embarrassment. She smiled her apology and the directorial frown became less ominous, entirely disappeared. She slipped quietly into

(Right) Although she has made her name as one of the smartest women on the screen, Claudette Colbert has inveigled Paramount executives to give her the rôle of a cabaret dancer in "Twenty-four Hours." (Below) The young man whom Madame Chauchoin, Claudette's mother, discovered had charm.

the vacant chair. She threw back her smart coat. She opened her manuscript to the first page and, like a dutiful child, waited for the reading to begin.

During the reading, Claudette managed polite glances at the juvenile. She felt it would be better for the love scenes if he were taller than she. But because of the way he squatted on the ottoman it was practically impossible to tell a thing about him.

If Norman Foster was conscious of Claudette's dark eyes upon him he gave no sign. He appeared to be entirely absorbed with his 'script. He read his lines beautifully.

At last the reading was concluded. Everybody stood up and as Norman Foster reached his full height Claudette Colbert breathed a little sigh of relief. He was sufficiently tall to hold her in the circle of his arms and tower above her. Claudette knows the importance of love scenes.

Weeks of rehearsals and then the play opened to score an immediate success. The company settled down for a long run.

Often after the evening performance one gentleman or another—a banker, perhaps, or a famous novelist, a king of industry or an artist—would stand at the Colbert dressing-room door, his flowers inside, his chauffeured cabriolet outside, waiting to take Claudette to supper.

IT'S nothing to wonder at that men always have sought her out. She has a smiling mouth and brilliant eyes. She has humor and a Gallic gaiety. However, in spite of all the charming gentlemen who peopled her life, Claudette insists that not until she met Norman did the thought of any man keep her awake at night. Then, suddenly, after "The Barker" had been playing about a month, no matter how hard she danced or how late the reading lamp burned beside her bed, it still would be a long time before she got to sleep. It was as if she had so much to think about that she couldn't bear to slip into unconsciousness.

Norman Foster hadn't gone out of his way to be pleasant. On the contrary, he was positively grouchy. But Claudette didn't let that worry her. She had been about, you see. She had read dozens of books on psychology. And she interpreted the gruff way in which Norman Foster treated her to her own glory and satisfaction. Had he been casual she would have been piqued, if not actually alarmed. But he wasn't casual, he was gruff. In this she found consolation, for it showed her very clearly that he was thinking about her more than he found comfortable. His grouchiness she saw to be defensive.

THEN Norman began writing poetry about black hair and laughing eyes, leaving it about where Claudette would be certain to see it. She was entirely satisfied it was her hair and her eyes he meant. No false modesty about Claudette. She's too modern for that.

"Finally," she told me, "Norman up and asked me to dinner. I knew he was going to. You know, he fumed and hedged and even talked about the war debt and the salt question of India before he came to the point.

"Now he insists he would have asked me much sooner except that he felt I was ritzing him. He says I spoke with an English accent and used frightfully broad A's. He's probably quite right at that. I'd been playing with an English company previously and I'm one of those awful unconscious mimics."

Claudette and Norman must have had a wonderful time over that first dinner table. With the orchestra playing the new love songs. With the headwaiter bending solicitously over them, aware of their importance on Broadway, sensing their budding romance. And then the hurry back to the theater because they had lost all track of time. The rush to get into make-up. It's quite possible they played their love scenes a little differently that night, a little self-consciously.

Norman asked Claudette to dine with him again and again. Together they began to discover how wonderful is New York. They found the old Egyptian tomb in the Metropolitan Museum. All lovers do. They discovered the hansom cabs at the Plaza and drove through Central Park in the mad starlight. They searched the most dimly lit cafés and restaurants until they found the most secluded tables.

"Ah, this is wisdom—to love, to live. . . ."

CLAUDETTE knew right from the start that the secret happiness that sang inside of her was this thing called love. And she tells of the day when, jubilant, she was satisfied that Norman loved her too. He didn't tell her so, or even hint at it. He simply suggested that she use a little less mascara and perhaps just a trifle less lipstick. And her dresses maybe just a bit longer.

"After that," she told me, "his proposal was anti-climactic. Whenever a man suggests less make-up or longer skirts it's obvious he's in love with you. Even though he may not realize it at the time.

"There's something about men that makes them want to temper, change, make more conservative if not less attractive, the woman they love.

"Of course, I didn't give in to Norman. I was smarter than that. If he'd been good enough to fall in love with me as I was I wasn't going to be foolhardy enough to risk any change."

Theirs was true love. And it didn't run smooth.

Claudette's mother, Madame Chauchoin, held up her hands in horror at the very thought of Claudette marrying an actor.

"C'est impossible!" bonne maman Chauchoin insisted. "Impossible! Un acteur pour ma petite fille!"

Claudette didn't know what to do. Her father was dead. She hardly could go off and leave her mother to live alone, miserable over what had come to pass. And she couldn't give up Norman. She realized she was only half alive now with Norman away from her. Life without Norman would be such a dreadful waste, a desperate business of marking time. The sound of his voice on the telephone brought that divine choking sensation to her throat. The touch of his hand . . . ah, she made up her mind, once and for all, never would she give up Norman.

So one day the two of them ran off somewhere—where is their secret—and under their real names of Chauchoin and Hoefler, they were married.

The best things in life come easily to Claudette Colbert. One of them was the honor of playing opposite Maurice Chevalier in "The Smiling Lieutenant." Don't miss seeing it.

THE weeks spun around. Never were there such love scenes on any stage as Norman and Claudette enacted—of course that's not the right word at all—in "The Barker."

And then, gradually, in spite of the deeply rooted prejudices of a whole lifetime, Madame Chauchoin began to change her mind about the dark young man who was always calling for Claudette and bringing her home after the theater. He had charm, that young man. And once she had admitted this, even to herself, there was nothing for Madame Chauchoin's prejudices to do but vanish. For no one places a greater importance on charm than ladies born and bred in Paris.

Claudette admits she had counted on this very thing. Inevitably, she felt, in the face of such graciousness and sympathy and humor, her mother's foolish prejudices must give way. Because of no other man had Claudette ever walked the streets not knowing where she was going or what she was doing. Because of no other man had she ever felt that if the telephone didn't ring soon she must stop breathing.

However, even after Madame Chauchoin had entirely capitulated and Norman and Claudette had told her of their marriage and received her Continued on page 169

Marriage à la Colbert

Continued from page 168

blessing, they continued to live apart.

"I might never have found the courage to start out, like this if we hadn't been married secretly," Claudette admits. "But now that I know how perfect it is, I wouldn't want it otherwise. Neither would Norman.

"It wouldn't be practical for everybody, of course," she said. "There's the economic side of things to be considered. But for professional people with individual incomes, separate establishments seem to me ideal.

"There are, unfortunately, bound to be some bad nights. Off nights at least. At such times—if either of us are tired from the day's work, say, or if we're preoccupied about the work we're to do the next day—Norman and I don't see each other. I know the old theory about love being a balm at difficult times. But I prefer to struggle through bad hours alone. I'd rather not tax love.

AND it's turned out to be such fun to live as Norman and I live. When Norman is in New York and he's coming over for the evening it's quite as exciting as if we were engaged. I dress up. And then I sit and wait for him and play wretched solitaire in my impatience for the doorbell to ring."

Recently Norman Foster has been working in California and last month when both he and Claudette found themselves with two weeks' holiday at the same time they arranged to meet in Chicago.

"It was like a rendezvous," Claudette said gaily. "It was fun getting our tooth brushes mixed up. But it probably wouldn't have been if we'd been living together in the same house and getting one thing or another mixed up every morning for three years.

"I suppose I'm an incurable romantic but I wouldn't want the thing Norman and I know to become less, to settle into a series of staid habits. If it ever should come to this in spite of our modern arrangements, or if Norman ever should cease to care for me I do hope I won't try to hold on, but that I will have the courage to call quits. Not spoil all that has gone before and ruin what might otherwise live as a beautiful memory . . ."

Her voice grew soft. "I can well imagine how very difficult it might be to do this," she said. "It is to be hoped I'll never have to . . ."

IT would be a girl like Claudette Colbert who, admitting love to be far and away the most important thing in life, would discard the traditions of marriage to work out a new pattern. Like her, her entire life is unusual. Overnight she made her name one to be reckoned with on Broadway. In one picture she proceeded to establish herself as a preëminent screen actress. She chose to spend a long holiday on a tramp steamer rather than on a de luxe liner. A product of this modern age, she, nevertheless, thinks people who keep on being divorced and married and divorced and married again are not happy. And rated one of the smartest dressed women on the screen, with her popularity based upon her appearance in society dramas, she finally has beguiled the monarchs of Paramount to allow her to play the cabaret singer in "Twenty Four Hours." Because it is parts like this that most interest her.

Oh, Claudette knows what she wants. And it isn't necessarily that upon which the world puts the highest price. She's the sort far more likely to set fashions than to follow them.

Separation of Joan and Doug

Continued from page 163

were married, Doug was a dreamy, poetic youth. He has changed into a sophisticated man of the world.

Joan, during the years of their marriage, has more and more sought simplicity. Today, her friends not only include the important people of Hollywood, but also a boy in the publicity department, the younger actors on the lot, a few underpaid writers and a script clerk as well.

And that brings us to Joan's friends. She still has a number of women friends —Claudette Colbert, Ann Harding, Helen Hayes, Doris Warner. It is the hey-hey girl friends of another period in her life who have not lived up to Joan's intense brand of loyalty.

Her closest friends are men—for Joan thinks like a man.

SHE has danced and laughed with Ric Cortez, Bob Young, Alexander Kirkland, Franchot Tone (one of her newest leading men).

Of course, that has all been grist for the gossip mill. But what the gossipers have failed to record is the fact that never has she been alone with any of these men on the dancing parties. Either Douglas or a party of other people have been along.

When Joan is "between pictures" she loves to laugh and she has an amazing sense of the ridiculous. She has found laughter with these bright and amusing boys.

Oh, she has tried to solve her problem. She has wandered through the rooms of her beautiful home trying, to think out every angle of the break with Douglas that was bound to come.

Naturally, she thought of her career. What would such a break do to her as an actress? Two people in private life grow apart and get on each other's nerves and they separate. But after such an important separation as this there is bound to be a storm of gossip, and Joan knew that she would be blamed for it.

But she knew that in remaining together they were not being fair to each other.

They talked the matter over quite calmly.

Seated in the quiet luxury of their enormous living room Joan said, "You know, Douglas, that we have got to face facts. You know that we can't go on like this—pretending to be happy when we're not."

"I know it," said Doug, "It is not fair to you nor to me. We have given it every trial."

And that was how they decided to separate.

"But we'll be friends?" Joan asked.

"I couldn't stand to lose your friendship," said Doug.

"And you never will."

And on that note they parted.

But remember this and this is the absolute truth.

There is no other man in Joan's life!

There is no other woman in Doug's!

Had there been they certainly would have chosen to get a divorce instead of this separation.

Perhaps one or the other may say that it is a temporary separation—but that is not true.

It is final—and there is never any going back with a woman like Joan. For remember that this is not so sudden as it seems to you. Remember that this has been coming on for many months.

They have tried—and tried hard—to make a go of it.

But it just wouldn't work.

And how does Doug Senior feel about it?

Before they made their final decision they talked it over with Doug, Sr. He is a wise and a kindly man and he said, "If you two kids can't be happy together, then there's just one thing for you to do."

And they've done it.

Of course, Joan will get the brunt of it all. Of course, the envious will be saying, "Sure, we knew it wouldn't last. Crawford is just reverting to type." Joan knew this, too, and it has given her many sleepless nights. That is why the separation has been postponed longer than it should have been for the peace of mind of both.

But Joan is brave enough and true enough to stand that gossip. She is big enough to face it—like the girl she is.

As I said before you'll be hearing and reading plenty of bunk about those two—but this is the absolute truth!

They were brides too soon

by Sheilah Graham

Rhonda Fleming was a bride at 16, a mother at 18, and a divorcée at 24.

June Haver, teen-age bride, knew unhappiness early.

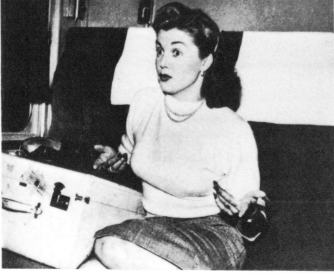
Esther Williams, married before 20, made a wise choice the second time.

They all married in their

■ How soon is too soon to get married? That of course depends on the man, the maid and the morals of the moment.

In India, for example, it's fine and dandy to marry the toothless baby of your family's choice. In points North, East and South, your relatives prefer you to wait until you can say "I do" without lisping.

In Hollywood practically anything can happen on the impatient marriage age front, and it sometimes does, sometimes disastrously.

Judy Garland was 17 when she sang her way into the Mrs. David Rose title. Shirley Temple was another sweet seventeen miss who wishes she had waited. Ditto Barbara Lawrence, now a young divorcée. Janet Leigh was 15 when she took the plunge that almost drowned her. Lana Turner was a head-strong 19 when Artie Shaw took her to dinner at 8 p.m. one night, wed her before dawn the same disenchanted evening. Deanna Durbin was 19 when she shouldn't have said "I do" to Vaughn Paul. And Rhonda Fleming, who didn't let many get ahead of her, says now, "I was a bride at 16, a mother at 18, a divorcée at 24. A girl is crazy if she marries *anyone* before she is twenty-something years old." Rhonda wants me to tell you her love story. "It may help some of your readers with theirs." That's what I hope anyway.

"I just about broke my mother's heart," said Rhonda, a sensible woman of 26, "when I ran off to Las Vegas to marry Tom Lane. She knew I was too young. But now I'm glad it all happened. Because maybe now I can help others *not* to make the same mistake. At 16 you think you know everything. No girl under 20 can possibly know the seriousness of marriage.

"But," continued Rhonda, leaning back in the arm-chair in my Beverly Hills living room, "the more my mother said 'Don't do it,' the more I wanted to. A couple of my girl friends were married so I wanted to be too. How silly could I get! Apart from my age, we weren't in any financial position to be married. And that's another reason why young people are fools to marry—they don't usually have enough money."

Wanda Hendrix had money. But Audie Murphy made her wait until *she* was 18 and *he* was more established as an actor. That didn't work out either. After champing at the bit for two years, their nerves were so on edge, the first angry word *after* the ceremony and Audie was hollering, "I quit."

Maybe that is the soft spot in young Hollywood marriages. Things go wrong and right away they scram to the divorce courts. What's happened to the old fashioned concept of stay married forever? Here, and in other big cities of course, the marriage plan seems to be "I'll have one husband while I'm a teen-ager, another for my twenties, one more for the thirties, etc." Anyway that's exactly what Bette Davis has been doing all these years. Will she get a new marital deal for her fifties?

"Tom and I," said Rhonda, *Continued on page 172*

Doris Day's two hasty marriages suffered.   Janet Leigh was a teen-age bride twice.   Jane Wyman wed Myron Futterman at 18.

eens, they all suffered in their twenties—and each one learned a lesson she'll never forget.

they were brides too soon

Continued from page 171 "went to live
with his family because we couldn't afford
a home of our own."

Errol Flynn did a turnabout on this situation. He invited ex-wife Nora's *stepmother* to live with them. He lost Nora,
kept the stepmother. Sometimes I think
Errol is 16—romantically.

"My in-laws were sweet, but if a young
couple wants to be happy and married,
living with your husband's family is not
the best way," Rhonda went on.

John Agar didn't exactly live with Shirley's family, but it was the next worst
thing, right next door within eye-view of
Mama and Papa Temple. You can bet
now that Charles Black will move the little
lady of his delightful dreams to a location
where in-laws will have to knock before
they look.

"Y ou're inclined to be confused when
you are married too young," said
Rhonda. "But look at Elizabeth Taylor,"
I told her. "I've never seen a girl so poised
in her marriage as 18-year-old Lizzie."
"Maybe she's different," Rhonda replied.
"She's been sheltered all her life. The decisions have all been made for her. But I
still think even Elizabeth would have in-
sured her chance of being happily married
if she had waited a little longer."

Some girls of course can't wait. They
want to set records—like Arline Judge
and her six husbands. Some girls like to
live happily ever after, every few years.
They shed husbands like snakes shed skins.
But these are exceptions of course. Most
intelligent girls enter the stage of matrimony with the fervent prayer that "This
is *it*."

"A girl friend of mine," Rhonda told me,
"asked my advice a few months ago. She's
19 but she wanted to know if that was too
young to get married. I didn't say 'No' because I remembered my mother saying
that. Parents have to be very careful with
their children when they have an urge to
get married. So I said to the girl—'I'll tell
you *my* story. If Tom and I had waited, we
wouldn't have married. When you marry
so young, you miss so much fun. You see
your girl friends running around having a
good time while you are so settled. Of
course, if he has a good sound job with
money in the bank that helps. If not, don't
let anyone fool you—love *can* fly out of
the window'."

"So what did the girl do?" I wanted to
know. "She married the guy," giggled
Rhonda. "And they seem to be happy. But
I'll tell you what happened with Tom and
me. I was only 15 when I met him. But
I thought I was quite experienced. I'd
worked as a show girl in Ken Murray's
Blackouts. I nearly won a 'Gateway to
Hollywood' radio contest from Jesse Las-
ky. I came in second. I'll never forget how
I cried and cried backstage, and Jean
Hersholt said, 'Some day you'll see that
losing was the greatest blessing that could
have happened to you.'

"I was pretty developed for a girl of
15, one year I was a child, and the
next I looked like a woman. I met Tom
on a New Year's Eve. I'd been going on
and off with a boy in the Beverly Hills
High School. We quarreled a lot. Girls
would ask me—'is it *on* or *off* this week?'"

This particular night we went to a party,
had an argument. I looked for him at midnight, but he had disappeared. I never did
find him. I was crazy about him. Another
boy said 'Come on—I'll take you home'. I
was crying. My life was ruined, but I let
him take me to a drive-in for some hot
chocolate. In those days I was so sensitive, if anyone said 'Boo' to me, I started
to cry.

"Next to us in the drive-in there was a
long convertible Buick. 'I want you to
meet Marilyn,' the boy with me shouted
to the man in the car (Rhonda's real name
is Marilyn Louis). 'Tom Lane has a fourteen piece orchestra and he's looking for
a girl singer,' he whispered to me. I was
still sobbing and I guess I attracted Tom
because I didn't pay any attention to him."
Do I have to tell you that Rhonda landed
the girl singer job? "I was never really
swept off my feet by Tom. I always have
to know a person well to like them. But
as I told you, the excitement of getting
married was too hard for me to resist.

"Tom was like a big brother to me. My
sister was married, my parents divorced.
I needed someone to talk to. We were
married seven years." The only good result, apart from the experience, was their
son Kent.

After the marriage Tom, for some reason
Rhonda couldn't remember, gave up his
orchestra and began interior decorating.

"I found I was earning more money than
Tom and that's bad, too. I was under contract to Fox, and to save the marriage I
gave that up and sold jewelry and luggage
at Coulters. Then when my figure came
back after the baby, I modeled at the May
Company and Magnins. Then Henry Will-
son said I just had to see Selznick. I was
wearing a little peasant blouse and skirt,
but he signed me the same day."

"How did Tom like that?" I asked Rhonda. "He didn't," she replied. "I was now
nearly 19 and growing up faster than Tom.
He was a few years older by actual count
but a boy of 21 is a baby compared to a
girl of 19.

"I was beginning to know what I wanted
to do. Until then it was just wonderful to
dance with Tom—we went to Catalina one
time and won a cup for a waltz. And we
had music in common. But even that
wasn't enough. I wanted to do more important things."

C ame the war, Tom went into the service,
and when he returned, he and Rhonda,
like millions of other war separated couples, were strangers across the breakfast
table.

"I didn't run around while he was away,
as some other war wives did," said Rhonda.

"I used to get phone calls, but I always
said 'no.' I stayed with his family during
the war. If a call came from the studio, I'd
rush with Kent to my own mother, then
pick him up late at night. I wanted so to
do the right thing. After the war, we took
a studio apartment on La Cienega Boulevard. I worked for every piece of furniture we got. There was only a couch to
sleep on, and no room for Kenny.

"I'm a Mormon and I started to do a lot
of church work. I went to Sunday School
to talk to the children about the importance of faith in God. A husband and wife,
I think, should share the same religion."

After the divorce Rhonda's name was
bracketed with A. C. Lyles', then with
John Hilton's. She almost married John,
who is an actor, but then she remembered
one of the causes for the bust-up with Tom
—financial insecurity. Now she is going
places with blond, 34-year-old, very handsome Doctor Lew Morrill.

"Is it serious?" I asked, adding, "I've
always wanted to marry a doctor myself."
"It takes a special kind of woman to marry
a doctor," replied Rhonda. "Lew's been
married twice. During the first marriage
he was away in the war and like me and
Tom got a divorce when he returned. He
says if he ever marries again, he'll choose
a woman who works." This is another
switch. Most successful men like the little
woman to concentrate on *them*.

"I always said I would never marry a
doctor," Rhonda revealed. "But Lew must
be quite experienced at being married by
this time. After two failures, maybe the
third will take." One thing is sure, whoever Rhonda does marry will have to be
successful at something.

"How about a very young girl marrying
a successful middle-aged man?" I asked
Rhonda. "I'm thinking of Lauren Bacall
and Bogart, and June Allyson and Dick
Powell, and Gene Kelly who isn't middle-
aged, but was considerably older than
Betsy Blair—he married her when she was
17." "No, I still think she should wait.
And no matter what, no one should rush
into marriage. There's no such thing as
love at first sight. You have to grow on
each other. It takes at least six months to
know a man well."

O f course, that doesn't always work out,
either. Jane Wyman and Ronald Reagan were engaged about a year and Jane
was in her early twenties, too. She was
only 18 when Myron Futterman, Ronnie's
predecessor, took her for better or worse.
It turned out worse for them both.

I don't know how long lovely Doris Day
waited to wed first hubby, Al Jordan. But
it wasn't long. She was 17. Husband number two, George Weidler, brother of Virginia, was a snap decision of 1946. But
fate has forced Doris to wait a year to
marry Marty Melcher, until he gets his
California divorce decree from Patti Andrews. Doris is now 26. Perhaps she is
not too young to marry now.

Nearly every star you can name was
married once before she was twenty years
old—Esther Williams, Elizabeth Taylor,
June Haver, Joan Blondell, Paulette Goddard, Ginger Rogers, Vivien Leigh, Ruth
Roman, Gloria de Haven. Some of the
hasty-hearted lasses have married again,
and again.

But who can really say when is the
right age for *anyone* to marry? You can
wait until you're forty, like Jimmy Stewart—and he's supremely happy. You can
be *married* for forty years like Edward
Arnold, then tell the judge it was all a
mistake. But for the record I'm stringing
along with Rhonda. I believe that if you
can wait until after you are 21, the odds
are in your favor for a happier marriage.
At least your eyes are open.

THE END

MODERN SCREEN

Courtesy Los Angeles *Herald*

Acme

While the marriage between Constance Bennett and the Marquis de la Falaise de la Coudraye has been set for December 2, in Arizona, rumor has it that they have already been married—in Paris. But it is doubtful if they would have been married before the Marquis' divorce became final—even in a foreign country. Friends of Gloria Swanson insist that Gloria will marry an older man than Michael Farmer—when she does marry. Nevertheless, the gossips insist that Gloria and Michael were recently married in New York.

THE NEXT MRS.

REAGAN?

Nobody's seen an engagement ring, but Ronnie is wearing his heart on his sleeve, and there's a 20 karat sparkle in Nancy Davis' eyes.

BY CAROLINE BROOKS

■ The San Fernando Valley moon hung like a big, golden grapefruit high in the sky, and out at Agoura —which sounds like an old-fashioned automobile horn, but is a hamlet not far from Hollywood—it bathed the shaggy oaks and whitewashed stables of Ronnie Reagan's ranch in a magically romantic light. To Ronnie and his best girl, Nancy Davis, who had come out after dinner for a peek at the horses, it seemed like a perfect time for a bareback ride in the moonlight.

They backed their favorite black mare, "Baby," out of the stall and started to climb aboard. "Do you think," ventured Nancy, who's a little leery of horses, "that this idea will be all right with Baby?"

"Don't worry about Baby," Ronnie laughed. "She's a lady, through and through."

Well, Ronnie was halfway up one side with a leg dangling, and Nancy had the same precarious hitch on the other, when Baby gave a snort and bolted. Ronnie tumbled without harm but Nancy whacked down flat on her spine with the wind knocked out of her. Ronnie lifted her up anxiously, dusted her off and patted back some breath. Nancy grinned gamely and gasped out a familiar line, like this. "Never—underestimate—the power—of a lady!"

Right now, Nancy Davis might well say the very same thing about herself. Because, at this point, the doe-eyed, gentle-voiced, sweet-faced young actress, who has Ronnie Reagan's heart tied up with love knots, is just about the most deceptive doll in Hollywood. To put it bluntly: the current conception of Nancy Davis around town is that she's a decorous, unexciting, and glamorless mouse, built for convention and not for speed. This idea—I can happily report—is about as cockeyed as Dean Martin and Jerry Lewis can sometimes get.

It's true enough that Nancy's a lady, through and through, like Baby. Often she's perfectly lady-like, but often, too, *Continued on page 176*

In public Nancy and Ronald are the picture of civic dignity. Her father is an eminent Chicago surgeon.

In private they are informal and ranchy. Nancy's been busy, too, has had eight roles in two years of Hollywood.

175

the next mrs. reagan?

Continued

from page 175 she kicks up her heels. Only you don't hear much about that—because in her quiet, charming way Nancy Davis can handle about whatever situation pops up.

For example, the other morning Nancy was scooting her Chrysler convertible over toward MGM, late for a studio call. It was six o'clock and traffic was clear and she wasn't thinking much about restraining things like speedometers. Les Paul and Mary Ford were swinging out "How High the Moon" on the radio good and loud, and Nancy was trying to drown them out with her bathtub coloratura, as she likes to do when she drives. So naturally she didn't hear the sirens.

The two traffic cops finally flagged her down, stalked over, tilted back their caps and wagged their heads ominously. "Where," demanded one of them, "is *your* driver's license?" Nancy said she was afraid she didn't have it with her. "Do you know how fast you were going?" She shook her head. "Sixty," informed the cop, "and did you see that four-way stop back there?" Nancy shook it again. "I didn't think so—you didn't even slow down. Well, Lady—" he sighed, reaching for his ticket pad.

It suddenly occurred to Nancy Davis that with a triple rap like that she was headed for Alcatraz, or at least San Quentin. She turned up her big, round brown eyes and stared in wounded innocence. **Pretty soon the police were speaking in honeyed tones and their anger had melted like butter. A little later Nancy drove away—slower and considerably quieter—but without a ticket.**

Now, a girl with persuasive charm like that is obviously going to get along. In fact, for one who has been around Hollywood barely more than two years, Nancy Davis gets along wonderfully. When she hit town, she had never gazed into a movie camera, and she couldn't tell you the name of one eligible Hollywood male. But by now her boss, Dore Shary, calls her, "as fine a young actress as we have on the lot," and Nancy has eight pictures behind her to back that up. In her private life, she's plainly heading for a wedding with Ronald Reagan, one of Hollywood's most attractive and most eminent citizens. But from these twin triumphs, oddly enough, stem the cluster of fuzzy ideas about Nancy.

Careerwise that's not too hard to figure. As Nancy sighs, "In every picture I've done I've either been true blue, noble, or pregnant." In fact, Nancy was wearing "the baby" a bulky contraption of cotton and net, no speck of makeup, and a baggy maternity gown when Ronnie Reagan first saw her on the screen. That was the night she took him to see her in *The Next Voice You Hear*, and after they wobbled out, he gave her a look. "May I make a suggestion?" he grinned. "Send out your laundry and tell them to lose it!"

But the way Hollywood adds up Nancy's romance with Ronnie is a little more curious. Only the other day a gossip columnist who should know better sized them up like this: "Ronnie Reagan and Nancy Davis are still carrying on their romance on a cerebral plane." Cerebral? Applesauce!

The reason Nancy was in such a hurry the morning she got tagged by the motorbike boys was because she'd overslept. And the reason she'd overslept was because she was out very late with Mister Reagan. In fact, he sees her every night of the world and they don't sit and hold hands. They have fun. Not necessarily

the kind that makes headlines, because generally it's far removed from the showcases where such news is made. "I used to get a charge out of the night club routine," Nancy will admit, "but it's boring now," which may be her way of saying when you're in love you don't like a crowd.

There's only one time when Ciro's or Mocambo's is a must, and that's when Nancy winds up one of her true blue roles and reverts to type by splurging on a dress. She went for a snaky off-shoulder red one after *Next Door Neighbor*, her last picture. The gown had a plunging neckline which would make Jane Russell grind her teeth in envy—so of course she had to go dancing to show that off, and at such times Ronnie's reasonable. But what happened this other late date I'm talking about is twice as typical of an enchanted evening with those two.

That night they'd accepted an invitation to a fancy dinner party at Jack's, down on the beach. It was high style, with champagne, caviar, and sparkling conversation to match. When the guests departed politely around 10:30, Nancy and Ronnie trotted off toward their car, with every good intention of getting home at a respectable hour.

But on the way they heard the inviting tinkle of honky-tonk music and spotted the beckoning lights of the Ocean Park Fun Zone down the way. They looked at each other, about-faced, and made tracks for the bright lights. Pretty soon Nancy and Ronnie were banging ducks in the shooting gallery, slamming baseballs at bottles, whirling dizzily on the Caterpillar, and collecting Kewpie dolls, cactus plants, goldfish, and scattered prizes of chance and skill on the pike. When they'd had their pictures taken, smeared their evening clothes with cotton candy, and bumped themselves groggy on the Rat Race, they thought they were ready to leave. But then they met a lonesome soldier just back from Korea, so they joined up with him and did the whole thing over. Nancy pulled in her Westwood apartment when the mockingbirds trilled around three o'clock in the morning.

Now, there are no news photographers prowling the plebian pike at Ocean Park, and you won't find Hollywood reporters hanging around little Los Angeles neighborhood movie houses, and certainly not at Ronnie's valley ranch where Nancy has wrecked a good dozen pairs of Levis painting fences.

Nancy explains, "In town my idea of a big, fat evening is dinner at Chasen's, then a movie—with popcorn." At Dave Chasen's restaurant—where they dine regularly—they don't let photographers in, nor do they come to the Bill Holden's parties. Sometimes when Nancy talks Ronnie into a night baseball game (she's a violent fan, but he's off the game ever since he busted his leg playing in an All-Star game two years ago) or the Santa Anita Races, or when she goes for broke with one of those new creations and they show up dancing at a glitter mill, people stare at them as if they'd staggered out of the Maine woods. But actually nobody's been in hiding or hugging a hearth.

THE simple truth is that both Nancy and Ronnie are having their fun as they want to, not as Hollywood expects them to. Anyone who knows Ronald Reagan knows he has a mind of his own, and the girl he'll probably marry stacks up exactly the same way and always has—even though she may not look it.

In fact, Nancy Davis has been somewhat of a surprise from the minute she was born. In an all-Nordic family where everyone has been blond from the roots of

the family tree on up, she turned out black-haired, brown-eyed and with a Latin complexion. This baffled the relatives for years until research turned up the fact that back in the mists of time one great-great-great grandpa had swept a dusky Spanish girl right off her feet. More up-to-date, there was a mixed family deal of another kind to give Nancy Davis a two-toned personality. Her father, Dr. Loyal Davis, is an eminent brain surgeon and a serious man of science; but Nancy's mother was "Lucky" Luckett, a glamorous stage actress of her day.

Nancy's godmother was Alla Nazimova, who cut quite a siren figure in the Hollywood silent epic days. And Walter Houston was "Uncle Walter" to Nancy until the day he died. Her first look at Hollywood was on visits to his house when she was still wearing Mary Janes.

So, while Nancy trotted dutifully off to the Girl's Latin School, where the nice Chicago girls went, she also haunted her mom's dressing room, backstage at the theater where a lot of them wished they could go. Even then it was pretty plain which way the wind would blow. While the pit orchestra tuned up, Nancy would rush dramatically out behind the curtain and take sweeping bows before imaginary throngs and generally ham up the vacant stage until her frantic mama chased her away to get the show started. When she was "a fast 13" she broke out professionally as a junior miss on some Chicago soap opera radio shows, and still sentimentally cherishes her uncashed first $10 check.

All this time, as today, Miss Nancy Davis preserved the Alice in Wonderland look of tender innocence which still gives people such mistaken ideas.

At Smith College, a very genteel ladies' institute in Northampton, Massachusetts, Nancy fitted in perfectly, and eventually graduated. But what really kept her interested those four years was the Dramatic Club. Summers, she took flings at stock around New England, and one season up at Gloucester, Mass., she lodged with the rest of the cast in an ancient, rickety summer resort. The nice old ladies who rocked on the front porch and whispered about those terrible actors upstairs, watched Nancy's innocent face bob in and out. One evening, as she raced down the steps, one of them touched her arm.

"My dear," she breathed in sepulchral tones, "I only hope you won't let this ruin you for the rest of your life!"

That only made Nancy more resolved to dare a fate worse than death in New York. There she almost wore herself out dog-trotting up and down Broadway hunting a job. She knew lots of show people through her mother. "But to them, of course," Nancy remembers disgustedly, "I was still just 'little Nancy.'" She might be chasing up and down yet, although it's doubtful, if one day she hadn't tried the office of Michael Myerberg who was preparing *Lute Song* for Mary Martin. While she gave him her sales talk he stared at her black hair and wide, slightly Oriental features and finally muttered, "You look Chinese!" When she recovered her poise, Nancy found herself promised a job on Broadway that fall and then—as breaks often go—she got another for the summer on the road in *Ramshackle Inn*.

But it wasn't *Lute Song* or the two brief-lived Broadway shows that brought Nancy to Hollywood, it was a TV presentation of *Ramshackle Inn* which she played on New Year's Eve. The Berg-Allenberg talent agency caught her in that and arranged an MGM test in Hollywood the next week. Nancy arrived as green about studios as the Pullman seat that carried her.

For instance, Nancy was thrilled to pieces because she thought she'd certainly run into her screen idol, Bing Crosby, the first day. She didn't know Bing worked at Paramount instead of MGM. And at MGM they still have a running rib on the poor girl which started the first day she stepped on the lot. She was ushered then into the office of Jack Dawn, MGM's famous makeup expert. He gave her a long look and finally allowed, "No—I don't think there'll be any particular problem—except, of course, your eyes are way too big for pictures!"

Of course, Jack was kidding—they don't make eyes too big for pictures—but Nancy took it straight, and being an eager beaver at heart, she started doing something about it. Her idea was that if she drooped her eyelids religiously they'd shrink down to the right size. That's what she actually did until people began to wonder if she was all there. One day, visiting the set of a Gable picture to see how the big-leaguers did it, Nancy arrived droopy eyed and looking like a chicken with the pip. Merv LeRoy, the director, came up and asked anxiously, "What's the matter, kid—are you sick or something?"

"Why, no," explained Nancy. "You see my eyes are too big for pictures." Merv called Clark over for that one and when they had picked themselves up off the floor and stopped howling, they spread the news around. To this day when she starts a picture the crew gives her a ride about special lighting for those oversize eyes.

But outside of a few tenderfoot trials like that, Nancy has had no trouble whatever getting along in her work. Producer Bob Sisk wandered accidentally into the projection room where they were running off the test she made with Howard Keel, and snapped her up for her first job, *Shadow on the Wall*, without even an interview. Dore Schary picked her for his pet faith film, *The Next Voice You Hear*, and took her into Director Bill Wellman, suggesting a test. Bill took a look and said, "I don't need to make a test." Then Bill, who has small time for lady actresses, scared her half to death by growling, "I want to tell you something. I *hate* to direct women!" But Nancy's winning ways tamed even Wild Bill, before that was over.

Beyond the studio gates, however, Nancy's adventures in Horrible Hollywood were a little more harrowing, until she found Ronnie Reagan to look after her. Nancy went to her first Hollywood party in a taxi, all by herself—and took one home the same solitary way. She didn't know anybody to take her. And trying to find the right place to roost for a respectable bachelor girl was an even more dismal experience.

THE first place Nancy landed was a one room apartment in Beverly Hills where the walls were so thin she had to sleep with a pillow over her head to keep from sharing the intimate secrets of her neighbors. When she got out of there, it was only to move in next door to a middle-aged wolf who kept his door open and invited her in every time she walked past. At the next place she tried, her neighbor had a girl friend who had a husband, and every night there were poundings on the door, hoarse whispers of "Joe—Joe—wake up—it's John!" and hasty exits out windows. With visions of bullets flying right through those flimsy walls, Nancy packed her trunk again. In fact, she moved around so often that half the time she was paying rent on two places and her business manager, Myrt Blumk, finally complained, "Nancy, I've never had a client who made less money than you do—but you're the first one I've had who could afford two apartments!"

By now Nancy's snugly settled in a trim, modern studio flat, screened by tropical plants and high, opaque glass with a sunny, private patio of her own in back. Indoors she's surrounded by her own blond, modern furniture she's had shipped out from New York, her own books and family knick-knacks. Her bedroom's tinted lipstick red and gray, and soft greens and yellows make the living room with its big fireplace smart and attractive. This haven is on Sorority Row in Westwood, out by U.C.L.A. and Nancy's neighbors think she's just a rah-rah girl herself. In fact, when a cabbie let her out one day last fall he said, "Well, I guess you girls'll be pretty busy now. School starts this week."

Nancy has left her schoolgirl days well behind—she's 27—but she's still a bachelor girl as this is written. She hasn't been exactly lonesome, though, not since the night almost a year ago when her telephone rang and a voice said, "This is Ronald Reagan calling about the Screen Actors' Guild," of which he was president. Someone had put Nancy's name up as a young board member but there was a little confusion. There were two Nancy Davises around Hollywood, and Ronnie wanted to get the right Nancy, also some facts and figures.

Nancy liked this stranger's voice and apparently Ronnie liked hers, which is low and sexy, and reminds you of Jean Arthur's. So when he suggested they could talk better over a dinner Nancy said, "I'd love it."

"It was a blind date, all right," she confesses, "but it was a lot blinder for Ronnie than it was for me." After all, Nancy had seen Ronald Reagan in pictures; he'd never even glimpsed a still of her face.

From that night on they've been as "steady" a twosome as you'll find anywhere around Hollywood. Nancy knits argyle socks for Ronnie although she doesn't cook him any meals, being the kind of girl who isn't handy with much in the kitchen that isn't canned or frozen.

Since they add up so perfectly as the same kind of character—smart but gay, too —and since their close association has been going on for a long time as Hollywood views courtships, the screen colony cupids have been getting a little more than impatient lately. They've been jumping the gun to get them married.

JUST the other day a newspaper reporter back in Chicago called Dr. Davis' house, and got Nancy's father. Was it true, he asked, that Nancy Davis was getting married to Ronald Reagan on such and such a date as was reported?

"I'm quite sure," replied the doctor calmly, "that if my daughter is getting married to anyone I'd know about it."

The truth is that nobody is going to hustle Nancy Davis and Ronald Reagan into a serious step like marriage. Reason: on Ronnie's part there are the serious considerations of his children, Maureen and Michael, and what his marriage would mean to them. What Jane Wyman does about her life may have some bearing on his thoughts that way, too.

When anyone asks Nancy about wedding plans she still smiles sweetly, "No plans," and tries to change the subject. Nancy is a lady, remember, and in her code keeping quiet about affairs of the heart is simply a matter of good manners and taste.

But in her forthright fashion she isn't cagey or coy. "Sure I want to get married," she'll tell you, "and have children of my own—not just in pictures. I'm ready."

Meanwhile Nancy is leading a whispering campaign at MGM to "Get Nancy Davis out of Maternity Clothes" and every time she sees Dore Schary she says, "Good morning—when do I play a comedy?" Meanwhile, too, she is keeping as happy as a clam in her private life, whether she's beside Ronnie Reagan banging nails into one of his corral fences, or flying off to New York by herself, as she recently did, to catch the World Series and the new Broadway shows.

But if and when she does become Mrs. Ronald Reagan one thing seems pretty certain, contrary to some very wrong ideas about a very right gal. There will be few dull moments for anybody including herself, with Nancy Davis around. And—unless everyone who knows a sometimes baffling Irishman named Reagan is a mile off the track—that will suit Ronnie just fine.   THE END

Tallulah Bankhead, Gambler

Continued from page 160

since they served together in the Senate. She asked the General to take her to luncheon. And over the luncheon table she told him her story.

"Never in my life will I do anything any harder," she said. "You just don't go to old family friends and ask for money. I knew that. But I also knew it was my only chance. I simply had to risk it."

As a matter of actual fact it so happened that before Tallulah got to the very asking, to putting into so many words "Will you lend me one thousand dollars so I can take a chance on getting this part upon which I've set my heart," General Dupont began figuring on the back of a menu card. He figured and he figured. And finally he said:

"I like your spirit, Tallulah. Do you think fifteen hundred dollars would see you through?"

He didn't lecture or ask her how it happened that she had not saved any money of her own. He knew Tallulah, you see.

TALLULAH didn't tell him that all she had hoped for was one thousand dollars. It evidently never occurred to her to keep her indebtedness down. With her love of luxury I'm sure that the minute she knew she could have fifteen hundred dollars, fifteen hundred dollars didn't seem one copper too much. She would be sure she would have no trouble in paying it back. She has that sublime optimism you must possess to stake everything on a single chance. She felt she was certain to make good. And to her then, even though she was without any money at all, five hundred dollars was a trifling sum.

She sailed on the Aquitania. In no mean cabin. With all the beautiful clothes she had bought. With her hair, oh, so golden against her pale fair skin. With dreams in her blue eyes.

And when she got off the boat train in London it was to the Ritz she directed her taxi chauffeur. The Ritz!

Continued on page 180

I'm yours!

"He's so right for her," they all said—keeping their fingers crossed. And now, at last, Elizabeth Taylor has given her heart to the man of her choice.

BY CYNTHIA MILLER

■ She stood there in her bridal gown, a dream in white, her face radiant in its glow of happiness.

Elizabeth Taylor was about to be married.

Spencer Tracy walked her down the aisle. He was her father, and he was giving her away. As they reached the altar, and Spence moved away, director Vincente Minnelli called, "Cut."

The company broke—all but Elizabeth Taylor. She remained fixed, her eyes focused on infinity, her mind carried away by the play-acting. She seemed to be saying to herself: "So this is what it's like. This is what it's like to get married."

A woman walked up to her. "How do you feel, my dear?" she asked.

Liz turned her head. "I feel so wonderful," she said. "I could cry."

This marriage ceremony occurred on the set of *Father of the Bride* which Elizabeth has just finished with Spencer Tracy, Joan Bennett, and Don Taylor. But a real marriage ceremony starring Liz will take place on May 6.

The cast of characters, of course, will be slightly different. For one thing, Conrad Nicholson Hilton, Jr. is scheduled to play the groom.

Twenty-three-year-old Nicky is the son of Connie Hilton, the hotel magnate who owns the Waldorf-Astoria (New York), the Plaza (New York), the Manor (San Diego), the Caribe (Puerto Rico), the Palmer House (Chicago), the Mayfair (Washington, D. C.), the—but why go on? I'm sure you get the general idea: Nicky Hilton, who's been going with Liz since early last December, comes from a family that doesn't have to be too careful about turning the electricity off.

And the attractive Nicky's family believes in young marriages. Nicky's brother, Barron Hilton, is 15 months younger than Nicky and is already the father of two.

A tactful and well-bred young man, Nicky would say nothing about his honorable intentions toward Liz when I asked him prior to the announcement except that "we're going steady. I'm more than fond of her, and anything connected with weddings, engagements, and formal announcements will have to come from *her* parents.

"I see that my father, when he was in New York, said that Liz and I were scheduled to be married on May 6th—but I can assure you that I'm a whole lot closer to Liz than my father is.

"I don't know. Maybe he has some inside information. Maybe Liz has been holding out on me. But if you don't *Continued on page 180*

A bit of perfume is the last touch as Liz prepares for a date with fiancé Nicky Hilton—who (*right*) brings his lady orchids.

Continued on page 180

I'm yours!

Continued from page 178 mind, I'd rather not say anything at all about a wedding. All I want to say is that Liz and I are still going steady. Any further announcement, Liz's mother will have to make."

This reluctance of Nicky's to discuss his relationship with Liz seemed understandable, since Liz has had a way of changing her beaux with alacrity.

Of course you remember how she supposedly was divinely in love with Glenn Davis. It turned out that she wasn't divinely in love with Glenn Davis at all. She was only 15 at the time and mildly infatuated with Glenn's reputation and record as an athlete.

And then she supposedly was enraptured with Bill Pawley, Jr. In this case, it was Bill who called it quits. He could see the handwriting on the wall. He realized after six months of "going" with Liz that she was never of a mind to renounce her acting career and settle in Florida. He knew which way the wind was blowing, and he resigned from Liz's heart before he was fired.

Then, who should advance to the fore of her love life but Vic Damone, the Bay Ridge lover from Brooklyn.

Vic was booked into the Mocambo in Hollywood. Liz went around to see him, well-chaperoned; and this is how those unfair stories of her being a night-club habitue originated.

Liz was so shaken up about "what those nasty columnists are doing to my reputation" that she called Vic when he was singing at the Flamingo in Las Vegas and asked him what to do.

the truth will out . . .

Vic advised Liz to write Walter Winchell the truth—whereupon she sat down and wrote Mr. Winchell that she had only been to Mocambo three times: once as Jane Powell's guest, once with her brother Howard and his girl, Mara Regan, and once just long enough to catch Vic's act and then go home.

Winchell set the public straight, and Elizabeth Taylor was acquitted in the eyes of her movie fans.

It was because of the previous men in her life, her extreme sensitivity, and her mother's hypersensitivity that people understandably refrained from publicly discussing Liz and Nicky.

An intimate friend of hers, for example, recently said to me, "I think Liz is head over heels in love with Nicky Hilton, and I'm sure she'll marry him. Only for Pete's sake, don't quote me."

A colleague of Liz's felt much the same way: "While we were shooting *Father of the Bride*," he told me, "Nicky Hilton used to come on the set often. I've been in love myself, you know, and if the love light wasn't burning in the eyes of those two kids, then all my experience has been for nothing."

"Look," said a young girl who knows both Nicky and Liz and has double-dated with them. "I think they're going to get married and get married quickly.

"Nicky has had all the education he needs. He went to New Mexico Military Institute in Roswell, to De Paul University in Chicago and to Loyola in Los Angeles. He studied business administration, and he's in the process of making some hotel deals just like his father.

"As for Liz—well, she's been in the limelight with different fellows for the past three years. A lot of writers have called her a siren and a femme fatale and all that sort of silly stuff. The truth is that she's just a normal, healthy American girl just like me. She likes to go out with boys, and so do I, only she

has to be very, very careful. That's the price of stardom, of being famous. I can go out with any guy I want. Not Liz. She needs a young man, handsome, good family, unblemished reputation.

"She's got to stay out of nightclubs, dance halls, jam-joints. She might as well be running for President."

A day after Nicky Hilton had told me, "any further announcement, Liz's mother will have to make"—Liz's mother made one.

She said: "Oh, Liz and I planned to keep it secret. We wanted to make the announcement at a surprise party—but you know how those reporters are. Mr. Hilton spoke to them in New York and asked them to keep the news back for a few weeks, but they released it. So I guess we might as well come out with it now. Yes, Elizabeth and Nicky are definitely going to be married on May 6th. It will be a very large church wedding with all the trimmings."

The engagement tea which Liz gave after her mother's announcement was attended by Jane Powell; Marilyn Hilton, her future sister-in-law; Mara Regan, her brother's girl; Ann Westmore, daughter of make-up man Wally Westmore; Betty Sullivan; Barbara Thompson, and about a dozen others.

Pete Freeman, the son of Y. Frank Freeman, Paramount Theaters executive and a partner in the Hilton Hotel Chain, is the one who brought them together.

"It happened over at Paramount," Nicky says. "I was on the set of *A Place in the Sun*, the picture Liz was shooting with Monty Clift, and Pete introduced me to her. And I sure was impressed with her. We asked her to have lunch with us and then the four of us—Pete's wife was along—went to Lucy's across the street. Then, not long after, I asked her for a date, well, we simply fell in love."

Nicky Hilton—he was called Nicky by his mother because his middle name is Nicholson and there had to be some way of differentiating him by call from his father—is as good-looking, charming, and prosperous as any young man Liz ever dated. He seems very right for her.

As one of Liz's friends put it, "After all, Nicky lives in Bel Air. He won't insist that she move away or give up her career. Liz can have a real full life —a husband, a home, a family, two or three Cadillacs, all the clothes she wants, *and* stardom. What more can a girl ask?"

And what more could a boy ask for than Elizabeth Taylor? THE END

MODERN SCREEN

BELMONT

LISA RAVISH IN "THIS LIFE TOGETHER" EDGAR BOOGLE | TONI LURCH

"Two, Please!"

Tallulah Bankhead Gambler

Continued from page 177

She had one thousand dollars left. That is a lot of money, if you don't stop at the Ritz, if you don't invite everybody you meet to drop in for cocktails.

The next morning Tallulah presented herself at the agent's office. He, of course, was flabbergasted to see her. He asked, hopelessly, if she had not received his cable. And she shook her head.

"I must have missed it," she said. "It must have come when I was down in Washington saying good-by. What a pity!" Not until later did she tell him the truth.

Well, the agent promised to arrange for Tallulah to meet Sir Gerald Du-Maurier, the actor-manager directing the new play. It seemed the girl who had the part originally considered for Tallulah couldn't lose an accent she had been using and, therefore, wasn't making good.

While Tallulah waited for this meeting with Sir Gerald, without the least notion how things would turn out, she continued to live at the Ritz and to invite everybody for luncheon or dinner and to entertain large groups at the cocktail hour.

It really was through DuMaurier's daughter, Angela, that Tallulah got the part. Angela met Tallulah at a dinner party, thought her pretty and urged her father to give her a trial.

MAKING good, Tallulah was engaged at thirty pounds a week, about one hundred and fifty dollars. Not nearly enough for her to live on. But the other girl had a contract for the play's run and her salary had to be paid even though she never appeared.

"However," Tallulah said, "I decided when I was a success I could ask for more money and get it." Not *if* she was a success, you'll notice, but *when* she was a success.

And as they always have and as they probably always will, things worked out just as Tallulah anticipated. She was an immediate success. The English theatre-goers loved her husky voice, her faint southern inflexions, her typical American ways. However, don't make the mistake of thinking Tallulah became the rage as a personality. She was that, provocative and colorful, but she also merited the great praise she received for her splendid acting.

She was raised to fifty pounds, about two hundred and fifty dollars. Not enough to permit her living on at the Ritz. So she found other quarters and made up for this economical move by planning how she would live later on when she became a great and famous star. And later on there was, as we already know, the charming house in Mayfair, luxurious holidays in southern France, at Cannes, parties, servants, a beautiful car and all the rest of it.

"With a third of my income taken from me," said Tallulah, "I was robbed of any incentive to save. Now, working in the talkies, it will be different. I hope to create a trust fund. But the little

Continued on page 213

HEDDA & LOUELLA

ollywood is quite famous for creating monsters: *Frankenstein* (1931), *Dracula* (1931), and *The Wolfman* (1941), to name some of the biggest. However, few could instill the terror that Hedda Hopper and Louella Parsons created with their poison-dipped pens.

Hedda and Louella were the undisputed queens of the gossip columnists. They were vain, vindictive, and influential in manipulating the public's opinion of the stars. In addition to their nationally syndicated newspaper columns, they both wrote for *Modern Screen*.

In the 1980's, in a Hollywood where the sexual goings-on, and drug and alcohol consumption, are out in the open, it is hard to imagine how a bit of innocent gossip could really harm anyone. But, in the 1930's, 1940's, and 1950's news of adultery, homosexuality, or drug dependence could ruin lives and careers in an instant.

Said Lana Turner later: "Let's face it. Hedda Hopper and Louella Parsons dominated Hollywood. They took bribes and gifts and played favorites, and God help you if they ever got mad at you!"

Hedda Hopper began her Hollywood career as an actress. In her eighty-one years she appeared in over eighty movies. She usually played snooty society women, as she did in *Alice Adams* (1935), *Topper* (1937), and *Midnight* (1940). After she became famous as a journalist, she often played herself in films, including *Sunset Boulevard* (1950). Hedda's first appearance in the pages of *Modern Screen* was

> "Oh hello, girls. My, but you look lovely. Got any 'dirt' for the column?"
> —Hedda Hopper, to Rosalind Russell, Norma Shearer, and Joan Fontaine, in *The Women* (MGM, 1939)

in the June 1939 issue, as a model for a fashion page entitled "Youth vs. Sophistication" (page 183).

Surprisingly, Hedda and Louella began as friends, with Hedda actually giving Louella exclusives from the movie sets she was working on. Louella's daily column was based at the *Los Angeles Examiner,* and it was syndicated to all of the newspapers in the vast Hearst chain. Hedda quickly decided that if "Lolly" could be so successful at printing her items, why not give it a go herself? After trying her hand at a successful Hollywood newsletter, in 1937 Hedda began penning her own syndicated column based at the *Los Angeles Times*. When the studios decided to pit the two of them against each other the cat fight was officially on.

Louella's "The Truth About My Feuds," from *Modern Screen*'s May 1951 issue (page 184), shows off grudge-carrying Parsons at her bitchiest. In the article, she gets a few jabs into Orson Welles for parodying her boss, William Randolph Hearst, in *Citizen Kane* (1941). Also, in this article you'll find that she's still complaining about being scooped by Katherine Albert's 1933 *Modern Screen* article "The Separation of Joan and Doug" (page 162). Her regular column for *Modern Screen* was entitled "Louella Parsons' Good News," and a sample of it from the October 1944 issue is on page 187. "My Predictions for 1950," by Hedda Hopper, from the February 1950 issue of *Modern Screen* (page 188), are pretty much right "on target." She correctly forecasted big things for young hopefuls Janet Leigh, Montgomery Clift, and Shelley Winters. She also proved accurate in predicting a wedding for young Liz Taylor.

YOUTH vs. SOPHISTICATION

KAREN
MORLEY

HEDDA
HOPPER

On our left, Lovely Youth—
Karen Morley, who made her
screen début in "Inspiration."
She wears a misty white gown
of mousseline de soie, with
airy petals crossing the hipline
and forming the flounce. At
the right, Triumphant Sophistication—Hedda Hopper—in an
Empress Josephine gown of
silver bullion on black tulle.

There are
some people I've never
forgiven, and others
who've become
my good friends after
our battles royal.
Now I want to
set the long record
straight.

GINGER ROGERS

the truth about my feuds

by Louella Parsons

ORSON WELLES

JAMES MASON

GENE TIERNEY

CORINNE CALVET

REX HARRISON

JOAN CRAWFORD

■ My friend "Chuck" Saxon,
Ye Ed of MODERN SCREEN, has asked me
to let my short hair down and give
with the truth about my feuds—real and
otherwise—with certain Hollywood characters.

It's an assignment I suppose I should
coyly sidestep and say, "Feuds, suh? Really,
I don't know *what* you mean."

But if I am anything, I'm a
truthful woman, let the chips fall
where they may—so here goes:

In my 25 years *plus* in this town, I have had
some hair curling battles that were dillys.

I've yelled and shouted over telephones telling
off stars, producers, directors and press
agents alike. *But,* in most cases, after
the smoke has died down a few days later, I
have forgotten the row. It just ain't true
that my memory is more relentless
than that of an elephant and that I never
forget! I not only forget—but forgive,
except in a few isolated cases.

In other words, there are what I
consider my minor "skirmishes"
as against four or five really major battles
which have flourished for years.

Conspicuous headliners in the latter
group are—Orson Welles and Rex
Harrison! Let's take on sexy Rexy first:

When Lilli Palmer and Harrison first
came to Hollywood, I, along with many of the
film colony, went all out to welcome the
talented British actor. Rex can be so
charming with the ladies and I confess I
found myself as gullible as the rest.

I was in Europe when Carole
Landis committed *Continued on page 186*

the truth about my feuds

Continued from page 185 suicide. That Rex had been her good friend we all knew. I had talked with Carole shortly before I left for Europe, and she had told me of her great friendship for Harrison. I had known Carole a long time and was very fond of her.

I cabled my syndicate stories about Carole, but was always very careful not to mention Rex in any unpleasant way. He was also helped through this difficult time by Darryl Zanuck's entire 20th Century-Fox publicity department.

So what does Mr. Harrison do? First, he goes to Canada and makes a speech in which he excoriates me and all other Hollywood columnists. The very people who had protected him, he called "the most evil influence" in Hollywood.

And this did not end Mr. Harrison's tirade. Oh, no—he wasn't content to let it die. Several years later, he wrote a series of articles for a London magazine in which he harpooned Hollywood with silly assertions like "butlers there arrive for work in Cadillacs." He also stated that he could never get five minutes alone with head man Darryl Zanuck, and was forced to make pictures he didn't like. These may not be his exact words—but it's the gist of it—this and unflattering things about Hollywood and its people.

But the *most* untruthful story he recounted was his distorted version of an incident long since forgotten between Gene Tierney and myself. As Harrison told it, we were all guests at a dinner party and our host, kindly Gary Cooper, asked Gene to leave his home because she had annoyed me!

Rex said it made him sick to his stomach, all the bowing and scraping and "fear" of me at the Coopers. No, he didn't actually mention names, but he didn't need to.

What actually happened was this: I was in truth annoyed with Gene for good reason. I thought she had done a very unethical thing (unethical in newspaper circles) and I'm a girl who speaks her mind about such matters. As we met face to face, I promptly told her off!

My quarrel with glamorous Gene was based on a "news" story. I had had the inside tip that although she and Oleg Cassini had separated, and she had obtained her interlocutory divorce decree, they had secretly reconciled and were expecting a baby. That's a good dramatic story with a lot of reader appeal, and as I *knew* it was all true, I could have broadcast and printed the news without calling Gene. But, as always, I checked my facts to make doubly sure.

I called Gene and told her what I knew. She very simply said, "It's all true." I thanked her, and asked her to keep it exclusive for me. It's an unwritten law in the newspaper game that "the story" belongs to the fellow who gets it.

That night, at Rocky and Gary Cooper's dinner dance, I walked over to the table where Gene was sitting and told her how glad I was that she and Oleg had refound their happiness; and I also thanked her for being so honest with me.

Gene looked at me with those great big beautiful eyes and said, "Oh, as soon as *you* telephoned and I knew you had the story, I gave it to another reporter on a rival syndicate. I can't afford to antagonize anyone, you know."

Oh, *no*! Well, she had antagonized *me*—and how! I swear, for a moment, I saw red. I was so mad I couldn't see straight,

and la Tierney knew exactly how blazing mad I was. When I'm mad (particularly when I feel I'm justified) I do not simmer or boil. I explode!

I might add that Gene has a temper almost as good as mine. If I had started the fracas, Miss Tierney most certainly finished it when we met in the hallway as we were departing. She told me off, doing as thorough a job as I had done earlier. But, as far as Gary's asking her to leave —that's applesauce!

It was a beautiful battle which Gene and I have both forgotten long since. Fortunately for Gene (and me) the reporter she had tipped to my story was too inexperienced to telephone the news to her paper immediately, and after a short dash to my telephone, the "scoop" was all mine after all.

All was well that ended well, and as far as Miss T. and Miss P. were concerned the incident was closed. But not to Rex Harrison who insinuated that I had *demanded* that Gene be ordered to leave the party; a request (he said) the host was "too spineless" to ignore. After that, Harrison piously concluded, he did not want ever to attend any parties where columnists were present. So with that, he took on the *entire* Hollywood press!

And that's that for Rex Harrison and Gene Tierney.

The amusing thing about my "feud" with James Mason is that we never exchanged a harsh word when we formerly met at Hollywood parties.

We don't meet any more. Mr. Mason fixed that. When one of my closest friends, Joan Bennett, gave a farewell dinner party for Mason and his wife just before they left for England last fall, he requested that my name be omitted from the guest list.

Joan, thoroughly surprised, asked, "Why?"

Mason said it was because of uncomplimentary things I had printed about him.

I have also printed some very nice things about him—but I suppose that doesn't count. I had taken him and Pamela to a party in New York, and had supper with them at the Stork. In fact, I had always admired him as an actor in English pictures, and would probably have continued to do so until Mason (who had never been to Hollywood) chose to write an article about Hollywood, blasting my home town in a national magazine.

I thought it was utterly ridiculous for a man who had never set foot inside the Los Angeles city limits to make such an attack—and I said so. I still think so, even though Mr. Mason and his wife Pamela, and their assorted cats have since settled here and are crazy about the life.

My point is, why didn't he find out about us before he made harmful attacks on the world capital of the movies?

But that's yesterday's squabble. So let's forget it.

I have saved Orson Welles for the last of my "major" dislikes because he is the one with whom I never expect to smoke the pipe of peace. On one horrible occasion since the beginning of my vendetta, I was forced to sit next to Welles at a dinner party given by Evelyn Walsh McLean when she was living in Beverly Hills.

Orson was then married to Rita Hayworth; and Rita's agonized look when she saw what the hostess had done in the seating arrangements would have moved a heart of stone!

I adore Rita and I couldn't bear that stricken look on her face. So Welles and I sat side by side, munching our food and

exchanging the necessary amenities during that entire embarrassing meal. Oh, well—if it wasn't so peppy socially, I suppose it aided digestion.

My anger at Welles stems from a deliberate lie he told me. If there's one thing I hate, it's for a person to be dishonest with me.

Many years back, I had heard that Welles was making a picture about someone I love very much. I telephoned to ask him if this were true. He said (and I shall remember his words always), "It couldn't be farther from the truth. It has nothing to do with that person, and it's about an entirely different character."

Then he called three other well known film critics and showed them the picture, which was so shocking to one of them, a friend of mine, that he called and said, "Do you know what this picture is?"

I demanded to see the film. Flanked by two lawyers, I went to the studio to find out if my worst suspicions were true.

What I had to say to Orson Welles after I saw that picture was plenty—a barrage directed straight from my heart. I could not have been more shocked or unhappy. Welles tried to brazen it out by sending flowers and writing me notes—which were promptly sent back.

And from that day to this I have never forgiven him. I can take darts directed at me. I have felt the sting of many of them. But I cannot bear to see anyone I love hurt.

And so—there are the "major" feuds in my life. As for the lesser ones—well, many of them have been exaggerated out of all proportion, and some of them are completely untrue.

For instance, one of the most thoroughly publicized feuds never happened! I was supposed to be carrying an undying "mad" on Joan Crawford (who is one of my closest friends) because at the time the story of her divorce from Douglas Fairbanks Jr. broke, Joan had given it to a close friend for a magazine article, instead of to me for my newspaper syndicate.

What really happened was: Joan *had* promised the story of the break up of her marriage to Doug to Katherine Albert, her close friend, for a magazine article. (Katherine is the mother of Joan Evans who was named for Crawford.) I did not know this. But I had heard that the young Fairbanks were having trouble. I didn't believe it—but still I did not want to ignore the scoop.

So I called Joan and told her I was going to do a sympathetic story telling how the rumors about her and Doug were not true and that they were still very happy.

"Please don't do that," pleaded Joan. "Please don't print anything about how *happy* we are."

That was enough for Parsons. I got on my horse and went directly to Joan's house.

She admitted to me the truth—that she and Douglas were parting. Then, in a panic, she called the MGM studio to tell them what she had done. Where was Parsons? In another room, my friends, calling the "beat" in to my newspaper. We beat the world by two editions, and Katherine Albert's magazine yarn by several weeks.

How the story ever got around that I would never "forgive" Joan I shall never know. If ever there was a "feud" which did not exist, it is my "supposed" fracas with Miss Crawford, whom I happen to like very much.

Equally silly is the old one about Ginger Rogers and me. Oh, brother, were

Ginger and I supposed to hate each other! We were said to be bitter enemies. There was so much printed about us, I almost began to believe there was some truth to it. But I could never get anyone to explain what Ginger and I were supposed to be hassling about. This nonsensical state of affairs went on for several very tedious years.

Finally, Ginger and I sat down and decided we were going to end this business once and for all. The funny part is—we had absolutely nothing to get off our chests!

So we had a good laugh about it, ending with my inviting Ginger to appear on my radio show. And later I did an interview with her in the paper, officially burying our non-existent hatchet.

THERE was more body to the misunderstanding that lasted a year or so between Corinne Calvet, the little French actress, and her "worst enemy"—as she looked on me. When Corinne was brought to this country by Paramount, she was given a big chance for which many girls would have slaved.

But instead of trying to learn English and improve herself, the pretty mademoiselle neglected her studies and dramatic lessons and was the belle of the nightclub circuit.

When Paramount let her go (highly impatient with her) I thought she was the most foolish girl in the world, and said so in my column. What a waste for a girl to throw away such a golden opportunity.

But being ignored by the studios and falling really in love were two developments which completely changed Corinne. John Bromfield, himself a fine actor, did much to bring about this change, for Corinne is madly in love with her handsome husband.

After she married him and got another movie chance with Hal Wallis, she became "Miss Diligence" herself. She also sent word that she would like to meet me.

I couldn't help being touched—she seemed so childlike when she said, "I am glad you scolded me. I deserved it. But now I am different and I wish we could be friends."

"Then it isn't true." I laughed, "that you once said you'd like to put poison in my soup?"

"Ohhhhhh," she squealed, embarrassed. "Oh, no, that is not true *anymore!*"

Corinne was a darling when she appeared on my radio show and she made many friends—including me!

In closing, I want to say one thing about these Hollywood feuds—mine, or any others. In this town, as has often been pointed out, every little action is magnified. A simple little misunderstanding or a few words spoken in good old-fashioned temper are made to sound like a battle royal.

As I grow older, I realize you only hurt yourself by holding grudges and enmity against others.

Hollywood has so many vicious attacks from the outside, I think all of us in the industry should stick together as much as possible, and try to understand the other fellow's "side" of any problem.

This I shall try to do—until somebody does me "dirt" again!

THE END

Louella Parsons' GOOD NEWS

When author Parsons visited Sinatra and Kelly on "Anchors Aweigh" set, they painted canvas chair, "Pen" for her. Tunesmiths Silvers and Van Husen wrote ballad "Nancy With the Laughing Face" for Nancy Sinatra's fourth birthday. Frank'll introduce it, and all royalties will go into annuity fund for her college tuition!

• • •

On the set of "Anchors Aweigh," Frank Sinatra calls Gene Kelly "The Feet." Gene calls Frankie "The Voice." And they both call Kathryn Grayson "The Body."

I was out watching The Feet, The Voice and The Body emote the day Frankie's four-year-old daughter Nancy, was paying her Pa a visit.

She sat like a little owl on the sidelines watching her old man and Gene run through a dance number. "What do you think of your father's singing?" I asked Nancy.

Without a word she went into a dead swoon!

After she had straightened herself again I said, "And now—what do you think of his dancing?"

With an equally dead pan Miss Nancy grasped the end of her nose between two small fingers, clothes-pin fashion, and held it a long time. There was no added comment.

RUTH ROMAN. Playing it smart, this ex-carnival girl took small parts in order to learn. Now she'll get roles planned for Bette Davis.

PAUL DOUGLAS. Plain-faced, 45-year-old Paul's warmth and charm have put him sol: ly in the glamor-boy class.

JANET LEIGH. A natural-born actress, Janet worked hard and kept her head after her Cinderella break. MGM has big plans for her.

MARIO LANZA. This sweet-natured boy from across the tracks sang his way to singing stardom with one picture.

KIRK DOUGLAS. Dynamic, virile and canny, Kirk followed up his sensational success in *Champion* with a million-dollar contract at Warners. Excellent roles will keep him rising.

MY PREDICTIONS

From her intimate knowledge of the Hollywood scene, Hedda Hopper ventures prophecies of things to come. What new stars will emerge in the next twelve months . . . which romances will flourish and which will fail?

■ Anybody got a 1950-model crystal ball handy? Or a few magic tea-leaves? Anybody around who's the seventh son of a seventh son? I could use you right now—and a transfusion of gypsy blood, too. Because the editors of MODERN SCREEN have just pitched this puzzler at me:

"How about telling what's going to happen in Hollywood during the next year, Hedda? How about your own private star-predictions for 1950?"

Me, predict the unpredictables? Prophesize filmland's Fantasia for a full year ahead? What do they think I am—crazy?

SUSAN HAYWARD. Her great triumph in *My Foolish Heart* was final proof of her top-drawer talent and appeal.

MONTGOMERY CLIFT. Matinee-idol allure and shrewd script-selection are raising him sky-high, but his performances must measure up.

BARBARA HALE. Friendly, sincere and wholesome, she seems set to succeed Myrna Loy as the perfect screen wife.

FARLEY GRANGER. He has the deep emotional insight of the great stars, has never muffed a part, gets one of 1950's strongest roles.

SHELLEY WINTERS. Colorful Shelley combines a socko personality with dramatic talent, which she's working eagerly to develop. Only her temperamental streak can jinx her now.

FOR 1950 *by hedda hopper*

They do. "Anyway," they say, "we dare you."

Well, could be they're right about my state of mind. Sometimes on my dizzy beat I feel ripe and ready for a strait-jacket. Also, I haven't taken a dare since I jumped off the chicken shed back in Altoona, Pennsylvania, with pretty sad results. That's sort of the way I feel now—set for a bump but willing to try. So out goes my neck—where it's often been before—and on goes my swami hat to peer into the future and up at the stars.

Let's see—which Hollywood Forty-Niners will strike 1950's bonanzas of fame, fortune and popularity at this momentous mid-

century mark? The prize nuggets are already uncovered and shining bright. They line up for me like this—with ladies, naturally, first:

Susan Hayward—Barbara Hale—Ruth Roman—Shelley Winters —Janet Leigh.

And the men: Kirk Douglas—Farley Granger—Montgomery Clift—Paul Douglas—Mario Lanza.

New? you ask. What's new about those? Most of those Hollywood hot-shots are already up in lights. Well, they're my New Year's prize babies just the same, because *Continued on page 190*

189

they've all got new deals, new prospects, new pictures, new promise. It's been slow going for some of them and fast for others. But right now they all stand at the doorway of their rich rewards. They're fit and ready for 1950.

Let's see why.

Personally, I'm mighty pleased to pick a redhead from Brooklyn to lead the grand promenade. I've watched Susan Hayward for a good many seasons now, and always I've thought, "If that girl ever gets the right part—watch her go!" All the time Susan was ripe as a pink-skinned peach for her big break—and now she has it. Her sad-sweet triumph in *My Foolish Heart* will, I predict, set her off toward a top-notch starring career at long last and someday an Academy Award—which she just missed once before, in *Smashup*. I'm not the only one who's betting on Susan, either. Darryl Zanuck—and they don't come cannier—has just shelled out an even $200,000 for the privilege of hiring her for seven long years, special scripts are in the works for Susan and her prospects couldn't be rosier.

Barbara Hale, after *Jolson Sings Again*, is my candidate to succeed Myrna Loy as the screen's perfect wife. In person, too, Barbara's the perfect wife—sweet and wholesome as they make 'em, warm, friendly, sincere. Those are qualities Hollywood has never lost on and they'll not lose a nickel on Barbara Hale from now on out. She's worth a million dollars in the bank.

stars are made . . .

Ruth Roman hit Hollywood with exactly $100 to her name, and not a friend in town. She lived in a tiny hotel over a drug store while she set out bravely to bat down the studio gates. Suddenly she showed up as the sleeper gal in *The Window* and came through with a solid smash in *Champion*.

Could it all be a flash for Ruth, and will that flash blind her eyes? Listen—Ruth grabbed at a small part in *Beyond the Forest* when her agent and all her friends told her it was too dinky. "Think what I can learn, acting with Bette Davis," came back Ruth. Next, she played a straight girl to Milton Berle in *Always Leave Them Laughing*, again not for a splash but because "I think the experience of working with Milton might be darn good for me." Then Ruth mixed her shots to play a dipsomaniac in *Rock Bottom*. What will the ex-carnival kid do next? It looks as if she'll be Gary Cooper's leading lady, no less, in *Bright Leaf*, and she'll be getting all the stories Warners had planned for Bette Davis, before Bette walked out. Ruth is on a ride to a star's throne where not even a bulldog will be able to shake her loose.

Shelley Winters is—let's face it—a screwball. But a talented, bouncy, cute and sassy one. And Hollywood has always had room for a girl like that, when she could act, since before the days of Clara Bow. Shelley caught on like the one-girl bonfire she is, when she played the sexy waitress with Ronald Colman in *A Double Life*. Since then, Shelley has scored bull's-eyes in *Larceny*, *The Great Gatsby* and *A Place in the Sun*.

Shelley's eager as a beaver to make a name for herself, dying to learn her job and learn it right. She's a member of Charles Laughton's Shakespeare study group, which means that every night, including Saturday nights, she works hard to gain real acting ability, because Charles doesn't fool with them a minute unless they do. Has it paid off? Well, George Stevens, who can direct any day for my money, picked Shelley for the tragic little factory girl in *A Place in the Sun* (the re-make of *An American Tragedy*), a part with twice the guts and opportunity of the role drawn by everybody's pet and bet, Elizabeth Taylor. I'll predict that Shelley will get right to the top—if she'll watch her step, which is inclined to be high, wide and handsome. Anyway, she's on my first team for 1950.

Now, what about Janet Leigh? The girl Van Johnson named and started off in *Romance of Rosy Ridge* has made more pictures this past year than any other young star in Hollywood—and every one with prize leading men, including Robert Mitchum, Glenn Ford, Van Heflin and Peter Lawford. I happen to know that Louis B. Mayer puts her right up with Elizabeth Taylor as his biggest bet for 1950. She's made the best of her opportunities, worked hard, kept her head. 1950's her great year for sure, with *Holiday Affair* following up *The Red Danube* and *That Forsyte Woman*, and *Jet Pilot*—with John Wayne—all set to send her zooming.

You can't overlook Elizabeth Taylor, of course—and *I'm* certainly not, with the whole world looking her lovely way. At 18, which she'll be in February, Elizabeth can never be more beautiful. Next spring she'll do *Quo Vadis*, in Rome, MGM's biggest picture from all standpoints since *Ben Hur*, filmed back in 1924. I, for one, can't wait to see Elizabeth as *Lygia* strapped to a bull's back and fought for by Roman gladiators.

There are others who can come through this year to make big names for themselves. I think Ava Gardner will make the really stand-out star grade with James Mason in *East Side, West Side*. You may hate her in that slutty part but if she clicks, Ava's in—and *Carriage Entrance* with Bob Mitchum can keep her there.

Virginia Mayo, whom Jimmy Cagney uncovered as a real actress in *White Heat*, shows signs of making a serious bid for stardom at Warners. And don't overlook teen-age Joan Evans, either, who came through beautifully in her first test, *Roseanna McCoy*. Joan is Sam Goldwyn's pet and Sam can pick 'em—and build 'em. *Our Very Own*, her latest, and *Edge of Doom* are Joan's big-time career insurance for 1950. I'll also place side bets on Ann Blyth, Audrey Totter and Betty Garrett.

Now, what about the men in your Hollywood life for 1950? The five I'm picking are loaded and couldn't miss if you aimed them in the dark. First on that list, of course, is Kirk Douglas.

Today, the movie world is absolutely Kirk's oyster. He has *Champion* behind him, the more sensitive *Young Man With a Horn* ready to tear at your heart and *The Glass Menagerie* shooting as I write. He has a million-dollar contract at Warners—which gives him the right to make other films for any other studio he chooses. Nothing can stop that guy. He's still calling his shots as cannily as he ever did. He picked a comparatively small job in *The Glass Menagerie*, when he could have had the biggest. Why? "Gives me a chance at a comedy character," he said—right after he'd played a brooding, complexed trumpeter in *Young Man With A Horn*. And *that* after *Champion*, which was all muscle and action.

Kirk hasn't a pebble in his path to the all-time Hollywood greatness I predict he'll reach in 1950. The only puff in his sky is a mixed-up marriage, and in 1950 he just might straighten that out, too.

all hits, no errors . . .

But who's next—Montgomery Clift? Not for my money. Before Marvelous Monty hits the top rung he'll have to climb past Farley Granger. So far, Farley hasn't given a bad performance, hasn't missed in one single flicker of film. I can't say that about Montgomery. He was swell in *Red River* and *The Search*. But he missed in *The Heiress*, especially in the scene that should have wrapped up his part in the picture—the important one with Olivia de Havilland's tough old pa, Ralph Richardson. Monty played that wrong and in so doing lost what might have been a decisive star in his crown. (Incidentally, right here let me predict that Olivia will cop an Oscar for her performance.)

I know Monty's shrewd about his scripts and I know he'll be a big rave with millions of girls everywhere. I'm not running him down as an actor, either, because he's good: I think he's a great star bet for 1950. But I think Farley Granger is better.

Farley's deeper and more sensitive and he's landed a role that could make 1950 an Academy Award year for him, even at his age. In *Edge of Doom* he'll play a man who accidentally kills a priest and then wrestles with his own soul. Farley will have Mark Robson, who directed both *Champion* and *My Foolish Heart*, to guide him. I'm betting on Farley to have the world at his feet when it's over.

Now, you can't exactly call Paul Douglas a boy—he's splitting his forties right now—but just a few years aren't enough to keep him off my glamor boy list for 1950. A lot of the younger charm lads could take a lesson from Paul—and borrow some of his youthful pep, good humor and virility. Ever since *A Letter to Three Wives*, Paul has romped away with female hearts from six to 60. Everybody loved him in that whacky *Everybody Does It*, he's got *Two Corridors East* coming up and Darryl Zanuck, a fervent Douglas fan, is going to throw his best scripts Paul's way. Why? Paul isn't good looking—in fact, he's a big, dog-faced Joe. He's got a voice like a buzz saw and manners you could call uncouth if you wanted to. He's a scamp for sure. When I was in New York last, Paul was also present, and in happy hot water as usual. He'd asked two girls to meet him there—one from Europe and one from Hollywood—and when they both showed up, Doug was having one heck of a time keeping them apart! Behind the brass,

MODERN SCREEN

"Get a grip on yourself, Mac, and kiss the dame!"

though, Paul's definitely a sterling actor.

But Mario Lanza is pure gold through and through, which makes it a thrill for me to include that wonderful Italian boy from across the tracks who made America's unbounded dream come true. Mario studied under Caruso's old voice coach—and he showed it in his first movie, *That Midnight Kiss*. I predict Mario will be Hollywood's new Nelson Eddy in 1950. *Kiss of Fire*, his next, looks too much like his first one—too frail a story for his golden voice. But when MGM digs deeper, as it will, and comes up with a real plot to mount Mario's voice, then watch for something which I, for one, have sadly missed—another golden age of song on the screen.

But I don't want to miss a mighty strong second string of fast-stepping young stars who'll sprint to glory in the year to come. Arthur Kennedy, for instance, whom Kirk Douglas calls "the best young actor of them all"—including himself. Richard Basehart, whose contract was worth $75,-000 to Darryl Zanuck the other day. Mel Ferrer, whose performance in *Lost Boundaries* was superfine. David Brian who's first-rate in another MGM bid for the Academy Award, *Intruder in the Dust*. Since Joan Crawford discovered David in *Flamingo Road*, every star in town has been dying to get him—but there's just not enough Brian to go around. And keep your eye on John Derek, Richard Conte and Scott Brady—they've all got big steps ahead and the stride to make them. One really hot picture and they'll be off.

Now, let's turn from careers to Cupid and see what the outlook is for the little guy in the months ahead. What romances look altar-bound and what couples will tell their troubles to the judge? Well, my crystal ball gets a little cloudy here.

To start off, however, I can say that Bette Davis and Bill Sherry look a very good bet to stay together after their reconciliation. Bette's trouble is that she has always taken her career too seriously. When she's in a professional stew she takes it out at home. When she comes to her senses, she's sorry. But Bette's never had a baby in her former marriages and I predict her baby's father, temperamental as he too may be (after all, he's an artist), is too real an emotional tie to give up. And I also predict that her peace and happiness will fluctuate along with the luck Bette has in getting the right roles.

state of the unions . . .

I'm not too sanguine, though, about Kathryn Grayson's chances with her Johnny Johnston. Betty Hutton's marriage with Ted Briskin has been saved once, but if the pressure of her greatest career year—which, with *Let's Dance* and *Annie Get Your Gun*, it's bound to be—proves too much for Betty, there could be another, and a permanent, separation. There are clouds of misunderstanding that Alexis Smith and Craig Stevens must fight free of, and the same goes for Linda Darnell and her Pev Marley. Don't worry, though—I'm not—about Dan Dailey and his Elizabeth. Dan has got whatever bothered him out of his curly hair and has come to his senses—I have Dan's word for that. The Sinatras are set to grow old together, now that Frank appreciates Nancy for keeps. All that Mark Stevens has to worry about with Annelle is that touchy temper of his. All's well with Rory Calhoun and Lita Baron. Guy Madison and his Gail Russell couldn't be cozier—Guy even took suspension from Selznick because he just couldn't tear himself away from Gail for a personal appearance tour.

There've been all kinds of silly rumors about Lana Turner and Bob Topping since they came back to Hollywood. But I happen to know Lana wants this marriage to last and she's dedicated herself to that. I've never seen her look lovelier or happier —and, by the way, I'll predict right here that her career will blossom bright again in 1950.

It's always orange-blossom time in Hollywood, and there'll be plenty of new brides and grooms by 1951 that you'd never guess now. I'll predict three who'll stay bachelors, though, in spite of all the moonlight and beautiful girls in the world: Lew Ayres—because he likes his fun with no strings attached; Peter Lawford—because he prefers freedom to play the field; Cary Grant—because he's too contrary, Betsy Drake or no.

But I have the word of one young man that he's mighty eager for the girl to say "yes." That young man is Farley Granger and the girl is Shelley Winters. They don't add up as a team, as they come at you on the screen, but I've a hunch they'd be mighty good for each other. At any rate, I'm doing my darndest to make a match!

And how would you like to see Ava Gardner become Mrs. Howard Duff, in spite of her protests, sometime before 1951? I know Howard will go for that idea and, while Ava's said she doesn't love Howard enough, when you don't love a person you don't keep fighting and making up and have him hanging around all the time, do you? You get rid of the guy—which Ava has never done. I'm predicting she'll weaken before next New Year's Eve. He's a mighty stubborn man, that Duff.

And what about Ginger Rogers and Hollywood's beau boy, Greg Bautzer—wedding bells for them? Not in 1950, I'm afraid—but only for legal reasons. Ginger hasn't got her divorce yet, and that takes time, even if Greg is a lawyer. But I'll say this: If she were free right now, at the turn of the New Year she'd be Mrs. Bautzer. Greg's a mighty hard fish for the girls to net, and dozens of our best sirens have tried unsuccessfully before. But I think he's met his match in Ginger.

That same legal barrier is Clark Gable's greatest protection against a married man's fate. Paulette Goddard is still married to Burgess Meredith—otherwise, I think that clever gal would have been the King's queen by now. I never sell Paulette short in getting whatever she wants, and it certainly looks as if she wants Clarkie. I'm keeping my fingers crossed there for a long time to come, because I think Clark secretly longs to be wed again and he's going to fall pretty hard when he does at last.

Joan Caulfield will marry Frank Ross, Jean Arthur's ex, that's certain enough. Janet Leigh and Arthur Loew, Jr. have wedding plans that can come true. And whenever Doris Day's manager, Marty Melcher, is free from Patti Andrews of the Andrews Sisters, Doris and Marty are fairly sure to make a home together. And what about Ruth Roman and Bill Walsh? Not from what Ruth tells me—but there's a hint of yes, yes in her eyes.

But there are others who might take that lover's leap in 1950, so I'll boost their chances along by holding the thought: Jane Wyman, because she's lonely and beautiful—to somebody, but not to Lew Ayres; Hedy Lamarr, if she can find the right man. And, for sure, a romance for lovely Elizabeth Taylor—it could well be Bill Pawley again. When he came out to Hollywood for Jane Powell's wedding, he talked long and seriously with Liz, and I do know that heart affair was very, very deep. They've never stopped their long-distance calls. But whoever it is, I know Elizabeth will fall in love and, if she can, get married. Her parents are for it and so is Elizabeth. I don't know any star who is more ripe-and-ready for mature life and a home of her own.

Well, there you are—that's how the movieland merry-go-round looks to me as I watch the chubby kid with "1950" on his diaper climb in the window and heave that wizened and worn 1949 character out. Another year of Hollywood history is written and the book closed for keeps on the stars' lives, loves, and luck.

But another is wide open and the pages blank. I'm just crazy enough to try to fill in a few in advance, when I should know better by now. Maybe I'll never learn. Oh, well—come along, 1950, and cross me up good. I double dare you! THE END

GROWING UP IN HOLLYWOOD

So many of the Hollywood stars were literally born into a show business life. Mickey Rooney and Judy Garland came from traveling vaudeville families who eventually gravitated to Los Angeles. Shirley Temple was born in Santa Monica, to aggressive stage parents. Lana Turner attended Hollywood High School, and Deanna Durbin was discovered by an MGM talent scout who came to visit her school.

On the MGM lot, Lana, Judy, Mickey, and young Liz Taylor were all tutored in studio classrooms. They tried to live their lives as normally as possible— which of course was impossible. All of these stars also grew up in the pages of *Modern Screen*.

Ever since she appeared in *Lassie Come Home* in 1943, at the age of ten, Elizabeth Taylor has been one of the world's favorite movie stars. When Liz was fifteen years old, her mother wrote an article for the July 1947 issue of *Modern Screen* entitled "Bringing up Elizabeth". Mrs. Francis Taylor shared with *Modern Screen*'s readers the story of Liz's first singing lessons at the piano, and the dilemma of whether or not her daughter should be seen in public wearing lipstick: ("I finally agreed to lipstick within reason, and I've just flatly picked two shades she's allowed to use, and no others—Hildegarde Rose and Seashell Pink, which are almost the color of her lips").

Liz's mom also revealed that her daughter may have won the battle to have a black party dress, but the young girl was positively forbidden to have a strapless evening dress! Long gone are those

> "Mother, I was the only girl at the game without lipstick on, and it made me look different. You wouldn't want me to look different, would you?"
>
> —Elizabeth Taylor
> *Modern Screen*
> July 1947

days. From *Modern Screen*'s February 1947 issue comes "Little Miss Breathless" (page 194), which is one of the very first articles ever written by Hollywood's newest ingenue. This look at young Liz brings back memories of a teenage Taylor whom most people have long forgotten. Forty years later, Liz is still one of the biggest stars in films, a status that few of her contemporaries can claim!

Farley Granger was just seventeen years old when he made his film debut in the strongly anti-war production *The North Star* (1943). His most memorable roles are as the star of two of director Alfred Hitchcock's classics: *Rope* (1948) and *Strangers on a Train* (1951).

In *Modern Screen*'s December 1949 issue, his mother, Mrs. Eva Granger, penned "He's Not My Baby Anymore!" (page 198). She talks about Farley's bachelor pad, and how he drops by from time to time to raid the icebox. Mrs. Granger also touches on Farley's on-again off-again romance with Shelley Winters, and his early screen successes.

The photos of "Hallowe'en," from the November 1938 issue of *Modern Screen* (page 201), show posed glimpses of several of Hollywood's young stars amid what many of them never had in real life: a childhood. This was especially true for Judy Garland and Mickey Rooney. Note the photo of Judy before the studio slimmed down her figure to play Dorothy in *The Wizard of Oz* (1939). Judy and Deanna Durbin co-starred in the 1936 short *Every Sunday*. Six months later MGM studio chief Louis B. Mayer gave the decree "Drop the fat one!" and Deanna was mistakenly fired. For Hollywood's child stars, life was oft filled with tricks and treats!

BETTE DAVIS' MARITAL VACATION

Modern Screen

THE LARGEST
CIRCULATION
OF ANY SCREEN
MAGAZINE

HUNDREDS OF INTIMATE PICTURES!

194   **February 1947**

ELIZABETH TAYLOR DREAMS OF BEING
WISE AND WORLDLY, BUT SHE STILL HATES
SCHOOL AND LOVES WIENIE ROASTS AND
THINKS FOURTEEN IS VERY "FEMME FATALE."

By Irene Kane

Liz, whose dad is an art dealer, got her first equipment and criticism from him, now has a "studio" just for littering up with paints, canvases, etc. She's semi-grown up for "The Rich, Full Life."

Little Miss Breathless

■ She patted her stomach in the black dress, and studied herself in the mirror. People would think she was at least sixteen, she decided, and turned to her mother.

"How do I look?"

Her mother said, "Gruesome," cheerfully, and they both laughed. She looked fine, and she was waiting for Fred, who was eighteen, to come and take her out.

It was all unbearably exciting. Her first unchaperoned date, and they would be going to the Starlight Roof of New York's glamorous Waldorf, and there would be beautiful people, and soft music, and white linen on the little tables . . .

"Mother," she said, "may I wear the jacket?"

The jacket referred to is a lovely little white broadtail affair of Mrs. Taylor's. "Certainly not," Mrs. Taylor said. "We're going to the Colony, and I'll need it."

At that point, Fred arrived. Fred used to be called Sonny, and after that Freddie, but he'd decided neither one of them had enough dignity. He listened *Continued on page 196*

Continued on page 196

LITTLE MISS BREATHLESS

Continued from page 195

politely, as Mrs. Taylor gave instructions that they were to be home by midnight.

Then he helped Elizabeth into the white broadtail jacket, and they left.

Mrs. Taylor went to the Colony in an old black coat she'd traveled with. After all, you're only *that* young once.

Miss E. Taylor and escort made a stunning entrance at the Starlight Roof, walked composedly to their table, sat down very hard on their chairs, and tried to look blasé. No go. After a minute or so, they gave it up, and peered around like mere children. They even grinned.

Once Fred looked down at her. "How old are you, anyway?" he said.

"Guess." She tossed the cloud of black hair back the way she imagined Hedy Lamarr would do it, and looked mysterious.

"Sixteen?"

At that point, she was feeling at least 25, so the triumph hardly even excited her. Her clear, 14-year-old eyes danced. "A woman should never tell her age."

After Fred brought her home she threw herself across her mother's bed, and sighed happily. "Such a wonderful vacation!" Wednesday night, she and Fred were going to this place on Long Island, to a ball, and then they were going to stay at this girl's house, and go yachting on Thursday.

same old grind . . .

Back home in California, life isn't nearly so worldly. For one thing, Elizabeth goes to school, which is ghastly unsophisticated.

When she's not in a picture, she goes to the studio school. Fourteen M-G-M kids are enrolled there, including Jane Powell and Dean Stockwell and Butch Jenkins. "And Margaret, only she doesn't come," says Elizabeth.

"Margaret" is Miss O'Brien, who's tutored in her dressing room.

Elizabeth loves her teachers, and hates school. All very normal. She detests homework and despises tests and wishes vacations would go on and on.

Aside from school, California is delightful. The Taylors are looking for a place now where Elizabeth and her brother Howard can have a real rumpus house, since they have lots of healthy young friends.

Mrs. Taylor loves them all dearly, but the wear and tear on the furniture is ridiculous. Elizabeth and Howard approach her sometimes with that party look, and her heart sinks. "Let them want a barbecue," she prays. "Let them want to roll eggs on the lawn. Just so it isn't a dance."

"Mother," they say, "we'd like to have a few of the kids over for some dancing—"

And she has to say, "But I'm still having the floor fixed from the last time, darlings. You left nineteen holes, just like a golf course."

Even before dancing, comes Elizabeth's love for animals. The Taylors have three horses—King Charles, Prince Charming and Sweetheart. They have three dogs named Spot, Twinkle and Monty. They have three cats named Jeepers, Creepers and Cuddles. They have a bird, a cockatoo, it is, named Chiquita Juanita Pepita Pedro Taylor. They stuck the Pedro in because they weren't sure of the sex.

And of course there's Nibbles, the chipmunk.

The menagerie was almost joined by a soft-shell crab, too. It was when Elizabeth was up at her uncle's place in Fairfield, near Westport, Connecticut, during the early part of her vacation.

She and Uncle Jack and a girl named Joy went crabbing, and they got a whole lot of fine husky hard-shelled specimens for dinner. And then Elizabeth caught this poor scared little soft-shelled character who was obviously in the wrong place or the wrong month or the wrong season.

She picked him up, and he didn't bite or anything. "Oh, you poor little thing," she crooned. "You cute, poor little thing."

And then when they got home, by mistake, he was cooked, along with all the others. Mrs. Taylor was delighted, since she had already begun to conjure up a trip back with, item: One crab.

Elizabeth refused to come to the table though. They all coaxed her, but she wouldn't come. She just stood there staring at them, and muttering, "You're just a bunch of cannibals, that's all!"

There was the time Elizabeth went to a party given by Atwater Kent. It was a fabulous party, with animals rented from a circus, and clowns, and other circus performers, and Elizabeth fell in love with a tiny lion cub.

He was so sweet, and so gentle. "May I hold him?" she asked Mr. Kent, and Mr. Kent gave him to her, and he nuzzled on her shoulder, and chewed at her dress, and stole her heart completely.

Mr. Kent, watching, said, "You can have him, Elizabeth. I'll buy him for you."

And Elizabeth, her heart pounding, said goodbye, and went tearing home to ask her mother.

Her mother said no.

Her face fell. "But Mother, he's so cute!"

Mrs. Taylor pointed out that he wouldn't stay so cute, and what in the world kind of household pet would a lion make?

wanted: spot remover . . .

So Elizabeth gave up. Later, when Mrs. Taylor took Elizabeth's party dress to the cleaner's, the man couldn't figure out what the stain on the shoulder was, and asked.

"Lion drool," said Mrs. Taylor sweetly.

The man shook his head. Such a pretty woman, and she looked quite normal. "Maybe you better come back next week, lady," he told her. "Next week we got a specialty. Lion stains removed free."

She couldn't convince him, either.

It pleased Elizabeth and Howard enormously. Elizabeth and Howard are good friends, which is fairly odd, because most guys his age think most sisters her age are swift pains in the neck. They've always been good friends, too, partly due to the fact, Howard claims, that he's had to save Liz's darn old neck so many times.

The first rescue job he ever did on her took place at the Taylors' country place in Kent, England, when Elizabeth was three.

Howard was six, and he and she both had whooping cough. They couldn't play with other kids, naturally, and they were out sunning by a pond.

The pond had been getting too full of water, and an irrigation ditch had been dug next to it, to drain some of the water off. The ditch was about three feet deep.

Howard and Elizabeth decided to explore for tadpoles. Elizabeth plopped herself down by the side of the pond. "I bet I find one first."

"Why, you're just a baby," said Howard. His eyes searching the muddy water, he stretched his hand across the narrow ditch. The slope on the other side was very slippery, he discovered.

"Don't put your hand there; it's slippery," he said importantly.

Elizabeth of course got up and waddled over and attempted to put her hand there. She went into the ditch, head first, and got stuck completely in the thick, grey mud. All Howard could see was two small feet waving frantically in the air.

He planted his fat six-year-old legs solidly in the earth, and grabbed at her ankles. After that, he hollered. Loud, too.

"Mother," he screamed. "Mother, Mother, Mother—"

Mrs. Taylor came tearing down from the house, got a load of the hysterical Howard, and the pitch-black Elizabeth, and told herself to be calm.

After a while, she got them both home, and gave Elizabeth a hot bath and put her in bed, and called the doctor.

When the doctor came, he said Elizabeth had a fever, but she'd be all right. At least no complications were going to develop with the whooping cough. "If Howard hadn't acted so quickly," he said, "the baby would have suffocated."

Howard was unimpressed by his own heroism. All he knew was that he'd warned Elizabeth, and she'd ignored him, and he kept talking about it in an aggrieved tone of voice. "I tole her not to put her hands there," he kept saying. "I tole her, Mother, I tole her."

And there was the time she was on her way home from school, thinking dreamily of the best way to talk an ice cream sundae out of her mother that afternoon, and she passed a gas station when a car was backing out of a driveway.

no men, no makeup . . .

Howard gave her a shove that almost knocked her over the state line and when she turned around to slam him back playfully, she noticed the car. "Oh," she said, in a small voice.

"Oh, what?" said Howard bitterly. "I'm going to make Mother raise my allowance. For being a bodyguard in my spare time."

Actually, he likes her. He likes her and all her girl friends, and she and her girl friends like him and all his boy friends, and the whole crowd chases around together, swimming and riding and fishing.

Elizabeth plays the piano poorly, and Howard does much better, which she will admit behind his back. To his face, she will make scathing remarks such as, "Excuse me, Mr. Paderewski."

"That's quite all right," Howard says smugly. "We can't all be talented. When I think of the sort of people they have in the movies now—tsk, tsk."

Lovely boy, Howard. Elizabeth's best girl-friend is Anne Westmore, Wally's daughter. Anne has brown hair and blue eyes and is pretty, and she and Elizabeth have long daily conferences.

Elizabeth thinks twenty-five is a splendid age for marriage, which is a perfectly safe thought for her to hold. She also thinks she will be able to combine a career with marriage (when she's twenty-five, that is).

"No man is going to boss *me*," she tells Anne.

And Anne grins. "You'd better wait and find out if one wants to."

Also, Elizabeth is given to sweeping statements. "I," she says, "will never wear any makeup except maybe a little lipstick."

And Anne, who is Mr. Westmore's daughter, smiles wisely.

Elizabeth's absent-minded to the point where she sat on her mother's best hat and almost demoralized that bonnet, and her favorite actors are Ronald Colman and Gary Cooper.

"For real acting, that is," she says. "But I guess my favorite person in the movies is Van Johnson."

Anne, asking about her New York trip, discovered the principal thing that had impressed Elizabeth was that so many women walked around with false braids on their heads.

"All that hair," she said, "and none of it their own. I guess they think they can fool people."

But they couldn't fool her. No sir, not Taylor. Smart as a chipmunk, that kid.

CLIMAXING WARNER BROS.' GLITTERING PARADE OF MUSICALS!

Glorious "42nd Street"—magnificent "Gold Diggers"—actually surpassed by the master makers of musical films!
. . . In this new show packed with surprising novelties! . . . Jimmy Cagney singing and dancing for the first time
on the screen! Stupendous dance spectacles with hundreds of glorified beauties, staged UNDER WATER! New
laughs and song-hits from Gold Diggers' famous stars . . . All directed and staged by the internationally famous
creators of "42nd Street", Lloyd Bacon and Busby Berkeley. CAN YOU EVEN *THINK* OF MISSING IT?

"FOOTLIGHT PARADE"

JAMES CAGNEY • RUBY KEELER • DICK POWELL • JOAN BLONDELL

GUY KIBBEE • RUTH DONNELLY • FRANK McHUGH • HUGH HERBERT

Mrs. Eva Granger and her son, Farley. He now has his own apartment, but still brings friends to the old homestead for dinner.

He's not my baby anymore!

by Mrs. Eva Granger

Seen through his mother's eyes, Farley Granger's a boy who finds joy in a rainstorm, who brings her flowers—and his socks to darn.

■ Anything written about Farley Granger, I'm likely to read. Sometimes I love the stories—but sometimes they puzzle me, and I hand the magazine to my husband.

"That's Farley?" I ask unbelievingly.

He reads it. Then he says, "Hmmmm. . . . Well, I suppose all of us look different to different people. Question of viewpoint. Whoever wrote this—well, that's Farley to him."

"Fair enough. I've got a viewpoint too. Why don't they ask *me* about Farley?"

But when MODERN SCREEN asked me, I didn't feel quite so brash. It's one thing to babble about your child in private, and another to make sense about him in print. "Where'll I *start?*" I asked Dad, slightly panicky.

"Just dive in," he grinned. "You'll come up with something."

I'm taking his advice. If this is a hodgepodge, blame it on both of us. . .

To me, what makes Farley tick more than anything else is his tremendous zest for life. There's no limit to his enjoyment of the world and its magic. For instance, I remember when he came home from New York where they went to make *Side Street.* He'd seen all the shows. Well, everyone sees the shows, though maybe they don't get as excited as Farley. But that was the least of it. What really steamed him up were the things a lot of us take for granted.

"I walked around town in the rain and saw those fantastic buildings under lightning and thunder. Boy, what a beautiful sight!" He talks quietly enough, but his eyes blaze and he's like a high-tension wire, giving off sparks. "I got a horse and rode in Central Park. I stood on Brooklyn Bridge, and looked down at the water. I talked to cops. In New York, even the cops are wonderful."

There's another story I'd like to stick in here, for no reason except that it's just as characteristic. You can imagine how he felt—how we all felt—the day Joan Evans' arm was badly burned when Farley accidently discharged a blank cartridge while on location for *Roseanna McCoy.* It was 8:30 before the doctors said Joan's arm would be all right. After the first burst of relief, Farley thought, "Flowers. She can't wake up in that bare hospital room tomorrow, and not have any flowers!" *Continued on page 200*

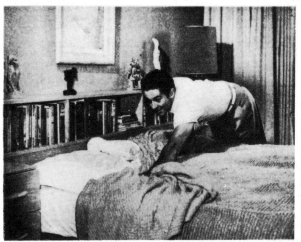

When Farley Granger makes the bed in his bachelor quarters it may not be thorough, but it's fast. His rooms are filled with books—one of his major passions.

Even before he could afford it, Farley was an avid record-collector—he began with modern music and is now gathering classics. He still sings off key, though.

His shiny black Chevvy is one of the joys of Farley's life. He's a few minutes away from his parents' home, no time at all from dates with—say—Shelley Winters.

You couldn't buy any. The whole little town was closed up. So Farley drove out and found himself an orchard and picked sprays of blossoms off the trees—whether with or without the owner's permission, I never asked. Back at the hospital, the nurses were busy, so he fixed them himself. And when she woke up next morning, Joan's room was bright with them. . . .

Farley's first love is his work. I can still see him, 17 years old, standing outside Mr. Goldwyn's office, the contracts just signed and none of us quite believing what had happened. Bob McIntyre, Mr. Goldwyn's casting director, put his hand on the boy's shoulder. "Well, Farley—d'you want to be a big movie star?"

"No sir, I just want to be a good actor."

That hasn't changed. But next to his work, he loves music, painting and books. One of his treasures is a painting of a little Indian boy by Diego Rivera, that he brought back from Mexico. One of my treasures is a picture Farley drew as a youngster, while lying on the floor in front of the fireplace. I had it framed not so long ago, and hung over the mantel. Farley had a fit. Nevertheless, it still hangs over the mantel.

"Some people," I tell him, "go for Diego Rivera. I have a taste for early Farley Granger."

Books he devours. "I've got so much to learn!"—that's his constant cry. If Farley's been away—though it's only for a few days—first two places he heads for are the bookstore and the Gramophone Shop. Straight like a thirsty horse for water.

I've seen mothers look at their dearly beloved children just the way Farley looks at a book. About music, it's funny. My father was a fine violinist, and I used to hope Farley'd be able to sing. He can't sing a note. Or rather, he'll cheerfully sing anything you ask. But you don't ask, because he's always half a key off. But this doesn't affect Farley's passion for music. That he was born with.

The way Farley got into films was this: Back in 1942, Farley—who'd been active in high-school play productions—landed a part in a little-theater production of *The Wookey.*

Lucille Reimer—she was working as a talent scout at the time—saw Farley in this little play and called us up. She wanted to take him to Samuel Goldwyn's for an interview, and since he was still under-age, she wanted Dad and me to go along. Naturally, we all went. "It's nothing," we kept telling each other over and over. "Things like this happen every day, and nothing comes of them." But I was shaking, and Farley's eyes were like coals.

Nothing definite happened that day. Farley was one of a hundred boys being interviewed for the part of Damian in *The North Star.* Bob McIntyre took him to Miss Hellman and Mr. Milestone. They took him to Mr. Goldwyn. All Mr. Goldwyn said was, "I like his physique." He was called back once to read, then we didn't hear and we didn't hear for a month.

Then one Thursday the call came. I was out on the front porch a dozen times before he got home. "Farley, you're going in for a test tomorrow."

P. S.—He got the job. And a Goldwyn contract.

He made *North Star,* he made *Purple Heart* and he joined the Navy. He was in the Navy two years, one month and one day. When he returned, we had 65 people in our little house to meet him and greet him. I invited all his old flames—Janie Withers, June Haver, Ann Blyth. "Have spaghetti and meatballs, Mom," he'd said on the phone. We had spaghetti and meatballs. And a champagne punch. They sat on the floor and played games till four in the morning. Me, I cried.

After that came what Farley calls the long drought. Eighteen months, and no picture. He wasn't the only one. It happened to lots of boys, whose careers were sidetracked by the war. In Farley's case, they said he was the wrong age. Too old for kid parts, too young for juvenile leads. "We're paying you to grow up," Mr. Goldwyn told him.

But Farley could stand not working just so long. I'm not sure I know just how to express this, and I don't want to express it wrong. He knew what a marvelous opportunity he'd been given back there in '43. He knew how experienced people beat at the doors of Hollywood for years, and how the doors had opened for him—a greenie—almost by magic. But he also knew that the cellar door can open as quick as the front door. Quicker. First and foremost, he still wants to be a good actor. He's much more concerned with working than with any glory that might come from a certain picture. "You can't learn to be a good actor," he'd say, "without acting." With every month that passed, he grew more tense and impatient. He went out and hunted for parts. And when he sold himself to Nick Ray for *They Live by Night,* no one was better pleased than Mr. Goldwyn.

Since then, it's been good sledding. *They Live by Night* to *Rope* to *Enchantment* to *Roseanna McCoy* to *Side Street* for MGM. Next comes *With All My Love* for Mr. Goldwyn, with Joan Evans and Ann Blyth. He's old enough now for juvenile leads. Even without the moustache he wore in *Enchantment.*

So much for Farley, the actor. Farley, the individual, lives by himself. Which is how it should be. For a year or so after he got back, he stayed with us. Kind of revelled in home cooking and being waited on. Then one day he looked at me out of the corner of his eye. "Mother, would you mind if I got a little place of my own?"

"I was wondering," says I, "when you'd get around to it." And that was the truth. Dad had brought up the subject with me more than once. "The boy's grown up," he'd say. "He's found a career, he's financially independent, he'll be wanting to fly the coop. It's only right and natural. You can't develop as an independent human under somebody else's wing."

So now Farley has his place, and we have ours. I think it's a perfect arrangement for us all. I keep his room as he left it, and he's free to come and go as he pleases.

Sometimes he'll drop by at 10, after a show. Raids the icebox. Rifles the preserve closet in the hall outside his old room. Ogles a cake I've baked. "I *could* be talked into taking half of that home." He still brings his friends to dinner whenever he feels like it. I'll be sitting here knitting, and the phone'll ring. "What're you having tonight, spareribs and sauerkraut? I'll be over at 6:30 with Arthur Laurents." If I don't have spareribs and sauerkraut—well, the market's close by.

After dinner, if the boys don't have dates, they'll stick around and gab. Farley lies on the floor and plays with Boots, same as in the old days. She's his dog and knows it. Minute she hears his car outside, she starts going crazy.

He still brings me his socks to darn and his pants to shorten. "Here's a job for you, dear." Apart from records and books, he splurges on gifts and clothes. To Farley, every day is Mother's Day. My garden's full of flowers, but Farley's always bringing flowers. Or perfume. Or a print he picked up. "Happy Thursday, dear," he'll say and dump it in my lap.

Farley's car is a black convertible Chevvy, and he's got a red cap that he uses just in the car. Likes the color combination. His house is just about seven minutes away. His maid comes in twice a week to keep it clean, and fix an occasional meal if he wants her to. Breakfast he fixes himself. That consists of throwing a teabag into hot water. In the morning Farley looks upon food with distaste. (But, I must add, it's the only time of day he does!)

Right now, he tells us, marriage isn't in the cards, and I can only take his word for it. Tomorrow's another day. Naturally I'm interested in whatever information he volunteers on the subject. But I strongly believe that people, including mothers, have no right to pry.

He goes out quite a bit with Shelley Winters and Vera-Ellen. They don't do much night-clubbing. Only time Farley cares about night clubs is when there's some top performer he doesn't want to miss—like Mitzi Green. As for dancing, he can take it or leave it. He's no Fred Astaire, not even the poor man's. They don't throw him off the floor, but they don't hand him any Arthur Murray cups either.

What he likes is dinner for two and a good movie. Or dropping in after dinner at the Gene Kellys' or the Saul Chaplins'. The Chaplins keep open house. Saul's a brilliant pianist and very generous about playing for his friends. They'll have music or games or gabfests or a combination of all three. That's Farley's idea of a swell evening. I imagine the girls like it too, or they wouldn't go with him.

Have I left anything out? Oh yes, his faults. Of course he has faults. Only trouble is, I can't seem to think at the moment what they are. Which leaves me wide open to other people saying, "That's Farley?"

I'm only his mother, folks. That's Farley to me.

THE END

MODERN SCREEN

"You're crying, see? Rodney brought you home with him but his mother won't let him keep you so you're crying, see?"

Jackie Cooper shows Deanna Durbin just how to bob for apples.

Freddie Bartholomew and Judy Garland try hard to keep the doctor away.

Hallowe'en

SCHMIDT'S PET SHOP

Granville "write" into the holiday spirit, soap and all.

Withers isn't frightened at all, she's just hide scared.

"I don't need a jack o'lantern," Mickey Rooney tells Ann Rutherford.

THE STARS WRITE FOR MODERN SCREEN

W hen *Modern Screen* in the early 1950's asked several movie stars to write their own feature stories for the magazine, it was a press agent's dream. It was also a brilliant ploy to let *Modern Screen* readers feel as though they were actually having a dialogue with their screen idols. These became some of the most revealing, and humorous, articles to have appeared in the magazine.

Take, for instance, "An Open Letter from Judy Garland," from the November 1950 issue (page 203). Judy had been heading for a collapse for quite some time. In one of Louis B. Mayer's 1938 memos to his secretary, Ida Koverman, he wrote about Judy, "Have her mother get the studio doctor's prescription for sleeping pills." So began the teenage Garland's perpetual roller-coaster nightmare of uppers and downers. It was speed every morning to keep slim and to stay awake during many long hours on the set. At night it was barbituates to get to sleep. By 1950 she finally broke down and had the long-overdue breakdown that had been years in the making.

Halfway through the filming of 1950's *Annie Get Your Gun,* Judy walked off the set and never returned. She was promptly replaced by Betty Hutton. Gossip columnists had a field day dragging Garland through the mud. In this "open letter," Judy confesses, "The honest answer is that I suffered from a mild sort of inferiority complex. I used to work myself up into depressions." Unfortunately, that was just the tip of the iceberg of

her problems. Here she thanks the readers of *Modern Screen* for standing by her side through this crisis.

Leave it to Joan Crawford to write "What Men Have Done to Me" for the November 1951 issue (page 204). At this point in her life Joan was between her marriage to Phillip Terry, and her eventual 1955 wedding (No. 4) to Pepsi Cola president Alfred Steele. According to Joan in this article, "If a girl wants anything in this world—and I still believe it's a man's world—she has to fight for it." Joan was always a fighter, and she usually had things her own way!

Who was Lana Turner kidding when she penned "Sex Is Not Enough" for *Modern Screen's* September 1951 issue? According to Lana, "I know because in my time I have dated some of the most handsome men this world has to offer. Sex appeal oozed from them."

Lana was known for her many loves, and sex just wasn't enough for a slick hoodlum stud named Johnny Stompanato, whom she became obsessed with in 1957. He also wanted to sadistically control her life. When Lana's daughter, Cheryl, fatally stabbed Stompanato in April 1958, to defend her mother, it became one of the hottest and sexiest scandals of the entire decade!

Promising young starlet Marilyn Monroe wrote a couple of articles for *Modern Screen* in the early fifties: "I Am an Orphan" in February 1951, and the delightfully questioning "Who'd Marry Me?" from the September 1951 issue (page 208). According to Marilyn, "I can broil pork chops or make a salad. I can make a bed." However, what she proved best at was making love to the movie camera. What's marriage got to do with it?

> "When I was a teenager I was known as whistle-bait."
> —Lana Turner
> *Modern Screen,*
> September 1951

an open letter from judy garland

Judy expresses her gratitude to Modern Screen's understanding readers

■ Dear Friends,

This is a thank-you note.

At a time when I've been gossip's victim and the target of a thousand lies, you people have stood by me. I won't ever forget that.

You've judged me not on the basis of headlines, rumor and innuendo but on my performances as an actress and entertainer.

Ever since the release of my last picture, *Summer Stock,* thousands of you have had the kindness to write me. You've congratulated me, encouraged me, and pledged me your future support. And for all this—let me repeat—I'm eternally grateful.

Inasmuch as it is impossible for me to reply individually to your more than 18,000 letters, I'm using this space in MODERN SCREEN to answer those questions you've most frequently asked.

I have a responsibility to you friends. Rather than let you be misguided by the flood of nonsense printed about me by reporters and uninformed writers who know none of the facts, I intend to fulfill my responsibility by telling you movie-goers the truth.

I am not quitting motion pictures. Movies are my life's blood. I love making motion pictures and always have ever since I was a little girl.

I do not intend, however, to make any films for the next six months. I'm just going to relax, take things easy, and regain my peace of mind.

For a while I expected to go to Paris with my daughter, Liza, and my husband, Vincente Minnelli—but his studio has decided to film all of *An* *Continued on page 212*

Judy, fully recovered, is shown on vacation at Sun Valley.

WHAT MEN HAVE DONE TO ME

by Joan Crawford

This is a man's world, and a girl has to fight for everything she wants. Men taught me how to fight; they taught me how to live.

■ The other evening I was going over a collection of movie magazines. Naturally, my eyes were diverted to stories dealing with Joan Crawford.

After reading three of them, I said to myself, "Is it *you*, actually *you* they're writing about?"

I couldn't believe it. Honestly! One writer quoted me as saying, "I've made three mistakes in my life—my three marriages, and I'm not proud of any of them."

Another reporter described me as "love-starved, man-crazy, husband-hungry, and altogether unhappy."

A third suggested that I was a domineering hermit who lived only for her career.

Bunk! Pure bunk!

I know the truth about myself, and I'm not afraid of it.

The basic truth about me is that I'm so normal it hurts, and that my character and personality are largely the result of the men in my life.

We all become a part of what we live with.

I have lived with three men, three fine men of character, integrity, kindness, and purpose. Some of it has worn off on me.

Douglas Fairbanks, Jr., my first husband, had been reared in style. I hadn't. I came from a poor family. I came up the hard way.

It was Doug who taught me graciousness, and introduced me to a way of life I had never known before, with servants and cars and secretaries. I brought to that life a great belief in equality—the feeling that our laundress was as good as we were, that wealth and position were not inalienable rights, that at best, they were the outgrowth of a lucky break or two.

I had never had people work for me before. To get along with them takes tolerance, perseverance, and understanding. I learned all those things.

I have the president of the Joan Crawford Fan Club *Continued on page 211*

September 1951

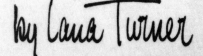

by Lana Turner

SEX
is not enough!

A STAR WITH SEX APPEAL TO BURN SAYS IF FACE AND FIGURE ARE YOUR ONLY ASSETS, YOU'LL GO BANKRUPT FAST!

■ When I was a teen-ager I was known as whistle-bait.
According to one writer, I possessed "the
kind of figure men looked at twice,
because they didn't believe it the first time."

I was physically precocious. Men found me
attractive; boys considered me pleasant; and my ego
found the combination completely satisfying.

More important still, my physical charms
were responsible for my getting into motion pictures.

Back in 1937, when Billy Wilkerson, publisher
of the Hollywood Reporter, saw me sipping a coke
in a drug store across from Hollywood Boulevard,
he was not impressed by my mind. He felt
that I had the kind of photogenic face and figure that
belonged in motion pictures, and he insisted
that I go see Zeppo Marx, an agent.

Zeppo thought I had possibilities, and turned me over to one
of his assistants. For five months, we saw the casting
director at every studio in town. They all turned me down,
which was when the *Continued on page 212*

207

who'd marry me?

He'd have to hold me awfully tight to keep me home. Because I'm a girl who wants to go places . . . and who'd put up with a footloose, fame-hungry female?

By MARILYN MONROE

■ As a wife I wouldn't be completely unprepared. I can broil chops or make a salad. I can make a bed. I can sew something simple and darn socks. I can iron a shirt, and I can actually bake bread. I can do all these things and would—if my heart were in it. But it isn't. The safest place for my heart, I have found, is all wrapped up in à breathless, interesting thing called a career. The boy would have to tear off all this wrapping . . . and probably without any encouragement from me at first. Who would take the trouble to marry me?

These are my reasons now, but right from the start of my life I wondered about it, it seems. I remember my first "romance" . . .

He was 22 and I was not yet 14. He lived across the street from me, and I know now that I was just a kid as far as he was concerned. I should have known that from the way he would pat me on top of the head when he came home and I *happened* to be standing near the fence on his side of the road. But I didn't. To me he was the center of my thoughts, my feelings, my whole world.

One day he came out of his house and was already in his car when he noticed me (there I was hanging around again!). "Hey! I'm going to a movie," he called, impulsively. "Ask your Aunt Anna if you can come along. It's a good picture."

Aunt Anna, who was my guardian, and who liked him, said yes, and I flew out to join him. When I sat down beside him my heart was pounding, my head in a whirl, and an inner voice kept whispering to me, *Continued on page 210*

who'd marry me?

Continued from page 208 "You shouldn't have gone. You won't know how to conduct yourself. He will never bother with you again."

That voice was right. I not only tried to act like an older girl and failed, but I was too far affected by being out with him to even act my own age. I was gawky. I was giggly. I was stupid. When I had been sitting too long in the car without saying anything I got nervous. Not being able to think of an idea of my own, I read an advertising sign we passed, read it aloud and mispronounced practically every word! When he made a driving error and I should have kept mum till the incident was forgotten, I laughed and earned an annoyed look. When we pulled up in the parking lot of the theater and he was coming around to open the door on my side, I not only opened it myself first, but closed it again quickly so he could open it after all! When we got inside my feet went rubbery and he had to save me from stumbling a half dozen times. And all through the picture I was in a daze.

He still said hello after that night, but no more smile, no invitations, not even a pat on the head! I cried off and on for weeks and that was the first time I thought—"Who'd ever marry me?"

Maybe my worrying about it that much was why I did get married when I was only 16. But that was so unwise and short-lived a marriage that it was as if it had never happened. So the old thought still comes back to me every time I meet someone I like. And now there are other reasons that keep popping up in my head making me wonder. When I was 14 it was silly to worry about it; maybe it still is silly, but I can't help it.

Of course, all girls get vague fears like this at times. I think something of this nature accounts for the fact that I had two periods in my life when I stuttered every time I tried to talk. Naturally shy to begin with, this affliction made me withdraw into myself altogether. I would start to say something and my lips would get fixed into an "O" shape, a lost feeling would come over me, and I would stand there frozen. One day when I was attending Van Nuys High School in the San Fernando Valley, I auditioned for a school play. I had memorized my lines perfectly. The other kids were standing around when the teacher gave me the cue. I opened my mouth—and nothing! There was a long silence and then curtain!

The fear was not one that I analyzed then as concern over being "wanted," but it certainly bore a close relationship to this. I worried about being left out of things, being passed up by the "crowd" as a goof and all that. I never could get over how glib the other kids could be, standing around the school yard and rattling away whole streams of merry talk. Like everyone else with a handicap, I worked hard to get the best of mine and I improved. But not sensationally then. And the other girls were fast to point up my deficiency whenever they could.

I'll never forget the little items in the school paper on this subject. Any boy who took me anywhere was reported as having "drug" me . . . the implication being that I was a dead weight, of course. Well, so I didn't talk the ear off a boy when I was with him! There were some, I found, who didn't mind silences between sentences. One was the boy who always played the lead in school plays. We could just stand or sit together, and have just as good a time as if we were yakking away.

I started dating by drifting into it. After that one bad experience with my "dream man" who lived across the street, I classed myself as a bad prospect for any boy. But there would be fellows who walked me home from school and we would stand outside the house and talk a while. Other kids would come along, and before long there was such a group of us that my Aunt Anna said we resembled a mob. She would invite us in just to get us out of the eyes of the neighbors. And sometimes one of the boys would suggest our going somewhere, and that way I sort of slid painlessly into going out.

I cured my stuttering, which was really an inability to get the opening word out. And after that I slowly learned to be myself and not act like a stick when I was out with someone. But there were other problems to lick. I remember that when I left school and got work as a model, it was terribly difficult for me to work in front of people. It was bad enough professionally, and it was awful for me socially. Suppose there was someone present who might be interested in me . . . what would his reaction be to a girl who could hardly hide her nervous state?

I remember modeling once at Bullock's big store. My job was to pull down little roller signs. Painted on them were illustrations of the wardrobe accessories a designer was discussing for some buyers. "Now here is a very versatile scarf that can be made to do for almost any occasion," the designer would say, and I would pull down an illustration of a leather belt!

The practice of putting women on pedestals began to die out when it was discovered that they could give orders better from that position.—Betty Grable as quoted by Irving Hoffman in The Hollywood Reporter.

I started going to cocktail parties. Next to me would be the fellow who brought me, and around us a sea of strange faces that would move closer and closer, and talk, talk, talk! What to say? What to answer? What were they thinking of me for my nervous laughter? What about the fellow who brought me? If he had had ideas that he liked me . . . weren't they gone forever? That little voice of mine used to give me the answer. "Better learn to live alone and pretend to like it."

I didn't want that. I kept going to cocktail parties and, by determining to conquer my fears, I did attain some ease of mind. A cocktail party is still not my idea of the best evening's entertainment in the world, but neither is it the worst.

Maybe the easiest feature of a cocktail party (or a dance) to handle is the stag line. That's probably because there is so little originality in the "approach." One night seven men talked to me and it was as if all seven of them were reading from the same script. Their lines (leaving out mine which probably were no brighter) ran something as follows:

"Well! The moment I saw you come in the door I knew I had to meet you."

"You know, you're like something I've never seen before."

"I'd like to call you up some time. If I had your number."

These days, now that I've been in some pictures, the only variation is:

"I saw you in *The Asphalt Jungle*. I'd call you up some time, if I had your number."

Or—

"I saw you in *All About Eve*. I'd like to call you up some time, if I had your number."

The future dialogue will be the same except that the pictures referred to will probably be my new ones, *As Young As You Feel, A WAC In His Life,* and *Let's Make It Legal.*

The barriers between romance and myself are still up. If I were a fellow, I don't think I'd be foolish enough to get serious about a girl like me. If it isn't one difficulty to overcome it's another, and now it's my work—or rather that I am just at the beginning of my career and so deeply set on making good. If there were a boy—where would we find the time to learn to know each other well enough to want to marry? And how could I be sure enough about our future to give up my career for it? Because . . . for the sake of marriage alone, I know I wouldn't.

One day a few weeks ago, I made a date for dinner and a show. I was to be ready at seven in the evening. On the morning of the date I was due in the studio at 8 A.M. to pose for publicity stills. Just before lunch I was interviewed in a session that lasted two hours. A car was waiting then to take me to my apartment for some "home" photographs for a magazine. At a little before five I was back in the studio to discuss a test with the director of my next picture. When we got all set on it the director called in the writer to suggest certain changes. He thought it would be a good idea if I stayed and rehearsed them right then and there. I did.

My date had just rung my bell for the twentieth time and I was on the way back to his car when I drove up. He took one look at my face and shook his head.

"The night is young," he said, "but do you care?"

I shook my head. I felt as I looked—beat.

Yet, I am not consistent. Sometimes I have a hard day, and when evening comes I want to go out. If I haven't a date I go out anyway—alone. And I like it this way. Just a few days ago when I left the studio I thought I would go for a little drive instead of heading home. When I saw a drive-in restaurant I stopped and had a hot dog and a coke. A little while later I was passing a tiny movie house in Hollywood which shows old time pictures, and went in to see an early Charlie Chaplin comedy. I laughed myself silly and went back to the car still feeling restless. I had no idea which way I was heading when I started off, but found myself stopping at Will Wright's in Beverly Hills for some ice cream. Inside I met a friend who told me he was just about to drop in on a farewell party for a couple he knew, and asked me to come along. That was the last event on the schedule for the evening, an evening I hadn't planned, and a very satisfactory one as far as I was concerned.

Even if I were married I think I'd have a yen every once in a while to spend some time like this by myself. What boy that I married would permit it? What would he say about the other things my moods sometimes drive me to? Sometimes if I can't sleep, I'll get up and play records in the middle of the night—or take a walk, or go out for a drive. I know this sounds as if I am spoiled, but all my life, because I was orphaned as a child, perhaps, I have had to be my own best friend.

When I am working I have to go to bed early. But when I have no picture I revert back to late hours. Sometimes the two different bedtimes are as much as six hours apart. It would be a habit I don't think I could change if I were married. Who would put up with it?

Oh, a lot of friendships begin these days but they never get anywhere. Most times when I go to a party there is someone who indicates he wants to see me again. If I don't encourage him, if I don't give him my phone number, it's not always because I don't like him. It's more likely because I can see far ahead, and the whole thing seems so futile. Men think I am playing exclusive. I'm really saving them a lot of time, and maybe trouble.

If I were married I would often be up and gone before my husband was awake. I'd be home ready for sleep right after dinner, while he'd be ready for a big evening. Then, suddenly, the whole thing would go into reverse. I would get up late and want to stay up after he got sleepy.

If I *did* marry, I don't think the boy I'd choose would be an actor. That's the way it seems to me now. And that, I notice, often spells trouble to Hollywood romances. It's hard for a non-professional to become accustomed to the ways of picture people, no matter how many times you read that it isn't. It's not only a matter of jealousy, it's the feeling that you really haven't full rights to the time and interest of your wife or husband if she or he happens to be in the public eye.

No, right now I have a one track mind—screen work. I want to be a real actress and I don't want to be causing anyone any pain or heartache while I am at it. Who would want to take a chance and marry me? Someone, someday, I hope. But he seems so far away now. THE END

what men have done to me

Continued from page 205 stay with me when she occasionally comes to Hollywood. I'm grateful for her interest in my career, and I try to demonstrate my gratitude.

Grips and gaffers and electricians who work on my pictures refer to me as a pretty good egg. I try to be.

Stories that I act like a prima donna on the set are laughable. I remember only too well when I myself worked in the line as a chorus girl. I am no haughty, snobbish social climber; no lonely, embittered woman obsessed with her career.

Thanks to Douglas, I try to live graciously. I work and will continue to work because I love it, and because I also have four children to support.

When I'm wrong about anything, I admit it readily. It took time to learn how to do it, but I learned. Only a year or so ago, I was making a picture with Vincent Sherman, a very fine director. Somehow, I couldn't follow his direction. I lost my temper and in front of the entire crew, cried, "I just don't know what you want me to do. I don't think you do yourself."

Five minutes later, I was back on the set. "Ladies and gentlemen," I said, "a little while ago you heard me blow my top at Mr. Sherman. In front of all of you, I should now like to apologize."

That's no great accomplishment, of course—but it was a man who taught me that the admission of error is an integral part of character.

When I'm wrong I up and say I'm wrong. I don't dilly-dally about it. I try to treat my associates with fairness and honesty. I pay my secretary and the children's nurse as much as I can possibly afford. I learned a long time ago that chiseling on help never pays.

I also learned from a man that there is more to marriage than sex—mind you, I'm not knocking it—but love is infinitely more than that.

It was Franchot Tone, my second husband, who contributed greatly to my intellectual development, and I don't mind admitting it one bit.

Franchot was a Phi Beta Kappa at Cornell. He came from a line of distinguished ancestors. Wolfe Tone, the great Irish revolutionary, was one of his forebears.

Franchot helped me cultivate a strong liking for literature and art and opera. When I was going through that stage, I used to have as many people of culture and taste for dinner and Sunday breakfast as I could possibly manage.

A few of the gossip columnists made fun of me. They mocked me, called me "Lady Crawford." I was burned up, but only for a while because I realized they had a job to do. If they wanted to kid me —well, I think the years have proven pretty conclusively that I'm one actress who can take it.

There is nothing shameful about the pursuit of knowledge. If my folks had been wealthy, perhaps I would have been sent to finishing school and a good university, and after that a year abroad. But they weren't wealthy; and I've always had to make my own way. It takes brain power to do that.

Franchot helped me develop that brain power, to channel it into a better understanding of the arts. I love to read. I now understand good music. Looking at a really fine painting means something to me. I perceive the artistic motivation behind the work. People aren't born with a sense of art appreciation. They have to learn, to be taught. I was taught by a man.

My house today is pretty well-decorated. I have some fine paintings. They reflect my taste. Taste doesn't come to a woman overnight. It's a gradual process compounded of trial and error and integration.

It was also Franchot who taught me a few things about a dollar. "Acting," he pointed out, "isn't a very secure profession, my dear. Save a few bucks while you can."

I listened and I invested some of my savings in real estate. I own an apartment house in Beverly Hills, and it's pretty good income property. During the years I wasn't working—after I left Metro and before I went to Warner Brothers—that income came in mighty handy.

I am not tight with a dollar, and so far as I can see or read—no one has ever accused me of that. I'm not going into a long list of my charities, but I believe money is meant to be spent, and I've spent plenty of it on all things, including dozens of worthwhile charities.

I've made bad investments, too—but there's no sense in crying over spilled milk. It was a man who taught me that, too. Forgive me, if I don't mention his name. There are a few things about my love-life I prefer not to share.

Practically everything I know I've been taught by men . . . not only the good things like kindness, humility, graciousness, and being a regular fellow. They taught me perseverance, and how to fight and hold on.

I remember how many people came up to me after I left Metro and said, "Joan, you're being foolish. What difference does it make? Suppose your parts aren't so hot. It's still money."

"If you believe in something firmly enough," I answered, "then you should be ready to fight for it." Well, I fought until I got the parts I wanted. I went without work for more than two years. Fair-weather friends left me by the dozen. Reporters ignored me. Gossip columnists said I wasn't news any more. I went all through that, but I hung on until I got the right role. It was *Mildred Pierce*, and it won me an Academy Award.

I've also fought to keep my marriages going. I remember the time an actor who, supposedly, was a deep friend of mine kept pumping such verbal rubbish into my husband's ear as, "Why don't you step out on Joan? I know some real cute girls over at the studio."

This actor proceeded to get my husband drunk. They went out on a double date, and I got wind of the fact. I wasn't worried about the actor. I was worried about my husband.

After all, the girl in question might have blackmailed him or involved us in a pretty huge scandal. I found my husband with this so-called "cutie." I took him home and sobered him up. He was apologetic and grateful. I myself was terribly hurt, but by holding on and fighting, I saved our marriage, at least for a while.

If a girl wants anything in this world —and I still believe it's a man's world— she has to fight for it. Maybe she doesn't show she's fighting. Maybe she appears sweet, simple, feminine, and naive but underneath she must be imbued with some sort of drive, some sort of push, or she will never get anywhere.

As I said before, I am in the position, fortunate or unfortunate—however you look at it—of having to support myself and four children.

This is a little rough. I should much prefer to be married to a millionaire, to sit on my south side most of the day, relax in the sun, and sport a beautiful tan. But no can do. I must work.

When you work in a man's world, you adopt some of the male accoutrement. I am direct. I call a spade a spade. I make decisions quickly. I keep my word. When I make a date with anyone, male or female, that date is kept. I value friendship too highly to endanger it.

If you read anywhere that Joan Crawford is not in the market for marriage, that she's had her fill of it, that she's been reported as saying, "No more husbands for me!"—it is pure poppycock.

I am not disillusioned with marriage. It is still the most perfect state for man and woman. I would marry tomorrow if the right fellow came along—so there!

The fact that I've been married three times in the past, I regret. I regret that they weren't lasting. Some of the blame must have been mine. I readily accept a share, and am wiser now. I know a little more about life and men and the birds and the bees, and if I walk down the aisle again it will probably be for keeps.

Actors generally don't make good husbands, so the chances are I won't marry an actor. But then again, a girl can never tell.

At the moment, I am not sour, embittered, man-crazy, money-mad, domineering, haughty, snobbish, or condescending.

I am a normal woman in the prime of life who works for a living as an actress. I love fans who ask me for autographs. I sign all of them. I love to pose with moviegoers. I love to answer their mail. I'm flattered when they go see me in motion pictures. I get a thrill when I buy a new gown. It does my ego a world of good when three men call up and ask for a date in the same evening.

In short, I am a normal woman with normal desires, and normal habits.

Anything said to the contrary is simply untrue. THE END

(Joan Crawford will soon be seen in Warners' This Woman Is Dangerous.—Ed.)

open letter from judy garland

Continued from page 203 American in Paris in Hollywood, and since he is directing that picture and plans shortly to direct the sequel to *Father of the Bride*, we all plan to remain in California.

I love to work, I love to sing, I love to act—I get restless when I don't—and it's entirely possible that I will do a few broadcasts with Bing Crosby or Bob Hope before six months are up.

MY health is fine. As I write this, I've just returned from a vacation in Sun Valley and Lake Tahoe. I'm sun-tanned, I weigh 110 pounds, and my outlook on things is joyful and optimistic.

Many of you have written and asked what was wrong with me in the past.

The honest answer is that I suffered from a mild sort of inferiority complex. I used to work myself up into depressions, thought no one really cared about me, no one outside my family, that is.

Why I should have ever gotten depressed, I certainly don't know. You people have proved to me that I've got thousands of friends the world over, that you care about my welfare and my career.

It's perfectly normal for people to have their ups and downs. I know that now, but a year or so ago, these depressions of mine used to worry me, and the more I worried about them, the lower I felt.

Anyway, all of that is gone and done with. The slate of the past is wiped clean. Insofar as I'm concerned, the world is good, golden, and glorious. My best years and my best work lie ahead of me, and I'm going to give them everything I've got.

MANY of you have asked if I realized how closely you followed my career and behavior. I certainly do, and that's why I want all of you to know, especially the youngsters, that I'm not in the slightest embittered about Hollywood and that I still think a motion picture career is one of the finest ambitions any girl can have.

It means hard work and it has its pitfalls but so has every other occupation.

If my daughter, Liza, wants to become an actress, I'll do everything to help her.

Of course, being a child actress and being raised on a studio lot is not the easiest adjustment a young girl can make. You don't go to baseball games or junior proms or sorority initiations, but every success has its sacrifices, and these are the ones a very young girl must make if she wants a career at a very early age.

The girl who finishes her schooling, however, and then wants to become an actress is facing a thrilling, rewarding career.

If I had to do it all over again, I would probably make the same choices and the same errors. These are part of living.

A lot of fanciful stories have depicted me as the victim of stark tragedy, high drama, and all sorts of mysterious Hollywood meanderings. All that is bunk.

Basically, I am still Judy Garland, a plain American girl from Grand Rapids, Minnesota, who's had a lot of good breaks, a few tough breaks, and who loves you with all her heart for your kindness in understanding that I am nothing more, nothing less.

Thank you again.

Judy Garland

sex is not enough!

Continued from page 207 realization first started to dawn on me that sex or sex appeal isn't enough.

The casting directors wanted to know if I could sing, if I could dance; what sort of dramatic training I'd had; what pictures I'd played in. Had I ever been in summer stock?

"Sure, you have loads of sex appeal," one casting man agreed, "but so have a million other girls."

Fortunately for me, Mervyn LeRoy at that point in his life and mine, needed a young girl for one scene in a picture called *They Won't Forget*.

This girl was to be a high-school girl dressed in a tight sweater. She was to walk down the steps of her high school, the camera panning with her, revealing her every curve. Later on, she was to be ravaged and murdered.

Mervyn gave me the part. I had the physical endowments to play it.

The role was a small bit, but from that point on I became typed. Lana Turner became synonymous with sex.

I AM neither anti-Freudian nor a debunker of sex. But I should like to go on record as saying that sex isn't everything in life, and that a girl who has only sex appeal to offer won't keep a man very long.

As a matter of fact, she won't keep a screen career very long, either. The best quality for longevity on the screen is talent. There is no other substitute.

I found that out during the making of *Love Finds Andy Hardy, Dancing Co-ed, Ziegfeld Girl, Johnny Eager, Honky Tonk,* and all the rest of the pictures that went to make up my apprenticeship.

I have also learned from my three marriages that there is infinitely more to love than physical attraction; love is basically a state of mind.

Every day I receive dozens of letters from young girls who are sick at heart because they lack beauty or sex appeal.

I'm not going to get into trouble by naming names, but here in Hollywood there are many actresses who have neither beauty nor high sex quotients. What they have most of all is personality.

Beauty without personality, sex appeal without substance, are tempting come-ons that upon examination, fade into nothingness.

I know, because in my time I have dated some of the most handsome men this world has to offer. Sex appeal oozed from them. They were built like Apollos, but they were about as interesting as laundry lists.

I remember one young actor I dated when I was single, largely because his studio thought the publicity might do him some good. We'd go dancing at a night club, and he'd keep asking, "How do I look?" When he wasn't worried about his looks, he was either running a comb through his hair or grimacing to attract the attention of other patrons. He suffered from a Narcissus complex, spoke only about himself, and while occasionally, he stumbled over the truth about himself, he always recovered and rambled on as if nothing had happened.

On the other hand, take a man like Spencer Tracy. Spence isn't the most handsome guy in the world, and maybe he doesn't exude sex—but what a personality! What warmth! What interest! What kindness! What gentleness!

These are qualities that last longer than sex, because a positive correlation exists between sex and passion, and passion as everyone knows, *Continued on page 213*

sex is not enough

Continued from page 212 fades with the years. But personality, warmth and gentility are enhanced by time.

These are the traits most young girls should cultivate. These are the traits I try to cultivate in Cheryl, my own daughter.

SEX appeal is important, sure. But as any married couple will testify, it takes more than sex to hold a marriage together.

It takes children, mutuality of purpose, self-sacrifice, understanding, a sense of humor, and the ability to put up with little idiosyncrasies.

I, for example, have more than my share. For some strange reason, I feel frightened at large social gatherings. Put me in a room with more than 10 or 12 people, and I'm uneasy. I know I shouldn't be, but I am. Invariably, the last thing I say to my husband before we step into a crowded room is, "Darling, don't leave me."

Bob understands my uneasiness and puts up with it. By the same token, I understand his love for deep-sea fishing. As a result, I've become a deep-sea fisherwoman myself. A few years ago down in the Bahamas, I pulled in a tuña that weighed more than 300 pounds. When I was a girl, you couldn't get me to go fishing for love or money.

I believe that a realization of the relative importance of sex is a part of growing up. When a girl is young, sex appeal is probably the most vital thing in life to her. She imagines that her face and figure are her paramount enticements. Boys, she will tell you, are not interested in her scholarly attainments, her athletic ability, or her knowledge of languages.

That, at least, is what I used to think. I know now that I was wrong. I know now that if I'd had the proper dramatic training to go with my physical endowments, my motion picture career would have progressed at a faster rate than it did.

Boys are interested in anything a smart girl wants them to be interested in. Girls with brains and personality marry men of stability and good will. Girls who offer nothing but beauty and sex usually wind up in the divorce courts.

I am not running sex down. I agree that it is an underlying motive in all human conduct, but I happen to feel that too much emphasis has been put upon it not only where I, personally, have been concerned, but in our day-to-day living.

Only recently, I read a book entitled, "The Folklore of Sex," in which the author said: "The American public will not take a work of fiction to its heart if the story does not imply that unconventional sex behavior is the nastiest and tastiest business imaginable."

Much the same thing has been said about motion pictures. I just don't believe it.

Sex alone will sell nothing.

Sex appeal is helpful in gaining entry either into a man's consciousness or a man's business, but sex alone will never capture any man's heart permanently.

Some of you will undoubtedly say that ever since Adam, men have been interested in sex, and that around your particular neighborhood that still holds true.

Maybe so, but it's been my experience that men fall hardest and quickest for girls who are pleasant, cheerful, witty, and good-natured.

You've all read a good deal about Marlene Dietrich, how even though she's past 50 she still has men pursuing her every Tuesday and Thursday. The reason Marlene is so attractive to men is because she's good-natured. She's always been good-natured even in the days when her legs were featured more than her wit.

Myrna Dell, a young actress who was recently married, is another Hollywood girl who always had plenty of beaux. And for that same reason, too. She knew how to swap gags with the boys and remain feminine in the process.

Janet Leigh, before she was married to Tony Curtis, was popular with most of the young Hollywood eligibles, because she, too, is sweet, perennially cheerful, and the possessor of a wonderful sense of humor.

Ann Sheridan and Ava Gardner are two more cases in point. Each of these girls offers charm, personality, and good humor before sex appeal.

I've seen Ava walking around Hollywood in glasses and blue jeans, looking as simple and plain and unrecognized as the girl next door. Despite her sex appeal —and it's considerable—men go for Ava because she has a mind like lightning, quick and flashing.

Even in Hollywood where sex supposedly is all-important, it has always taken a backseat to talent.

Give any casting director or producer the choice between an intelligent, not-so-pretty girl who can act, and a pretty, not-so-intelligent girl who can't—and the talent will always win.

Debbie Reynolds, Mitzi Gaynor, Pier Angeli, Leslie Caron—all of today's newcomers are young girls who have specialized talent.

It's not that sex has gone out of fashion, because it definitely hasn't. It's just that here in Hollywood, we've come to realize that the trouble with sex appeal is it's only skin-deep.

For lasting happiness, a girl needs something much more solid and enduring than that.   THE END

(Lana Turner can be seen in MGM's Mr. Imperium.—Ed.)

Tallulah Bankhead, Gambler

Continued from page 180

I had left after paying my bills in England was nothing more than an aggravation. When I figured how long it would take, putting that little by, before I'd get anywhere I went out on a tear and spent whatever extra I happened to have. It doesn't seem so foolish.

"So here you see me, with nothing!"

The talkies, in other words, offer higher stakes. And again the gambler, Tallulah has chucked her assured success and her assured income on the London stage to try her luck. Rumor has it that she receives several thousand a week.

I saw her in her luxurious suite at the exclusive Elysée one afternoon, with the soft gold sunlight streaming in the high windows. Lovely chintz covered sofas and chairs stood about, complemented by inlaid commodes and smoking tables. There were, as always, the loveliest flowers about . . . white lilacs and golden iris, purple anemones, scar-let gladioli . . . in bowls and vases of Lalique and silver. Charming lavender cushions and lamps. There was a personal maid. A secretary. There was a portable phonograph playing the record of a dramatic soprano. There was Tallulah's piano over which was flung a rich Chinese embroidery. There was milk white Maxmillian who had arrived that opening night ensconced in a basket of orchids. Maxmillian, however, was in frightful disgrace. That very morning he had chewed up a turquoise ring set in platinum and diamonds that had fallen from the dressing-table. Hanging on the wall was the famous and beautiful portrait of Tallulah by Augustus Johns which formerly hung in the Royal Academy.

Tallulah was very smart in black, a touch of rare lace in the neck of her gown. Her nails stained a deep red. Her long golden bob brushed until it shone.

Below, her big car with a liveried chauffeur waited to take her to one of the smartest and most expensive shops for a fitting. Even though her huge closet bulged with clothes.

And you'll remember Tallulah said she was broke. That's why she had to give up her bird in the hand, literally her assured success in England, for two birds in the bush, the hope of greater success in American-made talkies.

Thinking of Tallulah I cannot help but remember the lines:

"Live life today as though to-
    day were all
  As though this very morning
    you were born.
  Your yesterdays are days be-
    yond recall
  Tomorrow does not come until
    the dawn."

Tallulah, gambler that she is, does just that!

THEY HAD FACES THEN

Almost as important as the image up on the movie screen were the hundreds of publicity stills that the studios sent out for use in the press. Movie star portraits played a huge part in the creation of the screen-idol image.

Under the direction of still photographers, particularly in the 1930's and 1940's, an image of perfection that did not quite exist in reality could appear on an 8″ x 10″ glossy. The studios hired the most talented portrait photographers money could buy, and each subject was made up, lit, angled, and shot in the most flatering poses. After the shot was printed, each was carefully retouched to give the stars some of the features that nature had neglected to dole out. Joan Crawford would lose her hundreds of freckles, Claudette Colbert's shoulder would be airbrushed away to give her the long neck that did not exist in real life, and Errol Flynn would lose the creases under his eyes that too many late nights of partying had etched there. In this way, photographs of mere mortals were transformed into movie-star portraits.

From its very first issue in 1930 up through the 1980's, *Modern Screen* has always devoted ample space in each issue to full-page portraits of the stars. In the earlier issues there were sections of the magazine called "The Modern Screen Gallery of Honor" and "Modern Screen Portraits." By the 1940's, thanks to Betty Grable, they were to become known as "pin-ups."

Among the most famous still portrait photographers were

> "I loved photographing the stars.... The stars were electric, full of sexual qualities, alluring. Our world was a storybook—a romantic fantasy."
> —George Hurrell

Clarence Sinclair Bull and the incomparable George Hurrell. Examples of both of their work is represented in this book.

For the September 1933 issue of *Modern Screen* George Hurrell assembled nine of his favorite subjects for the photo spread entitled "A Great Photographer's Greatest Portraits" (page 215). According to Bette Davis, "The greatest photographs ever taken of the characters I played in films were the work of George Hurrell...his studies of me were an immense contribution to my career." Proclaims Barbara Stanwyck, "George Hurrell is more than just a photographer. His work always seems to go beyond the subject at hand—more into the depth of its character—and that's what makes Hurrell a fine artist."

That languishing look you see on Jean Harlow's face on the opposite page is classic Hurrell. He often posed the great screen goddesses in repose, lighting their hair as if it were spun gold. According to Hurrell, "Joan Crawford was for many years the most photogenic of the Hollywood group of actresses." He photographed her many times during her illustrious career. In addition to the portrait at the top of page 218 of this book, you will also find additional Crawford/Hurrell collaborations on pages 57, and 86–90. Other star portraits in this chapter include Katharine Hepburn by Robert W. Coburn (June 1933), Barbara Stanwyck by William A. Fraker (October 1931), and Errol Flynn (July 1938) and Tyrone Power (April 1940) by unidentified photographers.

To quote Gloria Swanson in *Sunset Boulevard* (1950), "We didn't need dialogue; we had faces!"

A great
PHOTOGRAPHER'S
greatest portraits

George E. Hurrell

THE PICTURES ON THIS AND THE FOLLOWING PAGES WERE SPECIALLY TAKEN FOR MODERN SCREEN BY GEORGE E. HURRELL

JEAN HARLOW—VENUS 1933

CONNIE BENNETT—SIREN WITH BRAINS | DOUG FAIRBANKS, JR.—A GOD TO HIS VALET

SALLY EILERS—IDEAL PROM GIRL   JOHNNY WEISMULLER—BRONZE GOD

CAROLE LOMBARD—AN ORCHID FOR HOLLYWOOD

JOE E. BROWN AND SON—CLOWN AT HOME

MODERN SCREEN'S GALLERY OF HONOR

Photograph by Robert W. Coburn

We honor Katharine Hepburn for her unique interpretation in "Christopher Strong."

Photograph by William A. Fraker

BARBARA STANWYCK

—whose dramatic power is one of the best in Hollywood. Barbara and husband Frank Fay are still as much in love as ever and spend most of their time at their Malibu Beach home playing tennis and swimming. Barbara very seldom talks for publication. She stands in awe of anyone in the movies who is making more money than she is. Her next picture will be entitled "Forbidden."

ERROL FLYNN

TYRONE
POWER

ABOUT THE EDITOR

The author of several books on show business, from 1983 to 1985 Mark Bego was Editor-In-Chief of *Modern Screen* magazine. In 1984 Bego's best-selling biography of Michael Jackson: *Michael!*, sold three million copies, and was published in English, French, Spanish, Portugese, Hebrew, and Japanese. *Publishers Weekly* proclaimed Bego the best-selling paperback biographer of 1984!

Bego is also the author of *Rock Hudson: Public & Private* (1986), *Julian Lennon!* (1986), *Madonna!* (1985), *On The Road With Michael!* (1984), *The Doobie Brothers* (1980), *Barry Manilow* (1976), and *The Captain & Tennille* (1976).

Mark has written for several national and international publications, including *Modern Screen, People, US, CUE/New York, Billboard, The Detroit Free Press,* and *The Pontiac Press.* He has also reported show business news on an assortment of radio and television programs throughout the world.

Originally from Detroit, Michigan; Bego currently lives in New York City.

Photograph by Marc Raboy